BEYOND BELIEF

JAMES
F. COYLE

BEYOND
BELIEF

THE ULTIMATE MIND-POWER INSTRUCTIONAL MANUAL

Copyright James F. Coyle 2010
Published by Vivid Publishing
P.O. Box 948, Fremantle
Western Australia 6959
www.vividpublishing.com.au

National Library of Australia data:
Author: Coyle, James F.
Title: Beyond belief : the ultimate mind-power instructional manual / James F. Coyle.
Edition: 1st ed.
ISBN: 9781921787171 (pbk.)
Subjects: Self-actualization (Psychology)
              Thought and thinking.
              Mind and body.
              Success--Handbooks, manuals, etc.
Dewey Number: 158.1

DISCLAIMER
This book is for entertainment purposes only and the author and publisher accept no responsibility for the use or misuse of the material in this publication. The author of this publication will not be held responsible for the individual readers personal mind experiments as he will have no first hand knowledge of the nature and format of the procedures being used by the individual.

CONTENTS

FOREWORD

Angela Thompson Smith Ph.D.
Professional Remote Viewer
Las Vegas

The human mind is an amazing thing and we are only just beginning to understand how, and why, it works as well as it does! Part of this understanding comes from our knowledge of how the mind and brain integrate as a complete unit. James Coyle, in BEYOND BELIEF extends our understanding of what our minds can accomplish, and offers exercises to train these expanded abilities.

James Coyle is a serious researcher, who has a background in hypnosis and electronic design. His research laboratory produced a large number of confidential reports over the years to his private subscriber list and these were released under his pen name of "Jim Francis".

He is a New Zealander, who now spends his time between Australia, New Zealand, and Vanuatu. James founded the Australasian Lateral Thinking Newsletter and was its editor for twelve years. At the same time he founded the Australian Mind-Power Research Foundation and was its CEO for many years. He has also been an active skydiver, writer, professional recording guitarist with several records on the charts and a fixed wing and helicopter pilot.

In BEYOND BELIEF James describes what luck really is (a personal, psychokinetic resonance with the environment), how it appears to operate in distinct cycles, and describes how, under certain circumstances, luck can be triggered at will. James also describes how our sixth sense (intuition) can be made available, and how it can be easily trained, to become as reliable as our usual five senses.

Remote influencing has become a hot topic, under discussion on several Internet sites. James describes how the human mind can easily influence other minds, to produce a win-win outcome. He also describes a unique problem-solving mechanism that can trigger answers to critical problems, during the normal sleep cycle - - and describes a simple method of dream control.

James writes about Remote Viewing or RV, which, in its simplest definition is "the ability to access information from a remote geographic location using something other than the known five senses." The term was coined by Ingo Swann at the American Society for Psychical Research in the early 1970s. Remote Viewing research has been carried out by Stanford Research Institute (SRI), Scientific Applications International Corporation (SAIC), Princeton University and the American Government, notably the U.S. Army. James has undertaken training in various forms of remote viewing, and shows how RV can be learned by anybody, and put into serious, practical applications.

Apart from James description of his mind discoveries and their application, he also points to the serious science that supports his concepts. For example, there has been a recognition and consensus, among scientists, that the two halves of the brain are not equivalent, either in proportion or function. The left and right hemispheres appear to play different roles in mediating behavior and processing higher mental processes. Generally, in right-handed males, speech language, and motor planning skills are dependent on the left hemisphere, while spatial skills are right-hemisphere dependent. James describes how individuals can take advantage of these scientific concepts, to understand how our intuitive mind works.

The idea that an altered state of consciousness can facilitate the retrieval of anomalous information is not new. This system of retrieval of hidden information has been termed ESP or Psi. Modern researchers have noted that optimal psi effects may be linked to certain attentional states. Altered states occurring during sleep, relaxation, hypnosis, meditation, and sensory isolation have all been found to be psi-conducive. For instance, hypnosis has been employed as a psi-facilitative state in experimental studies including card-guessing and ESP. Highly significant dream studies were also conducted at Maimonides Hospital in New York in the 1960s. James describes practical, altered state exercises that are based on these discoveries. By following these methods, which are described in great detail, individuals can gain a much greater use of their mind's potential.

I have known James for many years now and have been impressed with his energy, in pushing the envelope of what we know about our mind's capabilities. Not only does he research and document his discoveries, but he puts them into practical application. For example, after developing his Mind Surge and Luck Cycle concepts, he put them to practical use. He has won over 100 casino jackpots which were used to fund further research. James has an inquisitive mind - - he attends personal development programs around the world and these generate ideas that spur many of his new concepts. He writes extensively about his discoveries, and believes that they are for sharing with others, rather than keeping them to himself. James is a unique individual, who can help you understand and use your mind's full potential - - how you can win with Mind Power.

INTRODUCTION

The mind does strange things at times.

Have you noticed that occasionally when you are desperate to drive to a destination in the quickest possible time that most of the traffic lights turn green to help you? Or when you're driving down town and mentally focusing on a parking spot....one just seems to materialise for you.

Or you may be thinking intently of a friend and at that very moment they telephone you.

Similarly you might be in a casino environment and you've put a whole bucket of coins through a particular slot machine, which has paid you virtually nothing. In absolute disgust you give it one more spin as you start to walk away......and it promptly gives you a substantial win.

Have you noticed how young children these days appear to be developing a higher intelligence at a young age? When you really analyse this situation, it is not the intelligence that is improving...it is their conscious awareness. It is almost as if these young people were suddenly evolving to have a 360 degree "mental surround" vision as opposed to us adults who are stuck with the equivalent of a 180 degree mental vision....and this fades in and out at times!

Every adult individual can probably relate to the above from personal experience but until recently nobody had ever sat down and started a serious research project to find out how and why this happens.....and how to replicate these mind-effects at will.

Around 12 years ago a low key privately funded research project was instigated to search for answers. The discoveries literally stunned the small group of investigators.

If you were told that you could use your mind to influence a slot machine or dice fall....would you find this beyond belief? If you were told that you could use your mind in a telepathic manner to influence the thinking pattern of another individual or group of people......would you believe it?

Would you find it somewhat amazing if you learnt that while in the alpha/theta state you can communicate quite easily with dolphins?

And if you were further told that you could instruct your subconscious mind to produce a specific dream to help you solve a problem.....and use an unusual intuitional mechanism to decode this dream.......would you find this a helpful ability?

But what if you were told that you could determine your luck cycle in advance so that you could use it for dollar windfall situations......would this give you a sense of personal satisfaction?

But even better still, what if you were informed that you could use an easy-to-learn mental trigger that will tell you which slot machine to play, which scratch-it ticket to buy, which colour to bet on at roulette and which likely numbers to enter in the lotto....with a possible 70-80% chance of being correct? Then would you find all this "beyond belief?"

Well, you may be somewhat stunned to learn that all of this is now possible.....plus more!!

A handful of individuals in Australia and New Zealand are using combinations of the above mind-power techniques to improve their personal lifestyle dramatically.

But you won't hear these people talk about it, because it is an in-house secret.

The book you are about to read explains in detail how these extraordinary mental manipulations are achieved. The methods can be used by any open-minded individual of average intelligence.

All that is required is the ability and willingness to look at personal mind-power in a different way and the dedication to practice these procedures, some of which can be learned in one night.

This book is not a theoretical "mumbo-jumbo" document designed to merely titillate your interest, then leave you with no practical formula to follow. It is a hands-on instructional manual which has been developed by a group of serious businessmen in a dedicated research laboratory. It is designed to take you through the various mind-power disciplines step by step so that you can understand, learn and use them.

This might well turn out to be the most practical book on personal mind-power ever written.

WARNING: If for any reason you are nervous about exploring the full capabilities of your mind potential, then put this book down and walk away....it is not for you.

BACKGROUND TO
MIND-POWER TECHNOLOGY

Around 300 years ago at the end of medieval times a series of new scientifically based processes began to evolve and these eventually became known collectively as "technology".

From this emerged the steam and fossil fuel engines, electricity, electrical storage batteries, aviation, metallurgy, radio followed by electronic devices and rocket propulsion systems, to name but a few.

This was the turning point in human evolution but it may well have taken a different direction.

For example, psychotronic and zero-point energy devices could have been developed which would have taken society in a totally different direction. In this case there would have been no need for steam and fossil fuel engines to have been invented.

The human race moved in one direction but it could just have easily moved in another.

On the other hand mind power technology appears to have retained the same format throughout recorded history. There have always been clairvoyants and the like but little serious scientific attention has been accorded these nebulous personal mind effects. The main reason for this is that mental phenomena such as psychokinetic effects cannot be effectively measured and indeed cannot be reliably induced under normal circumstances.

But that is rapidly changing. Major breakthroughs have occurred in the fields of psychokinetics and clairvoyance (now referred to as "remote viewing").

Individuals with impeccable scientific credentials have tackled these nebulous subjects with results that have been somewhat encouraging, to say the least.

My own personal feeling is that the field of mind power technology today is about where computers and software were.........25 years ago.

There is massive public interest in media programs and movies pertaining to mind effects. There appears to be an increasing conscious awareness of this subject as evidenced by the rapidly growing human-potential movements springing up around the world.

I'm referring here to the western materialistic world which is orientated toward conventional technology. The Eastern world and the indigenous native tribes of various countries have always been aware of these unusual mental abilities. The Australian Aboriginals for example have long been known for their astounding psychokinetic and remote viewing abilities. The Aboriginal elders consider these abilities "normal" and have traditionally used them for tribal survival purposes.

Conventional western science is only now starting to suspect that there is a little more to all this than meets the eye and as more serious scientific research is promulgated through the centres of higher learning, then we might look forward to major breakthroughs in the not-too-distant future.

When my research team started on our earlier PK experiments we had no idea at all as to where it would lead us and in looking back over that period I am stunned at how one aspect of mind science led into another and how they all interrelated to produce a literal Pandora's-box of commercially applicable mind-science techniques.

In the earlier stages of the research we were publishing our ongoing results in the form of reports which were sold to a private subscription-only international customer base. We were operating in a small town near the eastern Australian seaboard but as various religious cults became aware of what we were doing they felt threatened and we received several serious death threats. We elected to move from Australia to nearby New Zealand and then on to another adjoining country.

The main problem we had at the time was in obtaining up-to-date information on overseas mind-power research. This was before the Internet and we had to rely on tracking down printed materials by mail, much of which was already out of date. As such we were fairly isolated and evolved our own particular research protocols and techniques. It was probably due to this forced innovative approach that we were able to obtain the results we did.

Advanced mind technology brings with it a need for responsibility and fair play.

I have observed that those who misuse these techniques tend to come unstuck, sometimes in quite a nasty way. There is an old saying "what goes around comes around" and this is particularly true when it comes to manipulative mental applications.

The idea behind this book is to supply mental tools that can be used to provide yourself and those you care about with a richer and more satisfying life. The ability to intentionally evoke your natural intuition and to remote view gives you tools that could prove incredibly useful in your future.

The remote viewing training course provided in this book is designed to provoke your interest and if you elect to pursue this subject further there are more elaborate commercial interactive training courses available, both for home study and in a teacher/student environment.

The real beauty about becoming involved in this new technology is that it will cost you nothing for hardware. You do not have to buy a computer or set up an expensive laboratory. You already possess all the equipment you need....your mind! In fact for many readers the total financial outlay will be the cost of this book!

However once you make a decision to learn one of the disciplines detailed in this book then you will have to persevere with the necessary practice and this, for many individuals will be hard to do. Fortunately that strange human ability known as the "novice effect" will probably manifest itself and you may have outstanding results on your first try.

Of all the disciplines explained between these covers Subjective Communication is probably the most rewarding to start with. There is no training required and providing you follow the instructions you should experience positive results the first time you apply the process.

Another easy-to-learn process is dream control. You can basically program up a specific dream to solve any problem. Newcomers often find this simple process quite stunning!

Perhaps the most difficult of the disciplines for beginners is the autonomous thumb twitch in the Mental Pendulum program. A few may "get it" almost immediately but for most it will require dedicated training. However the rewards associated with having your intuition available on demand will make it all worthwhile.

It is also highly satisfying for business individuals to be able to solve problems via dream control and inspiration. Business people applying the psychokinetic problem solving techniques might be amazed at the difference it makes and the sense of personal awe it evokes. After a while you realise that there is no problem that you cannot solve and this in itself imparts a feeling of supreme confidence in ones abilities.

The most nebulous of the concepts in this book is the psychokinetic luck program. Luck at the best of times is something that we normally accept as having....or not having. Most individuals realise that occasionally they have bursts of luck which usually makes them feel quite good about life in general and virtually every sane living individual would like to have more "good luck".

We have concluded that luck is *your personal psychokinetic resonance with your environment* and under various circumstances this resonance can be intentionally modified.

Likewise at times luck cycles can be plotted. Our research indicates that at any point the human mind is capable of altering this *resonance with the environment* to produce bursts of either bad or good "luck". We consider this to be quite a profound "discovery" and the implications are interesting, to say the least.

But this program is nebulous and tricky so it is important to follow the instructions carefully and not overdo your own experiments. If you are using your hard-earned cash in a gambling environment then be sensible and do not get carried away. You may experience a few spectacular wins but unless you are careful these could be followed by spectacular losses!

If you are using this **PK Luck** program for gambling then it is vital that you work to a specific financial plan. If necessary write this plan down before you enter the gambling environment and stick ruthlessly to it, no matter what happens. If you have a major run of "luck" be very aware of when this cycle starts to drop off. When you stop winning then walk away and try again another day. The idea is to take your winnings home with you.

The biggest problem you will have with these leading-edge mind techniques is your own belief system. Unfortunately your current belief system has probably evolved from what your parents and peer group members believe and when you think about it they probably obtained their belief system from their parents and peer groups. In fact the average person may well discover that their basic belief system has evolved from what their grandparents thought!

That is your current belief system may have been influenced considerably by what people believed to be *fact* several generations ago.

The facts remain the same but it is the "belief about the facts" that is modified from generation to generation.

Around 100 years ago it was considered a "fact" that heavier-than-air flight was impossible. The fact is that it was possible, but the belief about the facts in that era was faulty.

It is the same with mind-power technology to day. A fair percentage of the population "know for sure" that remote viewing cannot be possible but when these very same individuals are forced to examine the facts then they can only conclude that it is not only possible but actually works quite well.

There are those in our society who have a natural curiosity about new things but unfortunately there is a very high percentage who find new exploratory concepts outside their personal comfort zone. To many people consciousness is a bore and they would rather put it "on hold" while they watch the latest TV soap program. Under these circumstances they are floating along in a daydream state and are quite happy about this state of affairs.

But there are others who seek conscious stimulation and who will sometimes go to great lengths to attain new knowledge.

It is likely that you are one of these people!

May the psychokinetic forces be with you!

1

THE HIDDEN SECRETS OF
MIND POWER TECHNOLOGY

MY NAME IS JAMES COYLE.

I am about to explain the results of a research program that you might find astounding....or ridiculous....depending upon your own personal belief system.

What I would like to point out right at the start is that this project cost many hundreds of thousands of dollars and was funded by intelligent, serious business individuals. The only reason they kept the funds rolling for so many years was because the project was producing results.

Admittedly several of these people dropped out....they simply could not handle the implications of an individual being able to identify and change their own natural luck....and worse still......intentionally influencing people and events to produce extraordinary windfall situations.

Another developed religious conflicts about our developing a fully working 6th sense intuition process, which could be learned by any average individual. He felt that the 6th sense should remain "mysterious" and should not be able to be evoked at will.

But the majority of the investors remained involved with us and in the final analysis were very glad they did.

Let me start at the beginning so you can understand how this research effort evolved.

As a child I slowly became aware that I had strange mental abilities which other children didn't appear to have. For a start, I was always finding money on the ground. The strange thing was dozens of people might have walked over this ground before me yet I was the only one to actually see the money. It was usually always coins, not paper money. I regularly found florins and half-crowns which, in those days, were the largest denomination coins in New Zealand. A half-crown was 2 shillings and 6 pence and there were 20 shillings in a pound. I recall my father used to earn 7 pounds a week in those times so a half crown was a goodly sum of money for a youngster.

I used to go and stay with a couple of old spinster aunties during school holidays and this constant discovery of coins used to amaze them.

At one point I remember one of them commenting that I must be creating the money out of thin air.

This comment had quite a profound effect on me and I have remembered it all my adult life. It would explain a number of very unusual events that have happened over the past few years, whereby in a moment of quiet desperation material objects just seemed to have appeared....out of thin air. I will cover these later.

I also noticed as a youngster that I could influence the behaviour of adults to a degree that other children could not manage. It was almost as if I was using a mild form of hypnosis to influence older people. I eventually became fascinated with the subject of hypnosis and learnt to hypnotise my classmates when I was 13 years old. This almost got me expelled from the school. At the age of 18 I was an amateur stage hypnotist and was putting on shows around the Wellington (NZ) area where I lived.

The usual procedure was to have 5-6 hypnotised subjects sitting on chairs on the stage. I would then give them either individual instructions or occasionally give them a mass instruction....such as "everyone stand up". Very occasionally the subjects would suddenly stand up as I formed the instruction in my mind.....but just before I uttered it out loud. This happened often enough for me to realise that I was projecting my thoughts at these people....and they were receiving and reacting to it. The implications of this dawned on me slowly. It wasn't until I got into serious mind-power research that I recalled these incidents and started to work on the concept of remote influencing.

In 1985 I started a business which marketed the Australasian Lateral Thinking newsletter which produced creative concepts and taught its subscribers the protocol required to produce intuitive lateral concepts. I had personally been instructed in these by the creator of lateral thinking Dr. Edward DeBono.

Around about 1993 one of my staff members drew my attention to the research on psychokinetics and remote viewing that was being done by the PEAR laboratory at Princeton University. For some reason this struck a resonant chord with me and I decided to start a small research project to see if the applications of specific mind power techniques could be used by my newsletter subscribers.

The direction that this research took rather astounded us. We became involved not only in the investigation of PK (psychokinetics) and remote viewing, but also in remote influencing, altered consciousness and brain frequency states.

One thing more or less led to another.

At that point I decided to take a Silva Mind course then followed that by a trip to the Gateway program at the Monroe Institute in Virginia, U.S.A.

Both of these experiences combined to produce an awareness of what a human mind might be capable of.

But it wasn't until I flew from Australia to Las Vegas to do a basic remote viewing course with the well known remote viewer Angela Thompson, that the penny dropped.

The human mind was capable of vastly more then even I ever suspected.

Then the results of the U.S.Government military remote viewing program became public knowledge. What this team of dedicated people at Ft. Meade had discovered was nothing short of incredible.

Basically after 20 odd years of experimentation they uncovered an extraordinary human potential ability which can be summed up as follows:

When a trained individual relaxes into a meditative state, then focuses his or her thoughts on a specific geographically distant target, they tend to mentally lock on to it, as if they were being reliably connected by a universal telephone exchange.

They can then "sense" information about this target with an accuracy that sometimes takes the breath away.

But that is nothing compared to what they subsequently discovered.

They found that they could also access the same target in the past or in the future. There is no time zone at all when retrieving psychic information.

But even more startling is the fact that they did not have to know what the target was. They had only to work off a random group of numbers that had been "mentally attached" to that specific target by the tasker who had organised that particular remote viewing session.

That is, in the tasker's mind a specific group of numbers related only to the target in question.

The whole process was based on "Intent"

The remote viewer was then given that group of numbers....nothing else......and usually managed to access the correct target. The "universal coordinates" provided as a group of mentally attached numbers was sufficient to tag that particular target, sometimes with unnerving accuracy.

The implications of this mental process are enormous.

Further, the remote viewer sometimes connected with the target so well that he or she felt they were actually at the scene. That is, they could feel the wind, detect the smells, sense the emotions, etc. This became known as "bilocation" whereby the remote viewer appeared to have most of his or her senses located at the actual site.

As this formerly secret military knowledge slowly became public, various groups of fascinated individuals started Internet newsgroups and around late 1997 several experienced individuals started giving remote viewing training.

My research group became involved with this field in late 1994 when there was no instructional material available. We carried out all sorts of experiments and concluded that it definitely worked, but was not consistent.

It was also during this time that we discovered that luck cycles appeared to be a personal psychokinetic events and we were able to develop methods not only to track these luck cycles, but under certain circumstances to enhance them.

Later chapters explain precisely how this is done.

This was all new knowledge. There appeared to be no one anywhere researching this field.

As our research efforts evolved we presented our findings in the form of written reports which were sold to our subscriber base. We found that our members had a very high interest level in our discoveries and we were able to sell enough reports over the years to partially finance our mental exploration program. Investor funds from various business people kept our working capital topped up.

We ascertained that there appeared to be a direct subconscious mental connection at all times between individuals and this explained why a friend might call on the telephone just as you were thinking of them.

Research at one overseas laboratory found that if you happen to start thinking intently about a distant individual, then under certain circumstances that individual's blood pressure will change measurably. This can only occur if a mental connection exists between the two parties.

Further, the military remote viewers found that if they had two or three remote viewers "working" the same target simultaneously then a "telepathic overlay" could occur, whereby one of the remote viewers would erroneously described a target....and the other remote viewers would immediately describe the exact same target...which happened to be the wrong target anyway.

We struck this problem in our own remote viewing experiments when we had several people working the same target at the same time. It was genuine proof that a telepathic connection can exist between individuals.

What I am saying here is that there is enough scattered evidence like this to indicate that not only are individuals in subconscious mental contact, but also under some circumstances they can establish conscious mental contact.

Any mother who has had a sudden strong intuitional hunch that her child is in danger will understand exactly what I am talking about. There is a direct mental connection between the sibling and its' mother. Under times of stress and dire necessity this mental connection "kicks in".

What the remote viewers have found is that there is no need for a "dire necessity" situation to be present. This natural mental ability can be evoked at will after suitable training.

There are rare individuals for whom this is a natural talent, but because it appears to be an inherent latent ability built into all of us then it is considered that the vast majority of people on this planet could learn this procedure.....providing they had the interest and the belief system.

Under normal circumstances when a remote viewer locks on to a target the input "signal" from the target is buried in mental background "noise". The procedures that have been developed tend to raise the strength of the signal above the noise level so it can be mentally processed and decoded.

Under situations of dire need the signal appears to automatically break through this noise threshold so that it appears as a strong "knowing" in the person's conscious mind.

There appears to be an inherent human ability to set up a conscious mental connection with another person...or group of people. Knowing this it becomes easy to see how, under the right circumstances, an individual can project a strong focussed thought which impinges upon the other person's subconscious mind and can be easily designed to influence their behaviour in a mild manner.

This is called Subjective Communication and is covered in a later chapter.

This process is probably the easiest of all mind-power techniques to learn and has been used by rank beginners with sometimes stunning success.

One of our lady subscribers had been trying to sell her house for two years with absolutely no luck. After the Subjective Communication process was explained to her she was totally stunned to find that it worked so well that she had her house under contract of sale within 5 days, at a higher price than she expected!

I have heard this literally dozens of times from people who had absolutely no knowledge of mind power, but who were open-minded enough to give it a try.

As our research progressed, I became fascinated with the potential ability of the mind to either influence, or share information with, both micro and macro systems.

The term "micro PK" refers to the apparent influence of the mind over atomic structures too small for the naked eye to detect. Macro PK refers to apparent psychokinetic events that can be observed visually.

The majority of recent experiments in this field have utilised an electronic device known as a random number generator or RNG. This device has also been referred to as a random event generator. This mechanism produces a series of rapid yes/no, or on/off pulses and can be likened to rapidly spinning a coin in the air, several thousand times a second, and seeing whether it comes down heads or tails. The random number generator can therefore be considered as a high speed electronic coin flipping mechanism.

A fair percentage of PK experiments are based on influencing the pulse output of this random number device in an attempt to produce either a higher than average number of "heads"...or alternatively a higher number of "tails".

I originally set out to build one of these devices but found problems in finding simple electronic circuitry that produced truly random results.

Then during a trip to Las Vegas I picked up a book describing the inner workings of slot machines and realised that all slot machines have such circuitry all ready built in. In fact, the random on/off pulses are the very basis of the slot machine operation.

With this knowledge I decided to do a series of experiments using slot machines to see if PK could affect the outcome. I reasoned that if it could then the results would be immediately apparent in the form of winnings.

To say this was a success would be a gross understatement. Over the first 5 years I personally won more than 130 individual jackpots on slot machines. Most of these were small but there were several larger ones that created a profound impact on my rather skeptical belief system. Details as to how this was achieved are covered in later chapters.

On one particular occasion I was sitting in a casino with a lady client. She had just undergone some remote viewing training and had a fairly open frame of mind, due to her remote viewing successes.

She asked if I could demonstrate how this PK influencing worked. Well, this was some challenge. Here I was sitting in front of a slot machine which had a small $310 jackpot available (it was a small 5 cent machine) and I was being asked to "put my money where my mouth was".

I did a really deep PK focus and mentally blasted a burst of energy at the machine. I put in a coin and stabbed the spin button. To her total surprise (but not entirely to mine) the five winning symbols appeared in one of the paylines and the jackpot light flashed on the machine. I had won this small jackpot. To say that this client was impressed was a major understatement.

I concluded that my success in this case was due to the mental energy burst and also the <u>necessity for a PK event to happen</u>.

There were a couple of occasions when extraordinary PK events appeared to manifest themselves which reminded me of all those coins that mysteriously appeared when I was a child.

On one occasion I was playing slots in a large casino and had the feeling that I was somewhat "divorced" from all that was going on around me. That is, I was aware that I was in a different consciousness state. The machines were paying me brilliantly and all of a sudden I won a $3000 jackpot. I collected that and felt as if I was mentally floating on air.

I decided to take a rest for a while and went up to my hotel room in the casino to freshen up. I decided to change my trousers and shirt and returned to the casino. I converted a $100 note into 100 single dollar coins at the cash cage and proceeded to play the same bank of machines. So there I was with a plastic bucket half full of coins ready to fire up again. I put 3 of these coins into a slot machine that "looked friendly" and stabbed the button. (These machines required three dollars a spin to cover all three of the payout lines effectively).

Bingo! Another $800 jackpot on the third spin! As usual the machine locked up and couldn't be played until the attendant had processed the jackpot and released the machine for further play.

I pressed the call button which would attract one of the roving attendants and while I was waiting decided to light up a small cigar to celebrate. I had the packet of cigars in my shirt pocket but could not find my lighter. Suddenly I realised that I had left it in my other trousers.

There I was, with a cigarillo in my mouth, no lighter and I could not leave the machine to buy one. Worse still, as it was early morning there were no other players in sight that I could have borrowed a lighter from. My girlfriend at the time was standing near me and I commented that I had left my lighter upstairs. She looked at me strangely and said...."you've got a lighter on top of your coins". I looked down into the coin bucket which I was holding in my right hand and sure enough, there was a lighter. I picked it up and lit my cigarillo.

I was stunned. It was not my lighter. It was a very small ladies one and colored black. I don't buy black lighters as they camouflage themselves too well and can't easily be seen. Also I don't buy the small ones as they don't last long enough.

I looked around me to see where this object could have come from. I then asked my girlfriend if she had put it there as a practical joke. She looked somewhat offended and commented that I had probably materialised it as usual. I queried her on this comment and she said that since we had first met I always appeared to have things materialise just when I needed them the most.

This young lady was Chinese and had a deep inherent belief in mind events. I concluded there and then that this lighter had indeed materialised "out of thin air". In a discussion with my lady friend later it transpired that she had noticed this sort of thing happen often in my presence. She had always assumed that I was aware of these events but somehow they had escaped my notice.

The other PK event which really shook me to the core happened in yet another casino.

It was early on a Sunday morning and I had converted a $50 note into dollar coins. I was wandering around banks of $1 machines putting a coin in here and there but having no payouts whatsoever. I must have been doing this for 30 minutes or so when suddenly a realisation hit that stopped me in my tracks. The coin bucket was as full as when I started play, yet I had had no wins at all and had not put any coins back into the bucket. I was extremely puzzled.

The bucket should have emptied itself within 8-10 minutes.

I continued to play and sure enough, within less than 10 minutes the bucket was empty.

I went and had a coffee and ran all this through my mind. Maybe I had made a mistake and had bought another batch of coins. Maybe I had had a payout that had slipped my mind.

If so I couldn't remember either event and I put the whole thing down to one of life's
mysteries.

Another such event happened during a trip up a beach in my new 4WD vehicle. I had topped the petrol tank up before driving onto the beach as petrol consumption can be quite severe if the tide was in and I had to travel on soft sand. I spent the morning travelling to the top of the beach and then as the tide came in decided to travel back to a spot I had selected as a nice place to camp overnight. However the 30 mile trip back was second gear most of the way due to the tide.

By the time I had reached the camping spot I was seriously low on petrol. The petrol gauge was on empty. I figured I didn't have enough fuel to get back to the gas station at the entrance to the beach. I went to sleep that night worrying about this fuel situation. When I started the car the next morning I was puzzled to see that the petrol gauge indicated a full tank. As it was a new car I figured the gauge was playing up. I knew I had used a full tank of gas the day before and quite stupidly had forgotten to bring a spare container of gas on the trip.

With some trepidation I started a slow fuel-saving trip back down the beach and to my utter relief made it to the gas station without the engine stopping.

I inserted the gas pump nozzle into my fuel tank and started pumping. To my total astonishment the tank accepted only $4 worth of petrol....it should have accepted at least $30 worth.

It was clearly obvious that the tank was indeed full.

Now this actually shook me very badly indeed. It is one thing to have a small cigarette lighter appear but a totally different thing to have a full tank of petrol materialise.

As I had been parked overnight by myself, with no other human being within a couple of miles, I had to discount the idea of some kind good samaritan playing a prank on me. I suppose an airforce tanker aircraft could have quietly landed on the beach during the night and refueled my car, but if so I didn't notice it!

To this day, the episode remains a mystery and I shall leave it as such. I am simply not prepared to draw any conclusions.

Some time in 1996 I was invited to a "PK Party" in Menlo Park, California, run by an aeronautical engineer by the name of Jack Houcke. Now Jack has fairly impeccable credentials as a serious high-tech aerospace engineer, so I decided to accept this invitation.

But I should point out that I was somewhat skeptical.

There were about 60 people present of whom some were obviously profound skeptics.

The evening got underway with a preamble from Jack on what this was all about.

One of the lady skeptics who was seated next to me, was interjecting with under-breath acidic comments and obviously thought the whole thing was a waste of her time.

The procedure started and everyone produced their balls of mental energy and fed it into the spoon or fork they were holding. Within seconds there was a shriek from across the room. One of the younger participants had found his spoon significantly bending.

It was a "sharp" bend also, as if it had been hit by a blow-torch.

Immediately after that there was a chorus of excited exclamations around the room as others had success. I personally had no success at that point.

But the skeptical lady sitting next to me had her fork all curled up and bent sharply in several places. By the end of the evening a good 60% of the participants had successfully bent something and as for the lady skeptic....well.....she was sitting on the carpet with a dazed look on her face.... surrounded by at least a dozen items she had bent by mind-power.

The whole evening has stuck in my mind as an exercise in developing a common-consciousness emotional event designed to trigger macro psychokinetic events.

Since then I have been to several other PK parties, all highly successful. I attended one in Australia where of the 28 people present, 26 had success. One gentleman who was happy to admit that he was a professional skeptic (his wife had dragged him along) was so successful that he bent a thick iron bar to an acute angle. This bar was too strong to be bent even by maximum physical force over his knee....he had tried this earlier.

The look on his face when this happened caused considerable hilarity in the room.

In talking to him afterwards he told me that he didn't actually believe what happened, but he didn't know how to explain it either. In fact, he didn't really want to discuss it at all.

Like many others who are confronted with the unknown, he will probably block this experience out of his conscious memory and never refer to it again.

Another unusual event in a totally different area happened while I was doing the original remote viewing training course with Angela Thompson in Las Vegas.

Angela was doing an individual exercise with each of the participants which was designed to set up an altered consciousness scenario that gave the participant a glimpse of his or her previous lives.

I was lying flat on the thick carpet with a pillow under my head and some sort of drumming sound was being played on the cassette player.

I was in a deep meditative state (somewhere in the theta brainwave range) and was being "talked" back in time by Angela.

I described what I could sense which was a moving image of myself leading a donkey across the sand toward a large pyramid shaped structure. A lady, presumably my wife, was following with her donkey. Suddenly without warning the ground opened beneath my feet and the donkey and I started to tumble. At this point my body jerked so violently it startled Angela and the other students and I was immediately wide awake, shaking and perspiring.

This had been a very real experience and almost verged on the "bilocation" phenomena that remote viewers talk about.

This experience convinced me that our past lives are accessible, providing the right information-retrieval technique is used. Others in this seminar had similar experiences but I had apparently produced the most dramatic reaction.

At another point I was doing a controlled remote viewing training course with an ex US army military remote viewing instructor.

He gave me a set of 8 numbers he had chosen at random to represent the remote viewing coordinates of a specific target. He had a picture of this target pinned up on a blackboard facing away from me, so I could not see it.

He asked me to commence the procedure following the Controlled Remote Viewing protocol he had taught the class.

I sensed a wide open area and then a rock structure with an unusual shape. After a period of time this rock slowly transformed into a large rock archway through which people could walk.

I also developed a clear mental picture of some traditional Indians in the background, mounted on horses.

At this point he asked me to describe the surrounding scenery. I replied that I saw lots of cacti plants and that there was a large amount of pollen in the air. Suddenly I came out of my remote viewing state to a violent fit of sneezing. This went on for several minutes and I couldn't recall ever having had a sneezing attack like this.

When it was all over and we were able to discuss the reaction, it was concluded that I had remote viewed the correct target several hundred years in the past and had effectively bilocated to the point where the pollen in the atmosphere had severely affected my sinuses. Well, maybe I didn't actually bilocate, but my nostrils certainly did!

When remote viewing targets like this, it is important that "present time" be specified, otherwise the remote viewer can end up in the past or maybe even the future.

And the strange thing is that 5 years earlier, as a serious no-nonsense businessman, I would never have seriously entertained the idea of dabbling in psychokinetics or this new field of human awareness, called remote viewing. The whole lot sort of crept up on me. I guess my original background of hypnosis left a few mental channels open over the years.

I'm very glad it did!

A whole new world of personal mental manipulation has opened up.... something that would not have happened if I had retained my earlier skepticism.

The most important aspect of all this however, is that I have been able to use these "new found" mental abilities to enhance both my financial situation....and my lifestyle.

I can now remote view potential business decisions to see the likely outcome and find that these days there are few problems arising that cannot be handled, without all the stress and frustration that used to occur. Business orientated individuals reading this will easily recognise the significance of what they have read so far.

To round out this chapter I will now explain our research results on the human alpha/theta/delta states generally known as the "mind-awake-body-asleep" states.

ALPHA / THETA / DELTA RESEARCH

It is now generally accepted that the daydream, or alpha state opens up intuitive channels in the mind. Hunches and inspirations often come from this relaxed mind state. Under normal waking circumstances the brain tends to tick over in the wide-awake beta state which is an electrical frequency of 14 cycles per second and above.

When we mentally relax our dominant brain frequency can drop to between 7 and 13 cycles per second, which is regarded as the alpha state. This can happen while we are taking a shower, meditating, driving a car, etc.

Our research group explored this mind state and then proceeded to investigate the lower brain frequency range of theta, which is generally acknowledged as producing brain frequencies of 3-7 cycles per second.

Methods have been discovered whereby it is possible to intentionally induce this frequency range, while simultaneously maintaining a wide awake beta state. The human mind, after suitable training, can operate in both frequency bands at once. The theta condition is usually regarded as a light sleep state. While in this state, you can be lightly snoring but still have full consciousness of what is going on around you.

You might recall the odd occasion where you are lying in bed on a Sunday morning and having had a full night's sleep don't feel like moving. Maybe the sounds of rain on the roof have lulled you into a sleep/awake state and your muscles feel too relaxed to move. You are on the verge of sleep but are also alert and you probably feel delightfully relaxed. Under these conditions it is highly likely that you are in a mild theta state. So you can now understand why meditation enthusiasts are keen on developing the ability to induce this magical relaxed state at will.

Once this dual theta/beta mental condition is achieved the practitioner can use the conscious portion of their mind to give themselves deep mental reprogramming instructions. Rather like being your own hypnotist.

We experimented at length with theta and found it particularly effective while practicing remote viewing.

The lowest brain frequency state is the delta range. This basically covers from 3 cycles per second down to less than one cycle.

It actually took me 10 constant years of daily practice to be able to achieve a mind-awake-body-asleep state in the dual delta/beta range.

I used an expensive twin channel 5 electrode EEG machine to determine that I was predominantly operating at 2 cycles per second, which is about the middle of the delta range.

That was several years ago. Since then I have been doing experiments in very deep delta and a situation arose that was potentially quite dangerous. My health started to fail and various other side effects appeared. I suspected they might be caused by all the delta practice. I had a remote view done on my condition and I was told quite bluntly to take a long break from everything for several months, otherwise I might not be here to enjoy the rest of my natural life.

I took this warning seriously and apart from having a holiday, left delta practice entirely alone for 5 months.

The only drawback with the delta state is that when I come out of it I feel so incredibly alive that it is a definite encouragement to keep practicing it.

In the lowest ranges of delta it is difficult to move the body muscles and I have found that it is far easier to give my muscles a firm instruction to move, similar to a personal hypnotic command.

The problem is there is very little public data available about this state and as very few people have ever learned to access this dual delta/beta state, then feedback from other practitioners is generally not available.

The Monroe Institute, located in Faber, Virginia, has apparently been able to access this range but multiple differential audio trigger tones are required. That is, an audio/electronic aid is used.

The type of delta work we are doing requires no aids....merely the dedicated personal intent to achieve increasingly lower brain frequencies.

The ultimate aim here is to eventually install a self post-hypnotic command that will trigger this delta state directly from wide-awake beta.

We are starting to have some success in this direction.

However, I would like to caution my readers here and suggest that if you are experimenting with delta, you watch carefully for any signs of confusion, excessive tiredness or physical disorientation.

If any of these conditions appear, then give the process a rest for some weeks.

Some individuals hold the belief that a lowered brainwave state is the same as a shift in consciousness. This is, in general, incorrect.

If an EEG brainwave machine is attached to a subject who is then hypnotised, the machine often records no shift in brain frequency patterns.

The conclusion here is that lowered brain frequency states and shifts in consciousness are basically two different animals, but there will obviously be instances where a combination of both is present.

I would think that it will take our research group at least another 5 years to fully explore the delta state and even then we may find that we are only scratching the surface.

To sum up, the mind-awake-body-asleep state of alpha is fairly easy to learn. An instructional chapter later in this book explains how to make your own alpha inducing cassette tape.

The everyday advantages in being able to take a few quiet moments to drop to the alpha state will provide an instant recharge to your over-stressed system and can make daily activities far more manageable. A brief 10 minute alpha session can have the same beneficial effect as a 45 minute nap. Also in the alpha state you are liable to get spontaneous answers to current problems.......sort of inspirational flashes. There is no danger at all in using alpha at will, because you usually drop into this state "accidentally" dozens of times a day.

The simple process of alpha tends to induce a feeling of serenity and most people find this sensation highly rewarding.

Alpha is a safe natural state....theta requires some caution as you can inadvertently reprogram yourself....and delta is highly experimental.

I had a classic example of how effective the alpha/theta state was during a mental communication exercise recently with Dolphins around the big Island of Hawaii.

A whole team of us were in the water trying to attract a shoal of these magnificent creatures. We were having no luck at all as they would not approach us. I was floating in the water with a face mask and snorkel, feeling totally relaxed. The sun's rays were reflecting off the white sandy bottom about 40 feet below and the effect was almost hypnotic. I did a simple mental exercise that quickly caused my brain waves to drop to the alpha/theta region. As I felt the familiar theta relaxation wash over my body I started "sending" a mental picture to a dolphin pod only just discernible near the bottom. A few seconds later I was jolted wide awake by the immediate presence of three of these beautiful adult creatures, plus a calf. They swam past, slowly circled then descended back to the bottom. I was so overawed I almost forgot I had an underwater camera but I managed to capture 3 quick close-up shots before they swam away.

These pictures turned out beautifully and I shall treasure them as a classic example of direct mind-to-mind communication. This experience had a profound effect on me, as it would on any individual who was able to mentally communicate with another species. I'm told that dolphins are quite telepathic which would explain why they were able to receive my focused picture. The act of sending thoughts telepathically falls under the technique known as Subjective Communication and you will learn how to use this mind communication technique later in this book.

Our research has uncovered just how useful some of these mind disciplines can be in everyday life and the following chapters are devoted to sharing this knowledge with you.

Several of the programs featured in this book require the reader to produce a simple cassette tape by reading a short script onto a tape machine or Dictaphone. This cassette is then normally played back at night after retiring to bed. You can also use the audio program in a computer and add a small echo/reverberation effect, which appears to enhance the effectiveness of the message.

We discovered quite accidentally that if echo or reverberation is added to the tape then the message appears to have a more profound effect upon the mind. You might remember a situation where you were either woken from a sleep by a voice calling you or somebody spoke to you just as you were on the verge of sleep. On either occasion you may recall that the voice appeared to originate from far away, almost from the depths of a cavern. Your consciousness had trouble grasping on to this disturbance, as it appeared to reverberate up from a vast distance.

It is for this reason we think the human mind *equates a shift of consciousness with reverberation,* which is a deep smooth echo effect.

When you play a cassette message as you are drifting off to sleep any reverberation effect on the message appears to assist in the smooth transition of consciousness states. Our conclusion is that echo or reverberation on a message of this type is of considerable assistance in inducing an altered consciousness state. Details about how to achieve this echo effect are given in the appropriate chapters.

2

THE SPECTACULAR WORLD OF 21ST CENTURY MIND SCIENCE

In the same manner that it is not necessary to understand the technology behind a VCR or TV to be able to use them, so it is with the technology of mind-power.

Some of the advanced research institutions are starting to "suspect" how it works ...... it appears likely that the explanation will lie in the realms of Quantum Physics or Superstring theory.

But it is not necessary to understand - or even comprehend - this Einsteinien science to be able to use recently discovered advances in mind-power knowledge for your personal advantage.

In the same way that micro-electronics evolved from a couple of significant discoveries in Silicon Valley some 30 years ago, so it is with mind-power research.

There are now isolated scientific organizations all over the world doing research in this direction. At one point, in recent history the second highest portion of the Soviet budget was for mind-power research.

And the western world is fast catching up, because of the technical disciplined procedures and protocols being incorporated into the research methods.

This book gives an indication of what is now not only possible, but also what is now being used commercially.

WHERE IS MIND-POWER RESEARCH LEADING?

Most of it is aimed at isolating and controlling at will, our 6th sense: **intuition.**

Let me explain. We have all been brought up to trust our 5 normal senses - **sight, touch, taste, hearing and smell.**

But ..... any single one of these senses can be tricked! That is, under certain circumstance, they are not accurate. We normally trust our sense of sight because when we observe something with our eyes we know it to be true. However, a good magician can totally trick our sense of sight and what we <u>absolutely believe</u> we are seeing can be 100% wrong!

Likewise under hypnosis we can be made to see things that just don't exist.

For example, if somebody opens a jar of Vegemite and places it on a table before us, we can detect exactly what it is by using one or more of our 5 senses.

However if somebody placed the same open jar of Vegemite in another room and asked us to "intuitively guess" what was on the table in the other room, our chances of getting it right would probably be less than 1 in 10,000 ..... **under normal circumstances!!**

And this is where mind-power training comes to the fore via the Princeton University and Stanford Research Institute <u>remote viewing processes.</u>

People who have trained in intuitive remote viewing, would have better than a 50/50 chance of "guessing" that the object was indeed an open vegemite jar.

This 6th sense ..... **intuition** ..... is available to <u>all of us</u> but we have <u>never been trained to use it.</u>

This is what the commercial mind courses touch upon. They <u>make you aware </u>that your intuition can not only be trained ..... but can be **relied upon!** A recent survey of the top executives in the large American Fortune 500 companies revealed that almost without exception they had a highly developed 6th sense. (Intuition is measurable).

This intuition, or the ability of your subconscious mind to "know" something which is undetectable via your normal 5 senses, can also be taught to manifest itself via your nervous system. The term "gut feeling" is an example of your nervous system giving you a message from your subconscious mind.

The method that has been used for thousands of years and which is now exploding in popularity is the use of "dowsing" via a pendulum or divining rod. This is what water diviners use and a good diviner has a 90% success rate. The chance of the average person walking over a paddock and correctly "guessing" where the water is, at what depth it is, what the flow rate will be and how potable it will be is round about one chance in 20,000.

What these dowsing devices do is to convert a subconscious response via the nervous system into a hand "twitch" or similar involuntary movement. This "twitch" directs the pendulum or divining rod. Many top American businessmen and women have now learnt to use a pendulum as a **back-up** for intuitive answers. So instead of having the occasional involuntary "gut feeling" the same nervous response can be induced at will ..... **when required!** The accuracy of a pendulum when providing intuitive answers can be better than 80% which is about all we can realistically expect from any of our other 5 senses, when you think about it.

In other words, the scientific research into intuition has now reached a point where the average person can not only learn it .... but reliably use it!

The personal benefit of being able to induce triggerable and accurate "hunches" at will is absolutely enormous!

Also the intuitive side of ourselves, via the simple pendulum, is being increasingly used to locate and identify health problems, such as specific vitamin or mineral deficiencies. This intuitive business is merely one aspect of personal mind power. Another side is the psychokinetic control of our interaction with the environment ..... better known as luck!

Let us revert back to one of the most useful aspects of personal mind-power - **intuition.**

Imagine this scenario:

Since birth you have been blind.

You have never had the use of your sight during your entire life. Your total existence and interaction with reality around you has been restricted to only 4 of your 5 senses. But you cope well with this because you have never experienced anything better.

Then one morning you wake up and suddenly, you can see!! A whole new world of experience has opened up. Your 5th sense is now working as it was intended to!

For months, you are totally overawed by your new ability,

New dimensions are now available to you ..... **for the first time in your life!!**

NOW IMAGINE **THIS** SCENARIO - All your life you have been restricted to the use of <u>only 5</u> of your 6 available senses and suddenly you wake up one morning with the full use of your 6th sense ..... **intuition!**

The effect on your life will be about the same as suddenly gaining full vision!!!!!

After you have experienced the magic of your 6th sense for a couple of months you wonder how you ever got along in the world without it.

With this new-found 6th sense you find amazing things happen. For example, you suddenly develop the "urge" to go down to the local news-agency and buy a $1 scratch-it lotto ticket.

And ..... you find you have won the first prize of $25,000.

Or take the case of the Perth businessman (interviewed on a national TV program some years ago) who dreamt in <u>3 separate dreams</u> that he was going to win an overseas trip being offered as a prize by a local Perth Radio Station. He not only renewed his passport and told all his associates that he was going to win this trip but he arranged a baby-sitter in advance.

This was <u>before </u>the prize was drawn.

To everyone's total amazement (but not his) he won the trip! The radio announcer, his wife, and various associates were interviewed on this Australian made documentary - it was a 100% genuine case of highly accurate intuition.

Once you start getting your 6th sense to work for you, a strange thing happens ..... you always seem to be in the right place at the right time. It seems to manifest itself in the form of "urges". If you listen to these, good things seem to happen. Also a side effect of training your intuition to work is that you seem to have the occasional dream which is so strong that you can remember it for weeks afterwards and it seems to be directing you towards a certain course of action. One of the more amazing aspects of the Silva Mind Course for example, is the way they teach you to program up the dreams you want .....and then actually remember them.

When I have a business problem I simply program up a dream that will provide an answer. It never fails and I've been doing it for years. What happens is that you program your intuition, while in an alpha state, to supply an answer. It is yet another way to make your intuition work for you!

This intuition ability is incredibly handy. Imagine being able to walk into a casino and after looking at some of the poker machines, develop the feeling that one specific machine is just right for you. And you walk out with $500 in your pocket!

It works!

There are many other aspects to the use of the right-hemisphere intuitive brain including subjective communication. Intuition is tied in directly with our right-hemisphere brain that seems to be responsible for our 6th sense. The problem is that our entire society and education is geared to training and encouraging us to use our left-hemisphere brain. The normal schooling system does not teach us specifically to use our intuitive brain. However, it must be remembered, when talking about left and right-hemisphere brain activities, that these are generalisations. We use our whole brain, but some activities utilise more of one brain hemisphere, than the other.

This "intuition" ability of ours can be put to use in the form of **remote viewing**. You will hear a lot about this over the coming years.

Basically remote viewing involves a person closing their eyes, relaxing and visualizing a specific scene some distance away.

They are then read out a checklist and are asked to verbally identify a number of aspects of the pictures they are "seeing".

For example they are asked: *are there any trees ...... any animals ...... any water ...... any power lines ...... etc.* All these items are then correlated to produce a final "score". Amazingly enough after a little practice the <u>average</u>

person can identify up to 70-80% of these points accurately and geographical distance appears to present no complication.

Any situation, anywhere on or *off* the planet can be remote viewed.

Also the "viewing" can be done **precognitively!** That is, the viewer can see some scenes that will take place some days ahead! He or she "sees" them before they happen. Likewise the past can be remote viewed.

At least one group in the States used remote viewing commercially for looking at the silver commodities prices 3-5 days into the future. Their accuracy was such that they are reportedly made substantial profits. And remote viewing is a relatively easy process to learn! I have seen rank beginners achieve amazingly accurate results on their first try!

Yet another aspect of right-brain intuition possibly deals with psychokinetic abilities. This is the power of the mind to influence matter - either directly or indirectly. The Princeton University PEAR Lab experiments use both a random number generator (like an electronic heads/tails coin tossing device) and a mechanical cascade device. A cascade of small ping-pong type balls is dropped down inside a vertical glass panel covered with small pegs like golf-tees. The whole cascade device is enclosed in a box type frame with a transparent front.

Hundreds of these balls are trickled out of a hole at the top centre and after bouncing down through the pegs ended up in a heap at the bottom, in something like a small mountain shape. Obviously the top of this pile would normally lie directly under the hole from which the balls fell.

However it was discovered that mind-power could influence this pile to assemble either to the right or the left of the centreline by a statistically significant amount.

Repeated experiments over 8 years proved conclusively that mind power, **under certain conditions**, exerted enough pressure on these falling balls to marginally modify their vertical descent trajectory.

Similarly it is now well known that directed mind-power can affect computer devices and there are a small handful of people who are able to mentally influence the outcome of gaming machines such as slot and poker machines.

One of the most useful of the intuitive right-brain facilities is the ability to gently influence other minds at a distance. This is called **Subjective Communication** and I cover the techniques in this book.

This mind technique can literally change your life when used properly!

I used it years ago when I was selling Real Estate.

This was at a time in Australia when the property market was really depressed. However buyers for these hard-to-sell properties would appear as if by magic and I had unusually high successes. What I was intentionally doing was to broadcast subjectively, positive details of the property and at the same time I visualized a "sold" sign in front of it. I had some stunning successes.

If this process is handled correctly, the results can be totally phenomenal.

The potential ability to do this is something that everybody has but virtually nobody is aware of! After you read this book you will understand the basics of this form of communication. If you learn the techniques and use them your life will change for the better.

In fact after reading this publication you might find yourself in a state of mild shock because the implications of the knowledge you have gained is enormous.

Possibly there will be some readers who will find it all quite unnerving but just remember _you were born_ with these natural abilities. It is just that nobody has told you that you have them and shown you how to use them.

Until now!

And the serious scientific research in this field has not come from some fringe UFO group - it has come from some of the worlds leading educational institutions and universities.

It all boils down to this:
When you start training in mind power techniques you get your "6th sense abilities" operating - probably for the first time since you were a child and the end result is that you start having a lot of "hunches" which turn out to be amazingly accurate.

This is the result of your intuition slowly coming back to life!

If these "hunches" appear in your imagination in visual form it is a form of Remote Viewing.

If they appear in a gambling environment it is probably connected with psychokinetic manipulation which is basically your own personal mental resonance with the gambling mechanisms.

If these hunches appear in the form of "urges" it usually results in good luck.

The 6th sense can manifest itself in many different ways. As you get into alpha self-control amazing coincidences start to happen.

These days a series of apparently unrelated coincidences which all appear to have a common denominator, are termed "**synchronistic events**".

As you get deeper into personal mind control you will start to notice a lot of this synchronicity appearing in your life. Some of it might have been there before but the alpha training gives you a new awareness and you really notice these unusual events.

I tend to get it a lot these days and it sometimes startles me. But each and every event that I have consciously noticed has been positive. Nothing "nasty" at all. Without a shadow of doubt the more you encourage your intuitive brain to function as it was intended the more "luck" you appear to have.

You usually seem to be in the right situation where nice things happen!

Yet another technique you will learn in this book is the ability, not only to order up the dreams you want, but also to actually remember them.

A normal dream memory only lasts 7 seconds or so after waking up unless you pre-program your mind to transfer the dream memory to your conscious brain immediately. By programming up specific dreams to solve problems you can obtain "dream inspired" answers. They may be in symbolic form but when programming the dream initially you instruct your subconscious mind to present the dream in a manner you will easily interpret.

It works! And it works reliably! You can actually get to the point where you can program to remember every dream you have but you may not be comfortable with this.

The actual process is similar to light hypnosis but it is not the usual form of hypnosis where you give over control of your mind to another person. In this case *you* are in control.

AWARENESS DURING ALPHA

For many years the psychology field assumed it was impossible for a person to drop voluntarily down to alpha and **retain** conscious thinking control.

That is it was thought impossible to run both alpha and beta brain frequencies at the same time.

Alpha is the state where your brain rhythm tends to "centre" around 10 cycles per second (cps). I've used the term "alpha" loosely as a general term for simplicity. Twin hemispheric brainwave analysis is quite a complex discipline.

It was always assumed that once a person entered alpha (like the daydream state), they would be unable to direct their thoughts and probably fall asleep. This was until Jose Silva, originator of the Silva Mind Course demonstrated otherwise. He proved conclusively that people could operate intentionally in alpha and retain control of their beta thinking at the same time. These days there are people who can drop down to a lower level of Theta (3-7cps) - and still maintain conscious control! There are even a handful of people who can drop down to mind-awake-body-asleep in delta!

What is happening at this level is that your conscious and your subconscious mind are operating simultaneously, giving you an increase in mental capacity and opening up your 6th sense. Women tend to use both brain hemispheres when solving problems which may give them extra intuitive capacity.

It was also discovered that a person could drop to alpha with their eyes open (you do this when you daydream) which offered another major advantage for the business executive.

But to all intents and purposes the alpha state is considered to be similar to a light self-hypnotic state. At least the outcome with regard to positive and habit-transforming programming is the same.

The biggest overall advantage in business, of getting your right intuitive brain fully operational, is the ability to "intuitively know" what the other person is thinking and what their real objections are. Not their "professed" objections but the real unspoken ones. By using a special alpha technique, you can actually pre-program to find out what it is they really want in advance. This gives the businessman or woman a tremendous advantage when the actual "crunch" time comes!

And it is an observable fact that those who practice alpha/theta techniques tend to progress quickly up through the ranks - all else being equal.

The reason - you have developed mind powers that others simply do not have. And if you use these regularly you have a massive advantage that others are totally unaware of. This is why most mind-course graduates seldom ever mention their training to outsiders. They are usually told during their mind-course, instructional program to keep it to themselves.

And it makes sense ...... because mind-power knowledge is an exclusive club!

If you go to a lot of trouble to learn and practice these techniques, then promptly tell everyone what you are doing, you will end up with no personal advantage, only a lot of envious criticism. So all your effort will have been negated or compromised.

The whole field of mind-power in the western world is in its infancy. And because it will make a lot of people nervous there will not be too much media education about it. It will creep up on us in the same manner that computers have. Who would have believed 25 years ago that computers would become part of our lives? I didn't and I was deeply involved in the world of electronics!

The following information explains the state-of-art in mind-power today.

Ignore this emerging field at your own peril!!!

THE CONSCIOUSNESS REVOLUTION

The human brain has an estimated 30 billion neurons. Each neuron consists of a vast collection of atoms and even vaster collection of sub-atomic particles. It operates like a computer, except that if the processing power of every computer on earth were joined together it would still not match the computing abilities of **one single human brain!**

Most office computers have the capacity to communicate with outside computers such as vast data banks, through a "modem" connected to a telephone line. The human mind, **under certain circumstances**, appears to have this same capacity. It appears that it can be triggered to interact with other minds and universal forces. Famed psychologist Karl Jung called this the "Universal Consciousness." Dr. Peter Russell calls it the global brain. World famous Biologist Rupert Sheldrake refers to it as the morphogenetic field.

All living creatures appear to have their own distinctive energy field. As far back as 1940 Harold Burr, a Neuroanatomist at Yale University, conducted a study of energy fields around living plants and animals. He discovered that a young Salamander exhibited an energy field approximately the same shape as the adult it would eventually become. Also he found that the axis of the field could even be detected in the egg stage. When he studied seedlings he found that the electrical field around the sprouts resembled the adult plant. But it wasn't until the Russians discovered Kirlian Photography that these energy fields around living objects could be photographed.

A Russian experimenter, Kirlian, discovered accidentally that photographs taken in the presence of high voltage fields contained an "aura" around the living object being photographed. Kirlian was an electrician of some renown and lived in a small cramped flat with his wife. He had no credibility at all in the scientific world and it wasn't for many years that the significance of his discovery was realised. He persevered with this unusual photography for many years until it caught the attention of the Russian Agricultural Department. One day, a senior official visited the Kirlians with two identical plants and asked Kirlian to photograph them both to see if there was any noticeable difference. Both plants looked exactly the same.

The resultant photographs indicated that one plant had a normal healthy aura while the other was very sickly.

The Agricultural man reportedly leapt up and down with delight because some disease had been destroying vast areas of crops and up until that point they had no way of telling which crops were affected. Now they had a method, via this new advance warning, of finding out which crops were going to fail if not treated promptly.

Kirlian found that the same thing applied to human beings. A person about to go down with a disease exhibited a sickly aura. In fact at one point when asked to demonstrate his equipment to high ranking government officials, his stress level upset his equipment. He used to check its operation on his own hand to make sure it was functioning properly. The equipment starting giving blurred and false readings. He thought it was the equipment itself until he realized that it was his stress level that was at fault. This alerted him to the potential of "reading" human auras.

INTELLIGENCE AND ENERGY FIELDS

This concept of intelligence existing "outside" the physical confines of the living organism has been hard for the scientific community to accept. But over the past 10-15 years, hard evidence has been produced which is having its effect on the scientific skeptics.

Dr. Karl Pribram, a prominent American brain surgeon, sees the brains neurons "outpicturing" the physical universe, similar to the holographic process. He suggests that our brains are exposed to the entire concept of the universe in the same way that any minute part of a hologram contains basically the same information as the whole.

British scientist, Jacob Boehm came up with the same Holographic Theory and had it published in a prominent scientific journal. But probably most amazing of all is the theory that British physicist Rupert Sheldrake has proffered. If his theory is proven correct, it will rival Charles Darwin's Theory of evolution in its magnitude.

Basically he has proven repeatedly through laboratory controlled experiments that different species of animals appear to be "plugged" into a dedicated intelligence field which is universal to that particular species.

For example, when enough mice in a group have learned a maze, they ALL suddenly know the maze - **whether they have run it or not!**

It now appears, after a BBC television experiment, that if enough humans have learned something, then it becomes easier for all humans to learn it. Sheldrake calls this shared intelligence the **MORPHOGENETIC FIELD.**

There is an interesting parable about this called the "100th monkey" relating to an apparent observation made on a remote Japanese Island.

A very bright female monkey on a small island was taught to wash sweet potatoes in the seawater. She then taught other members of the tribe to do this. When approximately 100 monkeys had learned this procedure, many other remote monkey tribes started washing potatoes in the same manner. But the interesting thing is that these other tribes were situated on other remote islands and also on the mainland. That is, they had no possible way of acquiring this knowledge, other by some form of intuitive universal "sharing".

The BBC in London tried out Sheldrake's Theory on 8 million of their viewers. They showed on prime time TV, a difficult puzzle that only a very small percentage of their viewers were able to solve. Then the correct answer was also given on prime time TV. Shortly after the same experiment was repeated by a TV network in another country. A far higher percentage of these foreign viewers were able to get the puzzle right the first time. As the puzzle was in the form of a universal pictorial concept, language and customs were not considered to be a factor.

The BBC and Sheldrake concluded that as the correct answer was now existing within the human morphogenetic field then the human race now "knows" the answer. Basically Sheldrake's Theory explains "intuitive" functioning to a degree.

What Sheldrake is saying is that there is a "larger" mind for each life-form and each individual life-form "programs" that larger mind. The theory might be laughable except for Sheldrake's acceptance in the scientific community and also the BBC experiment.

But probably the most startling (and easily repeatable) experiments came from Cleve Backster, a polygraph (lie detector) expert. Operating from his San Diego, Californian laboratory he found that plants react - at a distance - to human thought. He initially connected his polygraph equipment to a Dragon Plant to test for possible "plant stress".

He decided to generate stress by burning the plants leaves and sure enough the polygraph machine registered a strong reaction. But he hadn't actually burnt the leaves - he had only **intended to do so!**

He had thought about it with emotion and intent!

Skeptics who tried the same experiment without genuine intent couldn't get it to work. Backster went a step further and totally shocked the scientific world. He scraped human cells from a volunteer's mouth and connected these to his polygraph and medical EEG equipment. He found to his utter amazement that these cells reacted instantaneously to the **donor's emotions**, even when they were geographically separated! White blood cells were found to be particularly susceptible to emotion. (This may explain for the first time why people with strong positive emotions have better health).

THE HOLOGRAPHIC THEORY OF THE MIND

Let's detour a little and look closely at the Holographic Theory of the human mind and then briefly, how your own mind "blocks out" things it is programmed to be uncomfortable with. Then we'll go on to actual applications of this collective unconsciousness/morphogenetic field and what researchers are currently doing in the new science of "consciousness".

In 1981 a Nobel Prize in medicine was awarded to Dr. Roger Sperry for his Split-Brain theory. Basically he concluded that our left brain was the analytical dominant one, while our right brain was the intuitively dominant one. This right brain is the one that 90% of the human race don't bother to use fully. (I'm referring here to the average right-handed person).

The 10% who do use it are usually the creative writers, artists, etc. It appears to operate in the middle range of the brain frequency scan, at around 10 cycles per second. Analytically orientated tasks show the brain operating in the beta range of 14 to 40 cps.

Let's now talk about the Holographic Theory and how all of the above ties together. I guess everyone is familiar with what a hologram is. It looks like a photographic negative but is covered in swirls and patterns. However when a white coherent light is shone at it a third dimensional image suddenly leaps out.

A hologram is produced from multiple reference points and sets of images of the object to be "photographed".

It contains different viewpoints and perspectives of that object. When triggered by a light source all these reference points coalesce into a discernible 3D image. When you cut a hologram in half each half still contains the full picture (with a slight loss of spatial definition), unlike a photographic negative. And if you cut the hologram into very small pieces you will still obtain a recognisable picture of the whole object from any one of the small pieces. The clarity depends on the original quality of the hologram.

One of the leading researchers, Dr. Karl Pribram of Stanford University, feels that the brain probably records information in the same holographic manner. That is, the information is stored over a "family" of brain neurons, not in any one particular small group of neurons. This would clearly explain why the brain has such an incredible storage ability.

That is, the brain might well be storing information "spatially" rather than in the standard three-dimensional patterns that we currently believe it is working in.

Likewise, if the theories of universal consciousness and the morphogenetic field are correct (and the indications are that they may be at least partially correct) then each individual human brain is acting as a tiny holographic part of a **total hologram.**

That is, your brain is part of a whole! It logically follows that your brain has access to the universal brain via this morphogenetic field - if you can figure out how to tap into it!

The initial scientific research on mind power was started many years ago at Duke University, headed up by Dr. J.B. Rhine. He was largely ostracised by the scientific community at that time, some of whom still believed that the earth was flat. But he did prove that some form of controllable extra-sensory perception existed and that some people were more gifted than others.

So when one of the world's most prestigious universities - Princeton in the USA permitted their engineering department to set up an "anomalies" division, the scientific community sat up straight and started to take notice. The results of these experiments also bought a new batch of skeptics out of the woodwork, but after all this time it is generally accepted that mind/matter interaction exists.

Two of Princeton's scientists, Dr. Dean Radin and Dr. Roger Nelson reviewed and evaluated over 800 experiments conducted under strictly controlled conditions. Their subjects were tested on an electronic random number generator - something like a computerized version of a heads/tails coin flipping device. When the subjects set out to influence the otherwise random results with mind power, they were statistically successful. The scientists concluded that under **certain circumstances**, consciousness interacts with random physical systems. The experiments went on for years and included the investigation of remote viewing.

The United States military became deeply involved in research in this area because of their concern about the possibility of mind power being used to influence the computer directed control systems of their defense network, missiles and satellites.

Now before we go into any specific detail of what is currently being done with mind power by the leading military and non-military experts, let's look at how your own mind works, with regard to "limiting belief" systems.

BELIEF SYSTEMS

The contents of your mind are the result of everything in life that has "impacted" upon it. Mentally, you are the result of a lifetime of cumulative influences and experiences. This is true of everybody, including the author of this book. So if, for example, you have been told as a child that mental telepathy does not exist then you accept this subconsciously as a fact. This might be your inherent **belief** about the reality of telepathy, *not* a statement of fact about it. But because you accept this belief as true (subconsciously anyway), you **consider** it to be a fact. Facts cannot be changed but the **beliefs** about the facts can! So if somebody actually demonstrates to you that telepathy exists your subconscious cannot accept it. This is a "mind-block" bought about by strongly implanted "facts" during your upbringing.

(In fact telepathy can be a considerable annoyance to professional remote viewers who can find themselves sharing spurious identical information with a fellow viewer).

The fact that an estimated 2 million commercial mind-power graduates world wide have proven to themselves that telepathy exists simply does not impact upon the skeptic's mind.

When proof is offered the skeptically-programmed mind simply blocks it out.

It is almost as if the listener flips into another reality zone. You will have noticed this on occasion yourself when trying to explain something new to other people. They develop a glazed look in their eyes and their conscious attention floats off elsewhere. I refer to this a the *thousand yard stare* !!

This is what 90% of people do when they are exposed to innovations in consciousness technology. But with the constant bombardment they are going to get over the coming years on this subject, they will slowly change their attitude and belief system. An example of this is the appearance of almost nude models on the front of newsagency "family" magazines. Twenty years ago, the publishers would have been jailed. Now, not too many people care. Our population has been trained to accept this as normal due to the proliferation of such material over the past few years. Of course, there is a minority who vocally object to this and the same will apply to the field of consciousness technology.

Whether we like it or not, it's on us! It happened in micro-electronics and it will happen with mind-power technology.

I am constantly running across people who tell me they have never heard of these new consciousness technologies before, but in actual fact, when I question them, they *have* heard of them. It's just that the concept did not get past their belief system. That is, it did not register.

This input of new knowledge was discarded at the receiving point - their conscious mind says "rubbish" - end of conservation. In actual fact, I notice some people develop a glazed look when this subject arises.

Some of the material in the rest of this publication, might well evoke these mind-blocks, but at least you are now aware of why your reaction to some items might verge on disbelief.

The trick is to suspend your disbelief system for long enough to permit the implications of this new knowledge have its impact. Then you can decide whether to accept or reject it.

COMMERCIAL MIND CONTROL

The whole concept of commercial mind control instruction appears to have started with some very basic but quite amazing observations by Jose Silva of Laredo, Texas. He was an amateur hypnotist and owned an electronics business. He apparently realized early on that hypnosis put the logical left-hand brain to "sleep" and left the right-hand creative brain open to fairly unrestricted suggestion. He experimented with manipulating this "alpha wave" right brain and evolved some interesting non-hypnotic self-control methods.

It has long been known that thinking while at the alpha level produces the best quality ideas because the intuitive creative component is added to the thinking process. However, most people, when sliding down to the alpha level (similar to the daydream state) tend to fall asleep. That is, they cannot consciously maintain sustained and controlled thinking in alpha.

Enter the Silva method!

Jose Silva found a simple way of training a person to drop to alpha at will and maintain this state for as long as they wished.

That is, a person could use *both* sides of their brain simultaneously instead of just the left-hand side.

(It has since been found that women tend to use both brain hemispheres when solving problems).

Furthermore, he developed a method of training a person to drop to alpha with the eyes open and apparently fully awake!

This has proven to be extraordinarily handy in situations like business meetings where you are expected to produce inspirational answers while fully coherent. Over the past 20 years it has been found that people who use this "twin-state" thinking tend to progress rapidly in their chosen fields, which makes sense, as they are consciously using far more of their standard brain capabilities.

In other words controlled alpha wave thinking while remaining consciously in control, gives people vastly increased mental capacity and enables them to communicate subconsciously both with others and with morphogenetic fields of all-pervading human knowledge.

In the following material I will disclose exactly what the mind-power experts have achieved with these alpha control methods and how you can use the knowledge to your own advantage.

THE CONSCIOUSNESS REVOLUTION - (PART 2)

Basically mind training starts with the ability to self-induce a meditative or "centred" mental state.

The common denominator to it all is the 7-14 cycle per second alpha state. I realise that some readers may be concerned that this could be construed as "fiddling with nature" but I would like to point out that the alpha state is a **natural human mind state!**

We drop into alpha automatically several times a day. For example we tend to be in alpha at the following times and places:

- As we wake up in the morning, we pass through alpha
- As we go to sleep at night, we pass down through alpha
- When we are sitting comfortably in the bathroom, we drop into alpha
- When we are having a warm relaxing shower
- When we are daydreaming
- When we use meditation techniques
- When we are driving a car, we slip into this automatic state

- When we are praying, we do so more effectively in alpha
  (This enables us to contact "higher intelligence")

In fact, a recent scientific study indicates that the brain produces micro-second "bursts" of alpha every 2-3 seconds. It is thought that our two brains are "updating" each other in the same way that your office computer gets updates from its mainframe computer.

It has been calculated that we are automatically in alpha for approximately 5 seconds every two minutes and creative people like artists are in it for much longer periods of time.

The point is only 10% of the population use a lot of creative alpha time - the rest of us don't! So obviously there is no danger at all in joining those magic 10%. All we have to do is to intentionally learn what comes naturally to them.

When you intentionally enter the alpha state by sitting down, closing your eyes and relaxing, you are quietening your mind. You are taking time out mentally and physically ..... and ...... you are drastically reducing your stress levels. So it makes good sense to spend a little more time in this alpha state for your own health and peace of mind!

REMOTE VIEWING

Remote Viewing is the technical name given to an intelligence gathering process which uses mental means other than the usual five senses. Any rational person can learn the process and the success rate can be extraordinarily high! Even average untrained people "off the street" have achieved success rates as high as 80% ..... after just a few quick lessons!

Basically, the remote viewer is asked to "mentally feel" a distant situation and describe in detail what he or she senses. This "situation" can occur in the next room ...... or across the continent. Distant is of no consequence.

One of the earlier experiments involved a distance of 6000 miles and the result was exceptionally accurate. Also time does not seem to matter. Some of the viewers were able to "see" a situation some days ahead of the actual event. These viewings also turned out to be reasonably accurate.

One of the first U.S Companies to study remote viewing was the well known Stanford Research Institute in Menlo Park, California (now called SRI International).

They sent an "observer" (or "beacon") out into the city who was instructed to stand in front of some easily identifiable landmark and gaze at it. The remote viewer back at the lab was asked to relax and draw his impressions of what the observer might be seeing.

The accuracy after some practice was remarkably high. Commercial operators use consensual decision processing to validate the remote viewing results. In this process several viewers are independently given the same target and the results averaged. Another group used a variation of remote viewing called "associated remote viewing". In this process, the viewer looks forward at an **associated event in time** rather than the actual event itself. He or she looks for a signal which would indicate a positive or negative outcome. The vehicle they used for their initial experiments (in 1982) was the Silver Commodities market that fluctuates daily. By using consensus associated remote viewing they were able to make nine forecasts on December silver futures.. Of these predictions, seven were traded on the price of silver, 3 days in the future. In each case, the **magnitude and direction** of the price movements were correct. The odds against this happening by chance were calculated as being higher than 50,000 to 1.

Uri Geller, the famous Israeli psychic, demonstrated remote viewing live on TV here in Australia. A highly skeptical lady interviewer drew a pattern on a piece of paper out of Geller's direct view. Almost simultaneously he correctly drew the identical object on his piece of paper. He thought it was an eyebrow but it turned out to be a cockroach. The only difference was that Geller's object was slightly smaller. The detail was the same. And that is one TV interviewer who now believes in remote viewing! (Geller was *not* using mirrors or any other "gimmicks"). Around 1 million skeptical Australians watched this program in various states of awe!

This ability is not available only to a chosen few - some commercial mind-courses now teach it. And it is a gift that everyone has been born with. You can learn to do it yourself if it is within your field of interest.

As with any new talent it takes time to learn. However a fair percentage of first-timers experience the "novice effect" and are often stunned by the experience. My first try at remote viewing was so stunningly accurate it left me sitting on the steps of a casino, puzzled and very shaken.

The whole basis of mind-power is to initially achieve for yourself a controlled alpha state. After that the whole field of mind power is open to you.

Remote viewing is one of the most extraordinary applications of personal mind-power but another one which can be equally impressive is known as "Subjective Communication". This is something that almost anyone can learn to do very quickly and can enhance your lifestyle considerably!

Subjective communication can be defined simply as mind-to-mind contact, without the use of the other usual 5 senses. We all have the inherent ability to communicate in this manner but only a very small percentage of the population are aware of it and it usually manifests itself accidentally rather than intentionally.

Let me give you an example of how it happens:

(I mentioned this event earlier but it's worth repeating)

Many years ago when I was practicing hypnosis, I used to give small "stage shows" for maybe 50-100 people, who belonged to various local clubs in the area.

I'd hypnotize 5-6 people and have them sitting in chairs on the stage waiting for further instructions. At some point in the show I would require them all to stand up so I'd simply tell them to "stand up". However occasionally one or more of the subjects would stand up before I spoke, but just after I had **framed the intent** in my mind to issue that instruction. This happened several times and always left me puzzled. I knew it was some sort of thought transference but didn't bother to investigate it.

In fact, Jose Silva, in his early experiments with hypnotic learning with his own children, found a similar thing happened. He would prepare to ask them a question about their homework while they were in a light hypnotic (alpha) state and the child would frequently answer the question before it was verbally asked, but immediately after the **intent had been formed** to ask that question.

It seems that when we relax and go into alpha our right brain comes into play and if trained, is fully capable of communicating with other minds.

And after a small amount of training this facility can become incredibly useful.

People who have taken mind training and learned subjective communication, often think back and wonder how they ever got ahead in life without it. It is rather like learning to re-use a muscle. Suppose you've led a sedentary non-active life for the past 10 years and suddenly you are forced into an active, high muscle-activity lifestyle. For the first few weeks those muscles tend to respond very slowly. It is exactly the same when you start to use your right-side alpha brain. You haven't used it since your logical left beta brain started to develop at 5 or 6 years old. So it takes considerable practice to get it functioning again. But when you get it fully operational a whole new world opens up! Most people are staggered at the improvement it makes to their life and the effect it can have on people close to them.

You've probably noticed yourself, that if you desperately and **emotionally** want some event to happen in your life, and you **live and breathe** this event day and night, it quite often happens ..... against all odds!

Think back over your life. It is highly likely that you will be able to identify such a situation.

What basically happens is that you spend a LOT of time "daydreaming" about this event, both during the day and during the night when you wake up.

And daydreaming occurs at the alpha level!

So while in the alpha state you are feeding thoughts and emotional energy out (into Sheldrake's Morphogenetic Field?) and sometimes much to your surprise you have an amazing "stroke of luck" ..... the desired event happens.

Sound familiar?

Enter Subjective Communication .....

This is where you intentionally (or unintentionally) implant a subtle, gentle impression in somebody else's mind, **during their alpha periods.**

The suggestion is that they follow a certain course of action which will be **mutually beneficial** and provide a win-win situation for both parties.

Jose Silva originally considered that this talent would be immensely helpful among emotionally close family members, such as a mother and child, to solve problems such as bed-wetting by subjective suggestions. But it was found to work between people who were even total strangers.

The actual process is amazingly simple and the technique is described later in this book.

INTERCONNECTEDNESS OF ALL MINDS

In the past decade strong evidence has developed suggesting that all human consciousness is interconnected at a very deep subconscious level.

In the same way that a magnetic compass is part of the earth's larger magnetic field, so is your consciousness part of a larger universal consciousness!

Twitch a magnetic compass and its magnetic variation affects the earth's field (admittedly this would be difficult to measure). Twitch your consciousness with a mental thought and you twitch the whole consciousness field!

But the big difference is that your thoughts can be "tuned" or "resonated" to react in a certain way ..... with another specific human mind or with sub-atomic particles of matter!

A physical analogy to the above "interconnection" theory is the simple fridge magnet you stick on your fridge door. If you suddenly pull it off the door its magnetic movement will have a slight immeasurable microscopic effect on the earth magnetic field. Admittedly the effect will be so incredibly small as to be incapable of detection on current state-of-the-art instruments. But the effect will **still be there!**

Likewise if the earth's magnetic field were to suddenly shift every compass in existence would swing slightly. This is because everything that is magnetically sensitive is part of one field - the **magnetic field!** Change one part of the field and you affect the whole!

So far so good. Now let us get back to the fridge magnet example and expand on the effect of magnetic field disturbance, which will then lead on to **mental field disturbance!**

The most spectacular form of human-made magnetic field disturbance is created by the explosion of a nuclear bomb. When one of these is exploded it not only flattens everything within a 10 mile radius and produces a mushroom cloud 10-15 miles high, but it also produces an intense magnetic field which disrupts radio communications for thousands of miles. The effect of an atomic explosion can be detected half way round the earth and nuclear warning laboratories have sensitive instruments manned 24 hours per day to detect just such explosions.

But, the core of this bomb, made of Uranium 235 (or whatever they use these days) could easily fit in the boot of your car and take up about the same space as a box of 2-3000 fridge magnets! The message here is that a relatively small portable object can produce, by changing its chemical/atomic state, **a measurable effect half way around the earth!**

When you have a "thought" which chemically modifies the brain cell structures responsible for propagating this neural activity it is scientifically possible this may affect other neural structures outside your physical body, but sharing the same energy field. After all the air around you is made up of atomic structures (called molecules) and from a scientific viewpoint should be capable of transferring messages, at an atomic level, over vast distances!

It may be that your thought forms, by changing the chemical balance in your brain can affect a multitude of other thoughtforms around you...... in other people, far away!!

Theoretically this might happen by chemical/atomic transference through the atoms and molecules in the air between your brain cells and those of the "receivers"!

So if you developed an intense "mental resonance" style thought-form it may impinge in a sub-microscopic manner in the chemical thought-form processes of other individuals. . . **some of whom may be sympathetic to your requirements!!!** (maybe this is how so-called cult "gurus" attract their victims?)

And without individuals knowing why they may tend to gravitate in your direction to help you achieve your aims, either directly or indirectly!

I guess if this happened directly it could qualify as some sort of miracle. If it happened indirectly it could be regarded as the "universal mind" fulfilling your "cosmic" order!

And that is about where the scientific community is at the moment, in the science of consciousness! All this opens up a few doors for experimentation, doesn't it? And the most fascinating thing is ..... you can do your own experiments free of charge, because you already own the necessary lab equipment ..... **your own mind!**

3

MINDSURGE

The ultimate in new-age controlled intuition mechanisms!

When you have a sudden burst of intuition......that is...you absolutely know something is about to happen.....you experience a strong mental surge.

Likewise if you develop an intense impression that you've just made a correct decision....you get the same mental surge.

This could be described as a *mental gut feeling.....* an absolute *knowing.*
We call this ...MIND SURGE.

This happens all too seldom in our lives but we just might have found a method whereby this marvelous inherent human ability can be developed.......to the point where a distinct impression appears in the mind, which may well turn out to be as accurate as our other 5 senses.

We have discovered a way to convert a dowsing-pendulum **yes/no** type response to an involuntary muscular twitch. This in itself is not new but the rest of our process is. Once this simple process has become imbedded in your mind, you can then extend it to produce a yes/no mind surge. The final step is to convert this on/off "digital" response to a variable "analogue" style signal...which indicates varying degrees of yes through to no. This has been done successfully.

We think that this might be the first easily trainable method whereby a person can eventually induce "full on" intuition. This would be the ultimate in human potential mechanisms. The process is now out of the experimental stage and is proving extremely practical.

Your subconscious mind appears to have access to knowledge that will give you answers to anything you are likely to want to know. Furthermore it appears to be connected to all other minds in a form of *common consciousness*.......so any answers you want may be available from external mental sources. The problem has always been how to tap into this knowledge.

Now.......this may be possible.

The process we have developed is in its infancy....but for most of those who have tried it out....it works!! It starts out as an extension of the age-old "deviceless dowsing" but it is much more intricate and involved than that.

In fact, anyone watching it demonstrated is usually somewhat awed. And when it is demonstrated to a serious dowser...they tend to "freak out"!

The potential applications are enormous. For example....one of the most consistent uses we put it to is in decoding dreams. This can be done while lying down in bed....no need to get up and search for your pendulum or L-Rods. Another spectacular use is in a gambling environment. You can't exactly hold a set of L-Rods over a roulette table.....but you can quietly use this mechanism........without anyone knowing. You can use it while you're driving a car...or in a meeting....or as an intuitive device when you meet your daughter's new boyfriend!

The initial process of generating an involuntary muscle twitch to get yes or no answers to questions quickly extends itself to produce..... a rapid yes/no.......a rapid no/yes (which means that there is both a yes and a no answer)........a slow yes.......a slow no (which we take to mean as "yes...BUT".. and "no...BUT").....and a rapid "twitching" when the mechanism is asked to count numerically. We can also get a response for a "stupid question" and likewise for "don't know". We can also program it to point to magnetic north or toward a lost object.

All in all we have isolated 7 different response modes... in the **yes/ no** digital response format. The best thing about this mechanism is the rapid response rate... there is no waiting for the mass of a pendulum to start rotating or moving. So there is less chance of a mistake. We have also evolved a self checking protocol so we know in advance what percentage of accuracy we are likely to achieve for each specific question.

The second stage of the learning process is to transfer this involuntary muscle reaction to other muscle groups in the body...such as the toes and the eyebrows.

The final stage is to transfer it directly into the mind so that a mind-surge occurs. That is, a feeling of *absolute certainty*.

The basic program we have prepared explains in detail how the process was discovered and goes on to suggest different learning mechanisms. As it is experimental at this stage, it is still being refined, but the actual process to date will probably startle you when you when you are first able to make it work.

For want of a better name we have simply called this intuitive muscle-twitch mechanism the MENTAL PENDULUM.

In the following subheadings the MIND SURGE programs are broken down into six separate programs.

#1   ALPHA PERSONAL MIND CONTROL
#2   SUBJECTIVE COMMUNICATION
#3   THE MENTAL PENDULUM
#4   REMOTE VIEWING
#5   PSYCHOKINETIC PROBLEM SOLVING
#6   DREAM CONTROL

These six programs are based on 21st century mind-power techniques that will not become common knowledge until at least 20 years from now. By utilising the techniques you are about to learn you will be able to manipulate everything around you.......including gambling mechanisms.

Sound impossible? Well...there is a handful of people in society doing just this right now!!!!

They are the "Superminds" of our planet......but ...they were ordinary people....just like you and me until they stumbled across emerging 21st century mind-power techniques that enable them to:

- Use mind-awake-body-asleep techniques to tap their subconscious mind (Alpha training tape)

- Access their intuition on demand (The Mental Pendulum)

- Influence other minds at a geographical distance (Subjective Communication)

- Psychokinetically solve any problem quickly and accurately (Psychokinetic Problem Solving)

- Manifesting information which causes them to "see" remote events.....either in real-time, past or future (Remote Viewing)

- Programming up the dreams they want...and actually remembering them (Dream Control)

Let's look briefly at each one of these extraordinary human mental potentials:

Program #1
ALPHA LEARNING PROGRAM

Normally during waking hours our brains are ticking along in the beta frequency range.....usually 14 - 40 cycles per second. When we daydream we drop down to the lower ALPHA range....usually around 7 - 14 cycles per second. This alpha state relaxes us and reduces our stress build-up.

Also in this state we appear to tap universal consciousness and highly inspired and intuitive concepts can materialise unexpectedly.

It was always believed that while a person was in the alpha state they would be unable to simultaneously use their normal left brain analytical abilities.

Wrong!!

It was discovered that it was possible for a person to drop down to this mind-awake-body-asleep state and still have both brain hemispheres operating simultaneously.

Further to this it was also discovered that an individual can drop down to theta and delta states and *still* retain a conscious beta thought process.

That is, a person can be apparently deep asleep and snoring and still maintain conscious thinking and full awareness.

This ALPHA learning program teaches you how to quickly achieve the alpha state. If you keep practicing this process you will eventually end up in theta states...and possibly delta. It is in these deeper consciousness states that you can basically "reprogram" yourself.

Program #2

SUBJECTIVE COMMUNICATION

This is the inherent natural ability of one person to influence the mind of another....over a geographical distance. This knowledge has been around for many years but for some reason most people are unaware of it.

It wasn't until the Silva mind course became internationally popular and touched upon this subject that people became generally aware of the process. It involves a very simple procedure that you can apply immediately after reading this instructional course. There is no conventional mind training required. It will enable you to influence the mind of any individual or group of your choosing, in a positive win-win manner. When used correctly it can increase business sales dramatically. It can be used to resurrect a dying marriage or modify a wayward child's behavior. It can get you that job you are after. In fact, there is no limit to what can be achieved by using this magical communication process. It is ready made for attracting a partner or casual relationship...in fact the response can be downright embarrassing at times. People who have used it for this purpose usually report an astounding...and startling...response. It can also work quite effectively if you happen to own an internet web page which is attracting little attention. When you transmit a blanket subjective communication message web surfers just seem to end up on your page...and they don't know why!

You will probably find that this knowledge makes a profound difference to your success in life...and your lifestyle in general.

Its uses are virtually unlimited. This process can also be misused so we have included a short item on how to negate this.

Program #3

THE MENTAL PENDULUM

You've probably seen a "dowser" working. They use a pendulum (weight on a thread) or some sort of "water divining" rods. What these people are doing is tapping into their own subconscious knowledge that manifests itself in the form of an involuntary muscle response. This then activates the dowsing device that produces a twitch or circling movement, depending upon the nature of the detecting device. Very occasionally a dowser is able to do away with this "detecting tool" and rely on surges or feelings in his arm or hand muscles to decode this subconscious knowledge. You will probably be familiar with this....it is called a "gut feeling". What we have done is develop a mental mechanism that enables you to experience a variety of "muscle twitch" responses to give a variety of intuitional answers. Initially we show you how to get "twitch" responses in your thumb muscles (the muscles that control a pendulum movement) then we go on to show how this response can be transferred to other muscle groups. In fact you can develop it to the point where an intuitive answer flashes directly into your mind. This might well turn out to be the world's first method of bringing on full working 6th sense...with approximately the same accuracy factor as your other five senses. Clients who have had a preview of this program all make the same comment..."astounding"!

Program #4
REMOTE VIEWING

This is the inherent human ability to relax..... close the eyes......and mentally perceive a distant event with remarkable accuracy. There has been a lot written about remote viewing in the U.S. press lately relating to the recent admission by the United States Government that they used these "psychic detectives" to provide information that was unavailable from conventional sources. Due to the "novice effect" beginners sometimes have remarkably success on their first try at Remote Viewing. This course outlines a procedure that you can use at home to learn the basics of this human-potential mind-mechanism. The research laboratories that developed the protocol for Remote Viewing discovered that virtually anyone could be taught the procedure. In fact it helped if the trainee had no inherent psychic abilities whatsoever! You might just totally astound yourself on your first try at this!

Program #5
PSYCHOKINETIC PROBLEM SOLVING

This is a simple procedure whereby you program to have a dream...via a cassette message that you record.... that should give you the answer to any problem you might have. It is basically an alternative to the Lateral

Thinking process, but produces the same result with far less effort on your part. Australian clients who have used this problem-solving method report spectacular results.

Program #6
DREAM CONTROL

A simple procedure which enables you to "program" up the dreams you want...and to actually remember them when you wake up. You can then use the Mental Pendulum to analyze them....then and there! As many dreams contain hidden messages this is the ideal way to generate and decode them. Our Australian clients report a feeling of tremendous personal satisfaction after successfully using this process. One client summed it up as follows: ....."*due to this dream control I now know where I've been....and where I'm heading. This gives me a tremendous feeling of self-confidence*".

The following chapters are devoted to teaching you how to learn these human-potential programs.

Once you have mastered them you will look back and wonder how you ever "made it" through life without them.

Also included in this book is the original PK LUCK program. This extraordinary program

explores the effects of personal psychokinetic powers in the gambling environment.

The leading edge discoveries made by our research department identify what "luck" really is and explain how to discover your luck cycles.... and how to enhance them.

4

ALPHA PERSONAL MIND CONTROL

The extraordinary world of ALPHA!!

An interesting thing happens when you learn to enhance your brain's natural alpha waves ....a whole new world opens up! Because you are adding intuitive activity to your usual logical neural activity you become more creative and aware.

And this makes you <u>feel</u> different......almost like a shift in consciousness at times.

Nothing bothers you so much! You sleep better! In fact you can go to sleep any time you wish, even in the most uncomfortable noisy situation. You can quietly slip out to the washroom and after only 10 minutes of alpha relaxation come out mentally and physically re-charged. Your intuition increases out of sight ...... you tend to *sense* what people are thinking and learn to *read* them like a book. Strange events happen. For example, you *think* about getting a parking space in a busy spot down town - and you get one. Virtually every time! You mentally *focus* on completing your journey as quickly as possible and for some strange reason all the traffic lights seem to stay green for you. You find that you tend to stay stress-free all day and when you get home at night, instead of collapsing into a chair you feel quite energetic. Your increased alpha wave activity causes you to radiate a sense of *serenity* which others notice. They tend to relax in your presence and find you easy to be with. You get "urges" to do things for no apparent reason - and this turns out to your benefit, like buying a scratch-it ticket on the spur of the moment and finding you've won $500. Or the phone rings and you suddenly "know" who it is before you pick it up.

The list goes on and on. There is absolutely no "downside" to alpha that I've ever heard about. In fact quite the reverse. People who learn to use alpha <u>all</u> make the same comments. They feel different. They feel more in control. They sleep better. They feel healthier. They don't seem to catch colds as often as the rest of us do.

And it is so simple to learn. If you're learning without the assistance of a cassette or mind machine it will take you 60-90 days. If you use one of these aids you can expect good results within 2-3 weeks. If you go to an alpha course such as **Silva** or **Alpha Dynamics** (basically the same course) then you get the basics in 3-4 days but must practice regularly to get the process "locked' in.

I learnt it all the hard way from a Silva Mind Course book. It took me about 90 days. Then I went to a Silva course that filled in the gaps. But it was still taking me 15-20 minutes to get down to a lower level of alpha. At that point I bought a mind machine and I found I could get to alpha in 4-5 minutes with the machine running.

These machines produce an alpha tone in the headphones and a pulsing light inside a pair of goggles (like sunglasses) that you wear. They immerse you in a world of alpha (or theta) input that can feel quite compelling.

If you haven't got the time, inclination or opportunity to go to one of these expensive commercial mind-courses the mind machine is the next best thing. But this is still costly. The cheapest way is to develop your own tape cassette program, which will cost you only the price of a blank cassette. This chapter explains exactly how to do this.

When using a mind machine both sides of your brain tend to "synchronize" with the rhythmic audio/visual beat from the machine. However if you have any form of epileptic problem pulsing lights might present a problem so the use of a light/sound mind machine is not advised.

A mind machine will take you down into the alpha or theta ranges without any effort on your part but it will *not train you to achieve these states for yourself.*

It is much better to learn to drop down to these lower brain frequency states without mechanical aids and a pre-recorded tape message is the ideal training tool. After a while you will not need to use the tape at all as you will be able to induce the required brain states by yourself.

When you drop into alpha (which is a brain frequency of 7-14 cycles per second) your left hand logical brain tends to stop working *unless* you have programmed it to remain alert.

This is the brain that ticks along at between 14-30 cycles per second. These are the frequencies you produce when you are under stress. If you were having a "panic attack", for example, you might find your predominant brain frequency up around 30-40 cps. The beta state is where you do your everyday, wide-awake, logical thinking. The beta state is not capable of producing inspiration or creativity.

As you descend lower in brain frequency, as in light sleep, you are in theta which is around 3-7 cycles per second. The lowest frequency is delta which is 1-3 cps and is the deep sleep state.

For many years the scientific community assumed that once a person dropped into alpha they would tend to fall asleep. (Alpha is the state you are in when you dream). Jose Silva proved otherwise. In a test in a major medical institution an electroencephalograph (EEG machine) was connected to his head via electrode sensors and he was able to demonstrate that he could drop into the alpha range and still maintain conscious control. That is, he had both brain hemispheres working simultaneously. These days there are plenty of people who can go one better and drop to theta while maintaining conscious thought. There are even individuals who have been able to train themselves to drop down to the delta range while maintaining a simultaneous beta rhythm.

On rare occasions while lying on my back and intentionally reducing my brain frequencies I have noticed that my mouth drops open and I start to snore ..... but I am fully aware of this. It is actually quite an uncanny feeling and gives one the sense of supreme confidence in ones abilities. When you reach this stage of control you become aware that nothing in life can really hassle you. That is .... you are in control! (It took me about

24 months of constant practice to reach this level of expertise). Some readers will be able to achieve this state much quicker than I did as I had no experienced person to guide me and I did not know what was possible or attainable. Now I know and I'm happy to pass the knowledge on.

Basically what happens when you start practicing alpha is that you open up your right-brain faculties, which haven't had too much use since the days of your childhood, when you were free to use your imagination a lot. Once you reactivate these channels they tend to remain open ..... all day long!

It is rather like doing a workout in the gymnasium. While you are working-out you burn off calories and the strange thing is you keep burning them off for some hours after you've finished the workout.

Alpha training seems to work the same way. Once you get this disused mental ability working again it stays up and running!

All sorts of amazing things happen when you've got it under control. You can program yourself to have specific dreams of your choice. You can program to remember these dreams consciously if you wish. You can program to communicate subjectively with individuals or groups to "get your point of view across" in a non-argumentative manner. You can program yourself to stay awake for 24 hours or more without feeling fatigue. You can program yourself to bring in imaginary "consultants" (in the same manner that Einstein did) to help you solve a problem! (And that works spectacularly!!!) You can program yourself to remain healthy and even remove such things as moles! (I've just got rid of my second one while visualizing clear skin when in deep alpha).

Some American mind-power practitioners have even been able to maintain a constant body temperature in freezing conditions such as during military maneuvers in New Zealand in mid winter.

Actually none of this should be too surprising because your subconscious mind controls absolutely all your automatic body functions. What you are doing is giving your subconscious new instructions. If you want to change the speed of your breathing or slow your heart right down you can by temporarily modifying your mind-program controlling these vital functions.

Likewise you can change the local temperature of any part of your body and block out pain such as migraines. But you've got to be careful here that you don't override some serious medical condition.

Alpha and theta are natural brain rhythms and you naturally pass in and out of these over a normal 24 hour period so there is no harm at all in bringing them on more often. It's when you get down to low theta ranges that you should start exercising a little more caution as you can tend to over-ride your subconscious control over the natural body rhythms. But you won't need to worry about this for a couple of years, even if you do practice it every day.

When I first started learning the alpha technique I was so fascinated with it (and most people are) that I grossly overdid it. I was going into alpha 7-8 times a day - akin to starting a physical exercise regime and overdoing it - your muscles hurt. You've got to give them recovery time. The same applies to the right alpha/theta brain - give yourself time out from intensive alpha occasionally, at least till this under- used "muscle" gets back into shape. If you're going to do heavy alpha practice, say with a mind machine, for a week or so then take a couple of days break occasionally, especially if you're practicing Remote Viewing or Out-Of-Body experiences. These two exercises get to the very core of your being and tend to *drain* you mentally if you overdo them. They might have been natural to the human race 10-20,000 years ago but thousands of years of mental neglect have put us back to square one.

About all that is left over from our original natural mental prowess are the strange abilities to daydream and experience Deja-vue. These appear to be closely related to RVing and OBEing and are probably a diffused leftover. When you really think about it daydreaming is a total anomaly. There is no logical reason for us to have this ability unless it is a left-over from something much more profound and useful. Deja-vue is another strange anomaly ..... it is almost as if we are remembering our future which is what a number of experienced mind-power professionals believe.

LEARN ALPHA - MAKE YOUR OWN ALPHA CASSETTE MESSAGE

Alpha is an absolutely magical state. Only 15 minutes relaxing in the alpha state is equivalent to at least 1 hours sleep. And you come out of alpha feeling fantastic ....not drowsy! You pass in and out of alpha naturally dozens of times a day so it is quite a natural state. It involves dropping your dominant brain frequency down to center around 10 cycles per second, so that you are in the "dream" state but aware of your surroundings at the same time. It feels rather like the situation where you wake up on a Sunday morning and realize you don't have to go to work. You can hear the rain on the roof and are too tired to get up but not tired enough to go back to sleep.

You feel incredibly relaxed but alert at the same time, something akin to a fabulous mental drifting feeling.

And the interesting thing is that once you learn the alpha technique you can bring on this beautiful mind-state ....<u>any time you chose</u>!

There are various methods of learning the process. You can read a book about it and learn the hard way....as I did. Or you can pay for a 3-4 day commercial mind course and get the basics ingrained quickly (but you will still need to practice consistently after this to get the process "locked in").

Alternatively you can make life really simple for yourself and create the following instructional cassette tape and learn alpha easily in your own home.

You make this tape yourself by reading the pre-written script featured below into the microphone of your tape recording device. You can also create your recording as a sound file on your computer.

In fact where you are asked to repeat the message a multiple number of times you might find it easier to record the specific message once into your computer microphone then use the software program to create multiple repeats. You can even add echo or reverberation to the message that has been found to enhance the effect on the mind. When you have fully composed the message on your computer it can then be transferred to cassette tape.

The quality of the recording is unimportant. Providing you can hear the words reasonably clearly it will work for you.

All you have to do is turn on a recorder and read my pre-written script on to the tape. Your subconscious mind trusts your own voice so you may find that this "homemade" tape is more effective than a commercially made one. Then you either play the tape at night as you go to sleep or play it during the day (NOT while you're driving) as a reviver. The chances are you might be quite delighted with the results.

The tape is recorded in two parts. The first part is the actual alpha message and the second part is a health/habit-changing message if you should need it. All you do here is record the alpha message first then continue recording and add the specific affirmation you require. Five different affirmation messages are supplied.

If you merely want to learn the alpha process ignore the habit changing messages.

The 5 motivational messages included are:
Giving up smoking
Reducing alcohol intake
Neutralising insomnia
Better health & self-confidence
Sixth sense awareness

HOW TO MAKE YOUR OWN ALPHA CASSETTE LEARNING TAPE

You can use any form of tape recorder for this....quality is not important. A Dictaphone style machine will do the job as well as a $1000 stereo recorder.

To begin, pick a location that is reasonably quiet and where you won't be interrupted. It will help to add a masking "white noise" in the background. The most effective "masking" noise is the sound of running water such as a waterfall or the seashore. A reasonable effect can be obtained by running a shower or a water tap. I have found that by putting a cardboard carton upside down on the floor of my shower and running a stream of water onto this (no need to use your hot water) then a semi-realistic waterfall sound can be heard, when played back through a speaker or headphones.

This resultant "white noise" behind your recorded voice tends to mask outside sounds so that you can focus without distraction.

If you make your recording in your bathroom you will get a slight echo effect off the solid walls which enhances your recording.

You can make your tape anywhere between 10 and 20 minutes long, depending on what you want to achieve.

The tape should start off with the relaxation suggestions then finish off with the health/habit-breaking affirmations if you require them. If you want to use it as a "refresher" message during the day then you must add the "wakeup" message at the end of the tape.....so that you end up fresh and alert at the end of the session.

THE RELAXATION MESSAGE THAT YOU RECORD ON YOUR CASSETTE

(A mind-influencing tape is always made in the "third party". The word "you" is used instead of the word "I".)

START YOUR TAPE OR COMPUTER AUDIO RECORDER RUN-NING AND RECORD THE FOLLOWING:
(Speak slowly and clearly at about one quarter of your usual talking speed:)

You are relaxing - you are becoming sleepy.
   (pause)
Every muscle in your body is relaxing
   (pause)
With every breath you take you are becoming more relaxed
   (pause)
Your body is feeling peaceful and relaxed
   (pause)
Focus on your breathing - it is becoming slow and steady
   (pause)
Your scalp is relaxing...your scalp is relaxing
   (pause)
Your forehead is relaxing....your forehead is relaxing
   (pause)
Your eyelids are relaxing....your eyelids are relaxing
   (pause)
Your eye muscles are relaxing....your eye muscles are relaxing
   (pause)
Your jaw is relaxing....your jaw is relaxing
   (pause)
Your whole face is now relaxed....your whole face is now relaxed
   (pause)
Your neck is relaxed....your neck is relaxed
   (pause)

Your shoulders are relaxed....your shoulders are relaxed
   (pause)
Your arms are relaxing.....your arms are relaxing
   (pause)
Your hands and fingers are relaxing....your hands and fingers are relaxing
   (pause)
Your chest and stomach are relaxing...your chest and stomach are relaxing
   (pause)
Your hips and thighs are relaxing....your hips and thighs are relaxing
   (pause)
Your legs are relaxing .....your legs are relaxing
   (pause)
Your feet are relaxing.....your feet are relaxing
   (pause)
Your toes are relaxing....your toes are relaxing
   (pause)

(Twitch your toes and take a deeper breath.......... as you do so you will feel the tension drain out of your body)

   (pause)
Your entire body is now relaxing ....you can feel the tension drain away
   (pause)
Your entire body is now relaxed....the tension has drained away
   (pause)

(carry on recording doing the following countdown)

Twenty .... you are feeling tired and relaxed
   (pause)
Nineteen .... every muscle in your body has now let go
   (pause)
Eighteen.....listening only to my voice - nothing disturbs you
   (pause)
Seventeen.....deeper and deeper
   (pause)
You will remain consciously aware and not fall asleep
   (pause)
Sixteen....deeper and deeper
   (pause)

Fifteen....your body is feeling peaceful and relaxed
(pause)
Fourteen.....nothing disturbs you - listening only to my voice
(pause)
Thirteen.....with every breath you take you relax deeper and deeper
(pause)
Twelve....your breathing is becoming slower and slower
(pause)
You will remain consciously aware and not fall asleep
(pause)
Eleven.....you are feeling peaceful and calm - and very, very relaxed
(pause)
Ten.....you are drifting, drifting, drifting
(pause)
Nine.....nothing worries you - nothing troubles you
(pause)
Eight.....aware only of my voice - listening only to my voice
(pause)
Seven.....peaceful -calm-relaxed -   going deeper and deeper
(pause)
Six....feeling incredibly pleasant .....feeling incredibly pleasant
(pause)
You will remain consciously aware and not fall asleep
(pause)
Five.....nothing disturbs you - going deeper and deeper
(pause)
Four.....feeling contented, peaceful and relaxed
(pause)
Three ...... too tired to move - too tired to move
(pause)
Two...... letting go - letting go
(pause)
You will remain consciously aware and not fall asleep
(pause)
One....Focusing now only on my voice - focusing now only on my voice

(At this point press the <u>pause</u> button on your recorder)

That is the hardest part of your tape completed. Easy, wasn't it?

The next part is where you read on the message of your choice.

If you don't want to insert a message then you are finished and your alpha tape is ready to be played when you are in bed, or in an otherwise relaxed situation during the day.

When you are ready to do this, release the pause button and speak in the same clear slow voice.

Examples of these messages are given shortly. Pick the one that is most applicable to you (or make up your own) and insert it onto the tape immediately after your relaxation message.

Remember small mistakes do not matter. If you stumble over a few words it will make no difference to the strength of the message, unless these mistakes consciously annoy and distract you when replaying the tape.

The earlier relaxation message is designed to be used at night as you are going to sleep.

However if you wish to use it during the day as a "re-charger" then you must add a "wake up" message so that you come out of your alpha session feeling bright and alert. If you don't give yourself the right wake-up signal you will probably feel drowsy for some time.

Here is the message you add on to the very end of the tape:

"You will wake up on the count of three feeling positive, cheerful and wide awake.....you will wake up on the count of three feeling positive, cheerful and wide awake.....
One.....waking up ....waking up
Two ....waking up.....waking up
THREE......wide awake.....deep breath.....wide awake!"

POSITIVE AFFIRMATIONS

Select the one you want and add it immediately after the relaxation message.

You can record two or three of these message consecutively if you wish but don't use more than three otherwise there might be mental conflict.

When you select your desired message simply keep repeating it over and over in a very slow voice. It should be repeated at least 10 times, preferably more, or until you run out of tape. This is where it is best to record onto a computer so you can use the playback mode to keep repeating the message while adding a little reverberation. Then you simply stand your tape recorder in front of the computer speakers and record the repeating message onto your tape. Quality is not important.

GIVING UP SMOKING

(Repeat the following message at least 10 times onto your tape)
"Smoking makes you nauseous......you find the taste unpleasant.......you annoy other people when you smoke........your health will be affected badly if you continue......... you know that you feel a lot better when you don't smoke...... you realize you could save considerable money by not smoking.....you are slowly losing the taste for cigarettes...... you keep forgetting to buy more........you forget to light up more and more often.........you are starting to wonder why you smoke at all......you realize it is a ridiculous habit."
(repeat 10 times or more)

REDUCING ALCOHOL INTAKE

"You realize that excess alcohol is causing you problems......... you are fully aware of these problems.......... you are losing the taste for alcohol......it is starting to taste un-pleasant.........you keep forgetting to top your glass up........you also keep forgetting to buy more..........you are starting to favour less alcoholic beverages........you are feeling more alert and alive and you know that this is because you are losing interest in alco-hol.......your health is improving as you drink less......people now like you more........you are starting to feel totally in control."
(repeat 10 times or more)

INSOMNIA

If you have trouble getting to sleep there is a highly effective technique you can use in conjunction with this tape. In fact it is so effective in many cases that it will even work without the tape.

It is this:

Just before going to bed do 3-4 minutes of stretching exercises. Any form of exercise that works your muscles will do. Then take a warm shower and a small glass of warm milk beverage. Get into bed, turn out the light, make yourself comfortable .....and relax. Turn on your tape cassette at this point if you intend to use it.

Now ...... <u>clench every muscle in your body</u>!!

Clench your toes. Clench your leg muscles. Clench your abdomen muscles. Clench your shoulder and arm muscles. Clench your hands and fingers. Clench your neck and face muscles. Clench your eyelids tightly shut. Screw up your nose. Clench <u>every</u> muscle at the same time and hold this <u>as long as you can</u>.

Then .... <u>LET GO</u>!! The feeling of "letting go" is the feeling of alpha. The chances are the next thing you will know is that it is morning! At the same time as doing all this you can be running your tape.

"You are totally relaxed....every muscle has let go..........you feel extremely pleasant....... your stomach feels calm and peaceful......your body feels calm and peaceful.......... you will have a beautiful night's sleep........nothing will disturb you unless it is life-threatening........you feel yourself drifting.......you are letting go and listening only to my voice...........your body feels fabulously relaxed..........nothing disturbs you.........you feel blissful..........you are letting your mind wander as you listen to my voice..... deeper..... deeper........deeper.......drifting off.....drifting off."
(repeat 10 times or more)

BETTER HEALTH AND SELF-CONFIDENCE
"As the days progress you feel better and better.....your health is improving daily....... you wake up in the morning feeling totally refreshed and inspired..........you are relaxed and cheerful all day and are free from stress at all times.......nothing worries you.....you know that you can easily solve any problem........this gives you confidence..........other people catch colds and flu....you don't because your body rejects disease and viruses....... you exude self confidence.....other people look up to you........you can sense this........... you feel great during the day and sleep soundly at night. Each time you hear this message this program will reinforce itself."
(repeat 10 times or more)

SIXTH SENSE AWARENESS
"You are becoming aware of things you haven't noticed before......you are noticing synchronistic events........your intuition is becoming quite remarkable.........you sense what other people are thinking........you can now detect the hidden meaning behind what people are saying.........you are alert to natural dangers.....accidents happen to others - not you...........you are increasingly receiving flashes of positive insight.......your mind is now operating at its full potential as it was intended to..........some of the things that now happen in your life positively amaze you.........you are aware of a whole new world that you haven't noticed before."
(repeat this above message at least 10 times)

The above are examples of the most frequently requested positive affirmations. You can make up your own quite simply. Keep your words simple and easy as if you were speaking forcefully to a 10 year old child.

Where possible keep your messages emotive because your subconscious understands the language of emotions.

5

SUBJECTIVE COMMUNICATION

This to me this is one of the most miraculous aspects of alpha mind-technology. It has been known for a long time under the heading of mental telepathy but it wasn't until Jose Silva started seriously experimenting with it that its possibilities and limitations were identified.

In the early days before he had developed the Silva Mind Course he was using light hypnosis to try and help his children raise their grades at school. When he was giving them homework lessons he often noticed that they would answer a question before he had fully asked it. He had not given them enough information to answer the question but they answered it anyway. He figured that this was some sort of direct mind-to-mind communication.

Some time ago I saw a television program about the "super minds" who win all the Wheel-of-Fortune prizes. One particular segment showed one of the highly successful participants during one of his many winning runs. Something made me pick up my dictaphone and record the audio from this show. When I listened to it afterwards I suddenly realised that he was answering the questions.....precisely and accurately....... without waiting for the full question to be asked. In fact, on several occasions he *did not have sufficient information to answer the question at all!*

I replayed the tape again to make sure I wasn't missing anything.

It was fairly obvious that he was getting the information from a source other than the show-host's verbalized question.

He would have had to be picking it directly out of the mind of the host or retrieving it from the minds of the people who wrote the quiz......or..... he was inadvertently *remote viewing* the correct answer. There was no other logical explanation.

Now back to Jose Silva. Jose figured that if this mental contact actually existed then it could possibly be used between close family members, such as mother and child, to assist the child with problems such as bedwetting. Jose was also an amateur hypnotist and thought that maybe via this direct mental contact post-hypnotic suggestions could be planted in the child's mind. After years of experimenting he found that this "subjective communication" could also be used between people who were total strangers and not only that, it could be used to affect the thinking of *groups of people.*

So Subjective Communication was born as a commercially trainable mind-mechanism.

And the technique for using it is extraordinarily simple.

All it requires is that you focus on the other person *while they are in an alpha state*! The best time to do this is while they are in a light sleep in the early hours of the morning.

The standard method of doing this, as taught by the commercial mind courses, is as you're going to sleep at night, program your subconscious to wake you up when your *mind is in contact with the other person's mind.*

It sounds too simple to be true, doesn't it?

Years of experimentation in our laboratory prove that the process not only works, but in some cases the results are almost *beyond belief*!

The easiest way to explain all this is to give you an example:

Let us suppose that you are going for a job interview tomorrow and you're somewhat apprehensive. You know that a Mr. Bloggs will be interviewing you.

As you go to sleep you instruct your subconscious as follows:

I will wake up when I am in contact with Mr. Blogg's mind and I will remember why I have woken up.

You repeat this statement 10-20 times to make sure your subconscious gets the message. When you wake up sit up in bed (so you don't drop back to sleep) and relax so that you're in that daydream alpha state. You repeat the following slowly and clearly in your mind:

Mr. Bloggs, you know I am the best person for the job. I have all the qualifications and by employing me you will make life easier for yourself. I am exactly the right person for the job and you will be very satisfied with my work.....etc.

Convey the entire message as if you were sitting there in front of him.

Finally see him shaking your hand and congratulating you on getting the job.

Then go back to sleep.

When you meet Mr. Bloggs the next day you will be somewhat amazed at the friendly reception you get providing you have subjectively communicated correctly.

A young student of mine got a job this way. There were 22 applicants and she was the least qualified. Not only that, they wanted someone around 10 years older with existing experience. Nevertheless she was offered the job.......right after the end of the interview.

I used a lot of subjective communication when I was selling real estate years ago. This was during a property slump and nobody in the office was making sales ...... except me!

The method here is to program your mind (as you go to sleep) to wake you up when it is in contact with the largest group of likely buyers. Then you mentally explain to them how great a particular property is and why they should buy it.

You *repeat your address and who you are at least 3 times* so that the message sinks in. Chances are, the next day potential buyers will contact you left, right and centre to view the house.

You then use subjective communication once again to help sell it to one of these people and you finish off by visualizing a sold sign on the property.

Please note that they will only buy this property if they are genuinely interested, but somewhat undecided. You help them make up their mind! You cannot use Subjective Communication to make an unwilling person buy the property. They have to be initially receptive to a purchase of this kind. What the subjective program does is to draw them out of the woodwork.

You can use exactly the same process to attract people to your advertisement in the Yellow Pages or in the newspaper. Individuals glancing through the newspaper or yellow Page ads suddenly notice your ad. It tends to leap out at them and they feel compelled to contact you. Without the subjective programming they would probably have ignored it.

I had a most extraordinary experience some years ago involving subjective programming. It left me absolutely flabbergasted.

At that time I owned a small restaurant which I had purchased cheaply with the intention of building up the customer base. I had some success in doing this but concluded that the restaurant game was not for me. I placed the business on the market and by using subjective programming quickly found a potential buyer. The problem I had was that another similar restaurant had recently opened nearby and my lunchtime trade had dropped right off.

These buyers were arriving from out of town and I had arranged to meet their flight at the local airport and drive them in to view the business. Unfortunately for me they would be viewing the operation during a Monday lunchtime which was our quietest day.

I had done some very heavy subjective work the night before to attract Monday lunch customers and I drove out to the airport with fingers crossed.

We pulled up in front of my restaurant just after midday and I could not believe my eyes.

The small shop was totally packed! There were customers everywhere. My two waitresses were run off their feet. To say that I was stunned would be the understatement of the century. In the 12 months that I had owned the business I had never had more than a dozen of so diners in for a Monday lunch. Afterwards we found that we had served 58 meals!

The potential buyers were highly impressed and before the afternoon was over had signed an unconditional contract of purchase.

Did subjective programming work in this case? It certainly did! I had the contract in hand to prove it. For those of you reading this who are professional skeptics..... please don't tell me it doesn't work - I've been using it for 20 years with spectacular results and I know dozens of people who are doing the same. On top of that, I spent 6 months doing A/B tests for my mail-order company. Advertising the same product and doing a week on and a week off with Subjective Communication.

I roughly tabulated the results. The subjective work bought in between 50-80% more clients, depending upon the effort I put in over the preceding 2-3 days.

During the non-subjective weeks the sales dropped back to normal.

It is an interesting fact that people who learn Subjective Communication usually always realise how "magical" it is but never actually get round to doing anything with it in the future. I'd guess that about 90% of all commercial mind-course graduates don't bother to follow it up. Strange isn't it?

You can use Subjective Communication for virtually any situation where you need to attract the attention of another person or group of people.

The only actual downside is that if you do a lot of Subjective Communication it becomes mentally draining, waking up night after night. It basically means that you have to go to bed early so that when you wake up you have had enough sleep to be able to concentrate on the message, without dozing off. If I have any serious Subjective Communication to do I go to bed around 9pm which I personally find an inconvenient time to retire.

And it is very important that when you are doing your subconscious programming while going to sleep, you tell yourself you will remember _why_ you have woken up. On many occasions I have come totally awake in the middle of the night and wondered what woke me. I have then gone back to sleep and forgotten all about the subjective program. This can be quite annoying if the subjective program was of personal importance.

If you have something really important to achieve (involving other people) and you just can't seem to get results then Subjective Communication is close to the ultimate answer. It is an absolute _must_ for any progressive business.

However if you are using this mental influencing process I'd _strongly_ suggest that you keep the knowledge to yourself! It's not too hard to figure out why........ the average person becomes rather apprehensive if they think they have been mentally manipulated.

Apart from all that you've gone to some trouble and expense to learn about it - why give away a personal advantage that has taken you some effort to track down and learn?

Subjective Communication works anywhere there is a people problem.

Use it wisely .... it is a potent force!

Following is the original student course I wrote on Subjective Communication:

THE MAGIC OF.......
SUBJECTIVE COMMUNICATION

THE AMAZING DISCOVERY OF A "PRIMARY" COMMUNICATION BETWEEN HUMAN-BEINGS WHICH IS ACCURATE, DIRECT AND CAN'T BE MISINTERPRETED!

In the 50's an electronic expert by the name of Jose Silva was deeply involved with experiments in hypnosis. He was trying to raise his children's "intelligence" and grades at school by teaching their homework while they were in a light trance state.

After years of experimenting he found that this "remote hypnosis" not only worked between close family members but also between total strangers!

In the world of psychology this was quite a profound discovery!

Around the same time, in 1966, the famous Russian psychic Karl Nikolaiev took part in an extraordinary experiment organized by skeptical Soviet scientists. In fact the experiment was so successful that it was widely published in the Russian news media and was the acknowledged catalyst for the upsurge in parapsychology interest among the civilian and scientific population of Russia. It was reported that it was due to this single experiment that the Soviet Government developed a serious interest in mind power research.

It had been arranged that a close working associate would send Nikolaiev "coded" telepathic messages. The "sender" was in Moscow while Nikolaiev was at Leningrad University, wired in to brainwave monitoring equipment. The sender, at a prearranged time was to think of something emotional like "punching up" someone he didn't like. He was to do this for 15 seconds as a morse code "dot" and for 45 seconds as a morse code "dash". The word sent in "mental" morse code was MIG, which was received correctly, much to the skeptics astonishment. The EEG monitoring equipment showed a sudden change in brainwave pattern while the "dots and dashes" were being received. When these were decoded the word MIG was spelt out. This was fairly solid proof of direct mind-to-mind communication. Nikolaiev was unaware of the content of the message, but was vaguely aware that a message was being sent. It was suspected then and has since been proven, that people communicate on this level consistently. So whether you like it or not, you are involved in Subjective Communication with other people most of the time.

It has long been suspected that your right cerebral hemisphere, when in the alpha state, operates in a realm where time and space are of no consequence. What you think affects others...... and what others think affects you !

It is rather like the invisible connection between the earth's magnetic field and every magnetic compass on earth. They are interconnected. If the earth's magnetic field were to suddenly shift then every compass in existence would swing in unison. Likewise, if you suddenly move a magnetic compass, or any magnet for that matter, this movement will have a slight effect on the earth's entire magnetic field. Admittedly this would be so small as to be unmeasurable but it would still be there.

Similarly, when you have a thought it "twitches" the entire human consciousness "thought field".

Rupert Sheldrake calls this the MORPHOGENETIC FIELD. Karl Jung called it COLLECTIVE UNCONSCIOUSNESS.

Jose Silva found a practical method of evoking and controlling this marvelous human ability at will.

The technique, which is amazingly simple, has been developed over the years but to this day more than *99% of the population are unaware of it.*

In the United States it is used extensively in business to "sway" the outcome of a business proposition in favour of the person using Subjective Communication.

In personal life it has been used to resurrect a dying marriage, to name but one of its many applications.

And one of the most extraordinary applications is to use it to make people aware of your advertisement in the Yellow Pages!

Its effectiveness appears to vary between 20% and 500%. That is the results can be up to 500% better than they would have been without it.

If you consider two identical competitive businesses both vying for superior market share then the one that learns to use Subjective Communication will forge ahead. This has been tested and thoroughly proven.

Car dealers in the US who use this direct mental contact technique have reported a sharp improvement in sales. The usual comment is *it brings customers out of the woodwork* and actually closes more deals. US real estate agents use it also - it makes a vast difference in their commissions when used properly.

And it is a strange thing that most people are using it continually without being aware of it. Unfortunately they are also conveying mentally their fears and apprehensions. So it can work against them. But used properly and with the correct protocol it can (and does) produce quite astounding results. Sometimes the results leave the practitioner somewhat startled. They almost seem too good to be true! Some beginners have had such amazing success that the result has literally left them "awe-struck!

A REAL LIFE EXAMPLE IS AS FOLLOWS:

Imagine this scenario: you have your house on the market at $360,000 and you just can't seem to get any nibbles. You've advertised it for the past 6 months and while everyone agrees that the price is fair nobody has actually bought it. Worse still, you aren't even getting anyone to look at it. Things are looking rather dismal but for some reason you decide to attend a commercial mind course which is giving a seminar in your town that weekend and for the first time in your life you hear about Subjective Communication. Not only that, the instructor tells you exactly what to do, not only to sell your house, but to actually get the price you want. One week later it is sold, at $358,000. You can't quite believe it! You tell all your friends what has happened.......and......you guessed it....... you receive looks of pity. After all your friends know that you were "just lucky". But you know differently!

You then decide to apply this magical mental technique to other areas of your life ......and things suddenly become much more interesting. You seem to be able to achieve anything you set out to and for some "strange" reason, even total strangers fall over backwards trying to help you.

Welcome to the world of direct mental influence ...Subjective Communication!

In reality Subjective Communication is extremely easy and you do not have to have any experience whatsoever in alpha techniques, but it will help if you do. The reason for this is that Subjective Communication is usually done in the small hours of the morning for reasons explained later and unless you've had alpha training you tend to drop off to sleep halfway through your program. However there are simple ways to overcome this so that even a rank beginner can use Subjective Communication successfully on their first try!

In fact the moment you finish reading this course you will have sufficient knowledge to make it work successfully and things will only get better as you gain more experience and practice.

If you have a genuine need then by using Subjective Communication you will be able to contact the right people to assist you in achieving your goal, simply by utilizing the knowledge you are about to read.

At my office the staff simply refer to it as the *magic process*!

And it is!

Imagine you were asked to give a speech at a function but when you got up to the microphone instead of joining all your words together to make logical sentences you merely spouted all sorts of words at random. Nobody would understand what you were talking about.

This is exactly what happens with your thoughts as you are interacting with other people mentally all day long (and during your alpha periods at night). You are projecting jumbled confused "ramblings" which can only cause confusion in others. But when you direct your thinking in a coherent manner others understand you clearly, even though you have never communicated with them in the conventional sense. Your thoughts are clear and concise and other people react in a positive manner by accommodating your unspoken desires.

Basically Subjective Communication gently encourages a remote person or group of people to do things your way in a mutual win-win manner. However it will *not* work if you are not genuine about that which you want. If for example you are a salesperson and you are trying to push a product that you do not believe in, then it is very likely that your subconscious doubts will transfer to the other person or people. In this case the process may well work against you.

But if you believe wholeheartedly in what you are doing then this will be communicated to the other party.

Critics claim that it is a manipulative form of remote hypnotism but this is not correct.

Hypnosis is a one-way action where the hypnotist issues precise instructions. Subjective Communication on the other hand is a subtle form of mind-to-mind communication which is accepted *only* if it is agreeable to the "receiver".

Having said that you should also be aware that there are circumstances where it *can* be misused. This is covered at the end of this course along with instructions for preventing it from being used against you.

But the correct use of Subjective Communication will not only influence others to assist in creating spectacular positive events for yourself and all concerned, but it will actually mould your environment in a manner you might find hard to believe!

It is the most important process you can learn next to reading and writing because .....it is the ultimate human communication process.

It is direct, precise and accurate. The written word and other "normal" communication methods can be easily misunderstood. (Which is why the legal profession exists!)

It is the way your mind was intended to work, but until now you have probably been unaware of this!

If you have something really important to achieve which involves other people and you can't seem to make any headway by conventional means then Subjective Communication is close to the ultimate answer. And the results are usually very quick! That is, you don't have to wait weeks for a reaction.

In many situations you will get quite uncanny results the very next morning after you use it.

So.... how is this extraordinary process achieved?

Actually it is extremely simple. Following is the process by which you can learn this magical mental technique.

THE METHOD

The only practical time when you will be able to contact another person mentally is when their brain is operating at the *universal communication frequency* of alpha.

This occurs during the day while they are day-dreaming or otherwise meditating but it is well known that people go through various cycles while they are asleep. One of these cycles is the alpha-stage whereby they might slide up from a deep theta/delta sleep into a period of alpha. It is at this brain frequency that they dream and this is when you are most liable to make reliable mental contact with them.

The simple trick is to program your mind as you go to sleep at night to wake you up when your brain neurons are resonating with their brain neurons. That is, when your minds have established communication. This is a lot simpler to do than it sounds.

It was rather like making an international telephone call in the old days before direct dialing.

You had to book your call in advance and when the operator finally raised the other party she would ring you and connect you both together. Subjective communication works the same way. Also if you want to mentally communicate with a group of people rather than just an individual you connect in the same way as the above telephone operator would set up a conference call.

Except that when you're using subjective communication the multiple connection is established instantaneously. All you really need to do is visualize the person or group you want to contact and your automatic right-brain neuron switching network will do the rest. And amazingly enough it never makes a mistake! It never gets the wrong connection!

(The remote viewers refer to this as *acquiring the signal line*).

HERE IS HOW TO DO IT:

As you go to sleep at night you keep repeating to yourself:

...........**"I will wake up when I am in mental contact with (whomever) and I will remember why I have woken up"**..........

You repeat this a dozen times or more until you fall asleep. This is the programming that I mentioned earlier. If you have trouble with this you can always pre-record it onto a cassette and let it play as you fall asleep. Except the wording is slightly different. You will record:

...........**"you will wake up when you are in mental contact with (whomever) and you will remember why you have woken up"**...........

This is because you are talking to yourself as if you were a hypnotist.... hypnotizing somebody.

The reason for reminding yourself why you have woken up is because if you don't pre-program this you are likely to wake up and wonder what disturbed you! This has happened to me more times than I care to remember.

You can also program to wake up to talk to a group of people. In this case you say:

..............**"I will wake up when I am in contact with the greatest number of my targeted group and I will remember why I have woken up"**..............

When you do awaken it is fairly important to arrange things so that you don't fade away and drift off to sleep while in the middle of your "alpha transmission".

The best way to organize this is to get out of bed and freshen up by splashing cold water over your face .....visiting the bathroom, etc.

Then when you climb back into bed ....make sure you are not too comfortable.

Prop yourself up in a slightly uncomfortable position and leave a light on. This will tend to keep you awake for the duration of your alpha exercise.

Now at this point it will help considerably if you have had alpha training but if you haven't, don't worry. The idea is to relax your mind and let yourself drift down into that dreamy state, while all the time telling yourself this : ....**I will remain awake until after I have finished communicating with** (*the subject's name*)

Keep repeating this over and over. When you feel yourself totally relaxed start "talking" with the person (or group) in a positive friendly way.

DO NOT UNDER ANY CIRCUMSTANCES PROJECT CRITICISM.

Mentally see yourself talking to the other person and explaining the problem to them. See them nodding their head in agreement. Visualize clearly a happy and positive outcome to the "meeting".

Thank them for listening to you and visualize the meeting closed. Let yourself drift off to sleep.

If you keep thinking about them as you're going to sleep *control your thoughts very carefully*. Any negative mental projection may get through and undo the good work you've just done. The best way is to drift off while seeing all concerned celebrating a happy outcome.

Now as soon as possible contact that person in real life and run your problem past them. You will probably be pleasantly surprised to find that you receive a very cordial reception and things go the way you want.

Here are examples of situations where you can use the subjective process to advantage:

You have a wayward child who is getting in with the wrong crowd and is rapidly heading off the rails. You subjectively communicate and explain why it would be to their advantage to "straighten up". See them agreeing and visualize their attitude improving. But whatever you do, don't preach at them.

You have a toddler who is wetting the bed at night. Communicate to them that it would be more comfortable if they got out of bed and went to the toilet. Explain this in a loving manner.

You are a minister and your congregations are getting smaller and smaller. (Possibly because your sermons are uninspiring). Subjectively communicate with your church group and suggest they attend on Sunday. Then you could suggest also that they give a bigger donation, which is fair enough because you're personally saving them from the twilight zone!

Somebody is hassling/bullying/intimidating you. Communicate with the person concerned and explain that life would be a lot better for both of you if he or she changed their attitude. See them agreeing. And if they don't modify their behavior visualize them being very uncomfortable or very unsettled whenever they think of you. This tends to get through to them subconsciously and they may feel inclined to leave you alone.

Somebody owes you or your business money. Communicate and explain how much better they would feel if they paid. See them nodding in agreement and writing out a cheque. Debt collectors who use subjective programming in this manner report quite spectacular results in some cases.

Your business is short of customers and it is becoming financially stressed. Subjectively communicate with a broad band of potential customers in your vicinity. Mention the name and address of your business at least 3 times and point out that you have exactly what they need. See them purchasing then walking out of your shop totally satisfied.

Suppose you have to give a public speech and you are extremely nervous. Simply visualize yourself standing on a stage in front of a microphone with your audience listening intently and giving you wild applause at the end. Subjectively communicate an outline of the speech to your "imaginary" audience and see yourself getting a standing ovation.

Maybe your marriage is breaking down and you would like to correct this situation. You can use Subjective Communication to convey to your partner the strong emotional feelings of love and affection that you both *shared at the beginning*. Visualize both of you holding hands and gazing fondly into each other's eyes. Visualize total happiness and contentment.

Perhaps you aren't married and would like to find a suitable partner. Subjectively "advertise" for someone. Picture the general appearance of the person you are looking for. Project your own general appearance and your requirements. Avoid all sexual overtones and project friendship instead.

There is one important point to remember here: the left-brain is usually the analytical one which handles all the complex "nitty-gritty" but the right-brain usually only deals with "overall concepts". When doing Subjective Communication do not try to "transmit" facts and figures. That is left-brain material. If you do, you will probably break the "neural connection". Merely project win/win concepts. You *must* treat the "receiver" as your equal .....do not criticize in any way .....merely offer mutually beneficial suggestions, which you clearly visualize the "receiving party" agreeing with.

Some readers may perceive all this as controlling others, but you control others all day long anyway. When you smile or frown you affect the emotions of others. When you drive slowly along a one-lane road you "control" the speed of the drivers behind you. And the fact that you are broadcasting subjectively all the time has a constant effect on others. It is just that in this case you are controlling and directing your subjective broadcasts. You were given this natural talent as a birthright .....why not learn to use it?

CAUTION: Like any other talent you can also use it to "bore people to tears". Don't overdo it. Use it for a few days then give it a rest. Don't hammer others with consistent subjective broadcasts. If you do, it may work against you.

You will usually find that this communication works almost instantaneously and that you won't need to keep repeating it.

Welcome to the world of direct mental influence ..... Subjective Communication!

Use it wisely .... it is a potent force!

PSYCHIC ATTACK

I have had second thoughts about including this following section in this book as it can be *unsafe* knowledge in the wrong hands. It is basically the misuse of Subjective Communication. However it will undoubtedly be in your best interests to know what psychic attack is....where it comes from......and how to avoid it. I have decided to explain to you exactly how it works so that you can defend yourself against it should the necessity ever arise. I will have to leave it to your sense of fair play not to misuse this knowledge. But just remember, in the world of mind-power...... events *always* turn a full circle. Things can backfire on you ....with *several hundred percent interest*!

Psychic attack can result from the misuse of subjective communication ..... either intentionally or unintentionally.

You have probably had the misfortune at some point in your life to come across someone who absolutely and maliciously hates you - probably for no reason at all...... except that they are totally psychotic.

When one of these individuals gets you in their sights they live and breathe malice toward you. And often their dreams are filled with malice and thoughts of revenge .... directed at a totally unsuspecting you!

And guess what happens? You start having strange disturbing dreams that appear to have no reason for occurring.

In actual fact they are probably *not your dreams*, but someone else's that have been transferred subjectively to you.

A well known American dream laboratory have proven conclusively that this transference takes place by using two subjects connected to sensitive electronic brain measuring equipment. When the equipment indicated that the subjects were in the alpha state and dreaming, they were woken up and quickly asked to recall their dreams. In a number of cases, both "dreamer" and "dreamee" reported almost identical dream experiences.

I carried out an experiment of my own with a lady friend and was able to successfully transfer my dream to her. Her version differed ever so slightly but it was quite a startling experiment.

If you receive strangely weird dreams or even nightmares night after night you start to think about seeing a doctor. A really malicious person can plant this type of interference in your mind week after week and month after month. It can have quite a serious effect upon your sanity and most often the "sender' of these dreams is unaware of what they are doing.

The first defense against psychic attack is to *acknowledge* that the strange dream input....... and resultant uneasy feeling..... is coming from *external sources*. The second defense is to program your subconscious while in alpha (or as you go to sleep) to ignore any unwanted input of this nature. Actually the best self-program you can run is to instruct your subconscious to wake you up immediately this unwanted input arrives with the full conscious knowledge that it came from an outside source.

Your program would run as follows:

.... **"I will wake up immediately my mind detects negative incoming subjective communication. I will be aware of exactly what it is, disregard it and drop immediately back to sleep. It will have no negative effect on me at all"............**

But please remember, a lot of this negative subjective material may be coming from a person who is not only unaware of what they are doing but may be quite horrified to learn of the problems they are causing. So it is not fair to treat them unkindly......... unless they are completely aware of the harm they are doing, then there are various options open to you. It is like somebody getting a little drunk and taking a swing at you. The first time, you probably shrug it off. The second time you might start to defend yourself. But if it happens consistently you take serious action to stop the attack.

The impact of one focused human mind upon another can be quite enormous so when you are doing subjective communication make sure to keep your messages positive and mutually beneficial to both parties.

You can easily use it to project healing, loving thoughts to a person you really care about. You will be amazed at the effect it has on them! Treat Subjective Communication with the respect it deserves and treat other people as you would want to be treated yourself!

Then you can use this most magical of mental powers to help yourself and others!

6

THE AMAZING
MENTAL PENDULUM

In the past 30-40 years there have been no new major innovations in the use of the Pendulum......the following may well represent a breakthrough.........

How it all began....

It started in a very unusual way.

Ever since I was a child I had been aware of the peculiar abilities of the pendulum. My Dad used one. Which was very strange because Dad would never believe that Man could land on the Moon. Until it happened! In fact he had trouble accepting any form of new technology at all. But he believed in the power of the pendulum and the extraordinary power of hypnosis.

I can recall on many occasions that neighbours would bring over eggs for Dad to "sex". (That means to find out whether they were fertile or not).

Dad used to take off his gold wedding ring and tie a piece of cotton to it. He would then let it hang from about 6 inches of cotton over the egg (which didn't seem to mind).

If the ring started to swing it one direction, it was fertilized. If it swung in the other it was not. And the accuracy must have been fairly good because the neighbours kept returning year after year.

This "weight on a piece of thread" is called a **pendulum.**

It wasn't until recently that I learned that most major Japanese chicken hatcheries use a pendulum operator to determine the status of each egg. Apparently it saves them millions of dollars a year. And as the average Japanese businessman is very profit orientated I cannot imagine them using a "mystical" technology like this.....unless it worked.

So....... how does it work?

The answer is, nobody really knows for certain.

All that is known is that it is controlled by the subconscious mind. The idea being that you hold this pendulum between your thumb and forefinger and wait until all movement stops. You then ask, either mentally or out loud, a straightforward question that requires a **Yes** or **No** answer. The pendulum will usually start to circle and the direction of this circle gives you the answer. Once you establish whether clockwise or anti-clockwise is your "Yes" you have a useful device which taps directly into your subconscious. Constant practice increases the accuracy of the results. This simple little device has been around for thousands of years but it is only recently that the parapsychology community is starting to understand how it may operate.

It does not matter too much what the actual pendulum is constructed of. I use a paperclip on a piece of cotton. As this is very light it has little inertia and tends to pick up rotational speed quite rapidly. A heavier pendulum takes a lot longer to accelerate and supply the yes/no answer.

There is a volume of material written about actual pendulum construction and some of it is quite elaborate, but as far as I can tell, **any** small weight on a thread will give Yes/No answers. After all, it is basically only the subconscious mind converting knowledge into a discernible mechanical movement. Whether it works or not depends on the ability of your subconscious to "trigger" off an involuntary muscle movement. The strange thing is almost everyone who tries it achieves positive results. Even some of the world's greatest skeptics have been astounded to find that it actually works for them!

Anyway....on with the story.......

As a boy I never paid much attention to this pendulum business. I was too busy with other things, like trying to figure out what girls were all about!

However during my high school years my English teacher re-introduced me to the pendulum. He was an expert at it and as I showed a keen interest he taught me how to find lost or hidden objects with this weight on a bit of string. He used some sort of fairly heavy crystal on a piece of thin thread. I've forgotten what it was, but he seemed to feel that the type of crystal was important.

I had considerable success with this and used to impress my classmates no end by finding objects that they had hidden. What would happen is that I would leave the room while an object was hidden. After I had returned I would pick up a similar object - made of the same metal - and hold this in the palm of my pendulum hand as a sort of "sample". I would then instruct the pendulum to swing and point in the direction of the "lost" object. I would do this from two different angles so that I could triangulate the position of the object. I don't recall ever failing to find it! The whole business intrigued my classmates no end. However there was one engineering teacher who told me that the whole thing was a load of garbage and I'd be better off focusing on my school work. As I grew older I realized that the world was full of these "flat earth" society members. He was actually a very good teacher but like a lot of these career people suffered from tunnel vision.

Anyway I soon became bored with this whole pendulum business and forgot all about it until a couple of years ago when I picked up a woman's magazine with a picture of a pendulum on the cover and a very constructive article inside. I had actually parked my car in a no-parking spot outside a newsagency and rushed inside to buy a newspaper. As I exited something dragged me back in and I walked around the back to a magazine stand. This particular stand was right at the rear of the shop and I would not normally have looked this far back, but I did. My eyes fell on this particular woman's magazine and within 30 seconds of entering I was back at the counter buying it. I pulled the car along to a parking spot and sat there to read the article. There was definitely something about this pendulum business that "grabbed" me!

So I started fiddling with it again. Which is very strange because one would hardly expect the editor of an international business-ideas newsletter to get himself involved in such a "fringe" activity.

But for various reasons which become obvious later it would appear that I am being "led by the hand" down a certain path which I find quite interesting, to say the least!

The conventional pendulum has major limitations. To use it properly you have to be sitting upright, or close to it.

And there is always a substantial time delay between asking a question and getting an answer. The pendulum has to start swinging and it may take 30 seconds or so before a definite Yes/No answer emerges. During which time you have probably started thinking about something else and will confuse the pendulum.

I figured there had to be a better way!

It seemed to me that the muscle between the thumb and forefinger was responsible for the swinging of the pendulum weight. This is a sub-conscious autonomous movement and the operator is usually unaware of it.

But anyone sitting watching can normally detect the movement.

I started to wonder if I could get a Yes/No answer directly from my subconscious without the mechanical assistant.

And this is what I meant when I said right at the start of this report that my interest in this subject started in a very unusual way.

The chain-of-events that led up to the present state of knowledge are quite unreal!

Here is what happened:

I was lying on my bed in deep alpha one lunchtime and I started to think about this pendulum business. I was wondering how I could get a "Yes" signal directly from my subconscious. And as I had that thought .....to my total astonishment..........my left thumb muscle gave a distinct twitch. I was absolutely startled! I then asked for a "No" and got a very weak twitch in my right thumb muscle. At that point I forgot all about doing the usual count up out of alpha and sat bolt upright.

I had been given the technique!!!

I promptly tried it again while I was fully awake and nothing happened.

It actually took 2 months of constant alpha practice before it happened again. I persevered only because I knew it was possible. After that I could bring it on when required. But.........the "signal" was very weak. That is, the "twitch" was barely noticeable and there was some time delay between asking the question and actually getting an answer. I then designed an alpha tape that I played every night instructing this "twitch" response to become stronger and much more rapid.

After approximately 12 months I had it going reliably and found I could even use it while I was driving the car.

Then I discovered by accident that I could get a rapid "Yes/No" response and also a "No/Yes". And I started to realize how incredibly useful this could be. This type of response means that there is both a Yes and a No answer.

A mechanical pendulum cannot give a response like this as it would have to circle both ways simultaneously. Any conventional pendulum operator reading this will probably be jumping up and down with excitement at this point!

If so, I've got even better news!!

More recently I've been able to get a "slow" yes which I have taken to mean as a "Yes...**but**." Likewise with "No". Sort of an uncertain Yes or No response.

And the most amazing thing about all this is the manner in which it can be used.

The most useful aspect is while I am in bed at night and I am using alpha to solve business problems. I come up with some alpha answers then "ask" the pendulum if one specific answer is correct. I ask for a straight Yes/No answer. Sometimes I am totally staggered to find that this "Mental Pendulum" response tells me none of the answers are right, even though at least one answer felt like the right one. So I keep coming up with ideas and use the pendulum to get a sense of mental direction.

I have slowly evolved a "protocol" which involves asking a specific train of questions which tends to put me on the right track. This is far quicker than "guessing" questions to ask. I have been able to come up with the most extraordinary results in this way ......that have converted to cold, hard dollars and cents! Some of the ideas are not what I would have expected at all, but in retrospect they have been absolutely correct.

This procedure has gone a long way to convince me that the subconscious mind has all the answers necessary for a person to achieve total success and freedom in life! The problem has always been ......how to tap the subconscious for answers. It is starting to look like this might be one workable method.

But better still, I have been able to use dream control techniques to program up specific dreams and then use the pendulum to help interpret them.....**there and then!**

Basically what happens is that I program to have a specific dream and at the same time program to wake up immediately after it. (The subconscious can easily be programmed to do this - it will do anything you tell it........ once you have learnt the procedure). I then analyze the dream using the Mental Pendulum. This way I seem to be able to get some reasonably accurate interpretations that have proven to be remarkably handy.

But more amazingly, I have found (and I found this by accident also) that when I am down in Theta and my thumb muscles are too relaxed to twitch, I can transfer the "twitch" to my eyebrows. Probably because these are closer to the brain. Furthermore, I was eventually able to transfer the "twitch" to other muscle groups such as my large toes!

Which brings me to one of the more helpful aspects of this Mental Pendulum.

If I have a question which requires the answer to be "counted" out my thumb muscle will give a series of fairly rapid twitches. Professional pendulum users will immediately recognize the implications of this.

When Divining for water or whatever the depth in feet or meters can be determined by the number of rapid "twitches". Likewise if you're looking for opal or some other precious stone the hidden depth in the mine wall can be determined quite quickly.

One of the more interesting innovations was the development of a "checking" procedure to get a percentage accuracy reading for a specific question. I was getting unreliable answers in the casino when asking which slot machine to play and devised a self-checking method whereby I would ask the pendulum whether it would give me better than 90% accurate answers. If the answer was No I would then ask if it would give better than 80% accurate answers.....and so on.

Initially with the slot machines it would not give any better than 60% accurate answers, but I found this to be better than nothing. The accuracy has improved lately but I get the impression the pendulum doesn't like these futile games!

It has proven to be fairly handy in the gambling environment because casino management give you a strange look if you start using a conventional pendulum around the roulette wheel or slot machines. With this Mental Pendulum nobody knows what you're doing. You can stand around with your hands in your pockets asking for Yes/ No answers. Except other players give you strange looks if your trousers start twitching violently.

I find this whole mental process quite uncanny at times. It is not an original discovery as there are *dowsers* (people who use divining rods) who work in a similar manner. This is called "deviceless" dowsing. But at least it is original with regard to the method being used to interpret dreams and solve business problems. Or win on the slot machines and Roulette! All you need on Roulette is a 5% advantage over the "house" to make money. With the Slots you only need to know which machine is likely to pay out. I normally use the Mental Pendulum after I have given the machine a couple of spins. For some reason I can get a more accurate answer this way.

The usual mechanical pendulum gives a Yes/No/Maybe response, plus a couple of others if you're really proficient. This Mental Pendulum so far has produced 7 different styles of response (possibly 8)..... all very rapid and definite.

I have trained a couple of friends to use this new method - it took several days in one case and 2 weeks in another. It involved some deep alpha suggestion and some unusual muscle training exercises. But I have been able to simplify all this and have finalized a training method whereby virtually anybody could get it "up and running" within a week or so without any undue effort. (Some people will probably be able to "trigger" it off on the first try).

This whole Mental Pendulum procedure has improved my business and personal life out of sight. And the strange thing about it all is this: I have the feeling it is a "half-way" method to be able to bring on the 6th sense of *intuition* at will.

The reason I say this is because I am now starting to receive mental yes/ no impressions before I even ask the Mental Pendulum for an answer.

That is ....I do not even have to ask the question......I just *know* the correct answer!

All I have to do is *think* about asking the question and a strong impression pops into my mind.

On the occasions when this happens I feel quite elated. It has become obvious that the whole procedure is leading somewhere.

If the procedure eventually brings on the 6th sense as a fully controllable, working human facility then this mental process will take on a rather important new dimension.

And this is where the problem lies.....in the meantime anyway.

You really just can't sit down and instruct your thumb to twitch in response to a mental question. There has to be a psychological trigger implanted. But I think we've just about solved this problem. It initially took me 2 months to get even a faint repeatable response but a simple new procedure should bring this down to less than a week.

But, once you've got it up and running .....you've basically got it for the rest of your life. It will become an automatic response when you get a problem.

You don't think about using it ..... it just happens! And as you get better at it I'm sure you will find, as I have, that you don't have to ask for a Yes/No answer at all .... you just "know" the answer!

I have the definite feeling that this is the road to bringing on a fully working 6th sense facility. But ......time will tell!

Thanks to this process, some of the concepts I have been able to generate have converted into substantial lumps of cash........solely due to using this Mental Pendulum technique. And that to me......business-wise........is the bottom line!

IT REALLY COMES DOWN TO A PORTABLE, FLEXIBLE METHOD OF RAPIDLY TAPPING THE SUBCONSCIOUS, WITHOUT THE AWKWARDNESS OF PHYSICAL MECHANISMS.

SUGGESTED PROCEDURE FOR LEARNING THIS TECHNIQUE

It appears that you must *tell* your subconscious quite forcefully that you want your thumb muscles to twitch in response to a direct question. The best way to do this is to *show it*! Sit there...relax....and intentionally twitch the thumb muscles on each hand to show it what you want it to do.

As you go to sleep at night feed the suggestion into your mind that "my thumb muscles will twitch in response to a direct yes/no question".

Keep repeating this as you go to sleep. Maybe you can do what I did and make up a simple cassette that repeats this over and over.

You may find that you have fairly quick success.....or it may take some time.

Once you have the thumbs twitching you can simply tell the subconscious to transfer this twitch to other body muscles.....such as your toes or eyebrows.

In teaching other people I found the best thing was for them initially to practice twitching the muscles intentionally, while all the time telling their subconscious that this is what they *expected*. Then I got them to totally relax and ask a question that gave a *yes* answer ....such as - "Is my name Jim" (or whatever your name is)......or...."Is grass green".

Eventually they got it working. The secret appears to be in relaxing totally (or dropping to alpha) and telling your subconscious forcefully what it is you want.

AN ALTERNATIVE METHOD

There is an alternative way to get a muscle reaction and that is by pressing the palms of your hands flat together, with fingers outstretched and holding them as though you were praying. By asking for a *yes/no* response your hands may twitch one way or the other.

For some people this may be the easiest method of invoking this Mental pendulum reaction. A lot of my clients have found this method quicker and easier.

If it doesn't work the first time relax back in a chair and after closing your eyes visualize your hands twitching in response to your question. It may work better while relaxed.

When you first try to achieve a twitch in your thumb muscles you may notice a tingling sensation...this is an indication that the process is starting to work.

After you have become proficient at this process you might like to project it on to a *mental movie screen* in your mind. That is, you "see" your yes/no answer on your mental movie screen.

Picture a "blackboard pointer" which is placed in the centre of your mental screen. A *yes* or *no* response will cause this pointer to move either to the left or the right, at varying speeds, depending on the strength of the yes/no response.

If you practice this for a while you may find that it becomes amazingly accurate and reliable....and evolves into an automatic response.

It might take you some weeks of practice to make the twitch work as an autonomous muscle reaction but if you are prepared to persevere with the process you just might end up with something that will change your life.

The average reader of a mind-power book (like myself) becomes rather impatient with practical exercises that the author recommends trying. When I read a book that requires me to stop and carry out some sort of exercise I normally give it a perfunctory try then carry on reading.

However in this case I seriously suggest that you bookmark this pendulum section and come back to it later when you have time to seriously try the process. The reason for this is that when you are able to activate and develop your "thumb twitch" you will be in possession of extraordinary new intuition powers that will literally change your life.

If you can get it working successfully and reliably then this is the start of a fully automated, fully functional, full-on intuitional ability, which in the end may well become as reliable as your other 5 senses.

If you can develop the full use of your **six senses** then your success and lifestyle will change in a way that you would never have believed possible.

7

THE EXTRAORDINARY WORLD
OF REMOTE VIEWING &
OUT-OF-BODY EXPERIENCES

Throughout history there have always been individuals who possessed the amazing ability to "see" things either at a distant place or at a distant time, both past and future.

But it wasn't until around 20 years ago that serious research was started by scientific and military groups in the U.S.A.

They found that the human mind had the amazing ability to "see" events at a distance even though under normal circumstances the "viewer" had no knowledge of these events.

They further found that under certain mind-states a person could "see" reasonably accurately into the future or into the past. Not only that but distance didn't matter.

Princeton University and the original Stanford Research Institute carried out extensive research into this effect, which eventually became known as REMOTE VIEWING or RVing for short.

In fact the results created such a stir in the scientific world that the United States Government took an interest in it and the matter of Remote Viewing was raised in congress in June 1981

The advances in Remote Viewing have been quite spectacular since then.

So what then is remote viewing?

And how similar is it to a controlled out-of-body experience?

Both appear to give similar results but require the application of different mental techniques.

Most people have had some sort of Out-of-Body Experience (OBE) during their lives. This may occur during a dream when they clearly visualize themselves flying or visiting different places. Usually the vision is extraordinarily clear and colourful and often can be remembered quite vividly. Also the person often has considerable control over the OBE.

The people who have learnt to have OBE's intentionally can usually induce them at will and obtain incredibly accurate information about something at a distance. Similarly people who have taken a Remote Viewing (RV) course can obtain similar information but the quality of the information is different to that obtained from OBE's.

Remote Viewers who want accurate information about an event in the future use a process called *Associated Remote Viewing* whereby the target being viewed is represented as an object such as a ball, watch, pen, fork, etc.

They then "view" to see which object appears in their mind and this object is then associated with the actual future event. At least one group has experimented with remote viewing the stock market.....apparently quite successfully for a while.

Specialized remote viewing organizations now do serious work for oil companies, big businesses and government agencies where every piece of information is considered valuable.

When I was learning associated RVing I used to visualize a series of traffic lights.

If I saw a series of red lights down the road ahead of me I took that as a NO answer.

But if I saw a series of green lights I took that as a YES answer.

I also developed a method of seeing a group of full Champaign glasses as a YES answer while a NO answer was represented as a group of empty glasses lying on their side.

This is quite an easy RVing exercise to practice and beginners often have considerable success with it.

The general public are basically unaware of RV and will probably remain that way for the foreseeable future, so any individual or group who goes to the trouble to investigate this 6th sense process will probably find they have a tremendous personal and business advantage over others.

Basically the RV process works like this:

The "viewer" spends some time relaxing to get down to the alpha or theta brain frequency state. They are then asked by their interviewer to visualize a certain situation, set of map co-ordinates, or whatever.

The interviewer is not strictly necessary but in a commercial/military situation is usually found to produce better results.

The viewer focuses and then either verbalizes or draws diagrams of what they "sense".

An experienced interviewer can lead the viewer to give detailed information about the subject matter that might otherwise have been missed.

The amazing thing about this process is that virtually anyone can do it! Particularly those who are already capable of personal alpha or theta control. But it takes constant practice and training.

To become proficient in Remote Viewing takes some years of constant effort but that extraordinary human quirk known as the "novice effect" generally means that RV beginners sometimes have quite startling successes. On one of my earlier attempts I was able to remote view the exact layout of an overseas casino (which was totally unknown to me) and furthermore was able to identify a particular machine which was due to pay a jackpot. During a subsequent overseas business trip I was able to visit this casino and found that the layout of the establishment was exactly as the RV information indicated. The concrete driveway was where it should have been .... so were the 4 concrete columns in front ..... the gardens on each side ..... the views of the harbour from the front steps.....all the reflective glass inside (which were actually glass showcases but RV'd as mirrors).......the giant chandelier..... and the actual layout of the poker machines which were arranged in a large curve (this was the clearest view of all). It came as no surprise when the targeted machine paid a small jackpot that was sufficient to cover airfare and basic expenses. I ended up with almost a free trip to this country which was Macau outside Hong Kong! This experience (which was slightly unnerving) went a long way to convince me that RVing worked!!!

The strange thing about RVing is that the size of the target doesn't matter. The Silva Mind course I went to had us remote viewing inside small cubes of metal. The experience was uncanny as I could actually sense the coldness and metallic taste of the metal. Most of the people on the course (all rank beginners) were successful in this experiment.

If you want to try this yourself try visualizing your mind inside a biro pen or a leaf.

If you suddenly become aware of the horrible taste of biro ink or chlorophyll then you have succeeded.

During an OBE experience involving a small target most viewers reported that they appeared to be able to observe the atomic structure (or something similar) of the object. They also reported that an OBE view of a target gave a much clearer and detailed picture than a Remote View.

One of the easiest ways to practice Remote Viewing by yourself is, as you wake up in the morning (in the alpha state) and before you open your eyes, to picture your bedside clock and the exact time shown on the dial.

After a little practice you will probably be quite amazed to find that you get it exactly right more often than not. It took me around 2 weeks to achieve my first success. As you get better at it (and gain more confidence) you will find yourself able to do this at any time of the day or night. These simple experiences can have quite a profound effect upon you, sometimes even causing your "disbelief" system to kick in.

The strange thing is....you were born with this natural mental ability but if you have been unaware of the concept of remote viewing until now then this inherent ability will not have been nurtured.

It makes you wonder where all this human-potential knowledge has been hidden, doesn't it?

And when the US Congress takes an interest in it and the scientists at such institutions as Princeton University spend a fair portion of their working lives and funds on the subject you get the feeling that remote viewing is not going to go away merely because the skeptics say it can't work!

The interesting thing about RVing and OBEing is that your mind usually "connects "with the target required, even if it is presented to you only as a set of map co-ordinates. It is almost like a highly efficient universal telephone exchange. You mentally *dial the number* and get connected.

I can see enormous advantages for the serious business person in this field in the same manner that computer technology has changed the way a lot of businesses work. Twenty years from now RVing might well become part of standard business practice.

The more you practice this type of mental activity .... the more you open up your right-brain intuitive channels. There is no telling where it might lead to and it is 100% safe because that is how your mind was intended to function. Until now you have probably been unaware of that fact!

THE ORIGINAL REMOTE VIEWING TRAINING PROCEDURE

The original learning procedure as used at SRI International (formerly the Stanford Research Institute), during the 1970's and up until the mid 1980's, is as follows:

The viewer and his/her interviewer would be closeted in a room without windows in the lab.

Another team of 1 or 2 people would go and visit a preselected target. This group was known as the *out-bounders*. The target was selected at random from a pool of targets. The envelope containing the target information was opened in the car by the out-bounders only after they had left the grounds of the laboratory. They arrived at this target destination at the time specified in the instructions and spent 15 minutes *visually soaking* up the target.

Meanwhile the viewer was being monitored by the interviewer to give details in either verbal or pictorial form about the target.

When the out-bounders returned the entire team including the Remote Viewer returned to the target for the necessary feedback. The accuracy of the viewing was then accessed by a team of judges, who were separate from the viewing and beacon teams.

A more elaborate version of this procedure is where several independent teams work on the same target. The results are given to an independent judge who forms a *consensus* opinion.

Sometimes physical objects are substituted for the target - this is known as Associative remote viewing. The most elaborate kind of RV is *consensual associated remote viewing*. This is reported as sometimes being reasonably accurate, especially when viewing future events. This is the type of process used by the professionals to predict future commodity and stockmarket shifts.

In fact one of the better known RV groups actually financed their start-up operation with RV wins on the silver commodities market and horse races.

One of our subscribers has reported achieving top results in horse racing by using alpha/RV techniques. He has successfully *visualized* the first 3 letters of the names of winning horses ....in advance! And he had absolutely no knowledge of RVing until he read our material.

It is now suspected by an increasing proportion of the parapsychology community that remote viewing is a normal capability of mankind but has fallen into disuse compared to how it may have been utilized in earlier historic times. In actual fact RVing has been likened to **controlled daydreaming**, which is really what it is.

When you daydream you change your current reality and project your mind into an alternative situation. This is exactly what you attempt to achieve during a remote viewing session.

Several years ago I developed a basic remote viewing training program for my students. It enabled people with absolutely no knowledge of remote viewing to try it out for themselves.

(Eventually professional RVer Angela Thompson from Las Vegas and myself developed a much mote elaborate RV101 home training course.)

Here then is the original basic training program which you can use to get started............

THE EXTRAORDINARY WORLD
OF REMOTE PERCEPTION

INTRODUCTION

Remote Viewing is the name given to the gathering of geographically
displaced....or temporally displaced....information by senses other than
the conventional five that we normally use.

The process has been available to the human race for eons.......but
over the past 1000 years has been suppressed and discouraged.

A few secret societies such as the Rosicrucians were aware of it...and
encouraged their followers to learn the process.

Cultures within our society who were able to sidestep mainstream
belief systems over the last 1000 years...such as Australia's Aboriginals.......
have basically retained this historic remote viewing (RV) ability. It is part
of their inherent tradition and is considered a *normal* mental ability. That
is...among the Elders. Their young people who have been influenced by
western values, do not appear to share the same belief system.

There is generally nothing that <u>cannot</u> be remote viewed.

Any object, event, thoughtform or concept can be viewed in the past,
present or future.

Around 20 years ago a very perceptive physicist by the name of Hal
Puthoff started a series of investigations at what was then known as the
Stanford Research Institute.

He used as his subject a person who had demonstrated considerable
talents in mentally "seeing" geographically distant events and sequences.

That person was New York artist Ingo Swann.

The meeting of these two unlikely individuals changed the face of
psychic research completely.

It is now more acceptable for serious scientists to research psi abilities....back then...it definitely wasn't.

Hal Puthoff put his name fairly well on the line when he encouraged the nations second largest "think tank" to fund this new psi "science".

The result was the creation of a "new" mind-science....they called it REMOTE VIEWING.

The rest is history.

The US Military got wind of this research and eventually poured millions of dollars into it. It was eventually found that virtually anyone could learn RVing...and in fact the learning curve was short!

Some astounding discoveries were made. Swann startled the Stanford research team by telling them that he could identify a site merely from the latitude and longitude coordinates. He was given a set of coordinates and correctly identified the area.

He even described in detail what the weather was like......the shape of the buildings, etc.

Tests on RV students indicated that after a little practice this *coordinate RVing* was fairly easy to accomplish.

It was then discovered that RVing could be done just as accurately in the past and the future.

There appeared to be no time restraints at all.

Over the years the RV learning process has been refined.........and procedures and protocols have been developed that enable students to experience sometimes quite profound results quite rapidly.

At this point in time RVing has evolved into two separate camps.

The first is the military style **rigid-protocol** Controlled Remote Viewing (CRV) while the second is the non-military **elastic-protocol** generalised RVing.

It is this latter protocol that we are dealing with in this instructional course. The military version cannot easily be learnt at home......it requires an experienced moderator to guide the student at every step. Both methods have their place in the scheme of things but the "free-form" method is quicker and easier to learn.

You may find right at the start that you score some impressive *novice* hits but on the other hand you may find (like myself) that it takes several weeks of persevering before anything noticeable happens.

Your own progress will depend entirely upon your belief system and your own personal mind-set.

But one thing is absolutely certain.........you *will* learn to Remote View...if you are prepared to practice.

PREPARATION FOR RV TRAINING

RELAXATION

It appears that most successful RVing takes place in the alpha/theta state. It is very easy to learn to drop into alpha....which is really a relaxed meditative state. You probably drop into this state naturally 10-20 times a day.

Simply sit back in a comfortable chair (or lie down) and let yourself relax. Make sure you are totally at ease, with shoes off. If you're using a chair make sure it is of the armchair type, that supports your head. I personally prefer to lie down flat.

Now focus on your breathing. Simply become aware of yourself breathing in and out. Each time you exhale, say to yourself...."I am relaxing". Keep this up until you feel yourself on the verge of a dream state. By thinking about your breathing you are thinking inwards...rather than focusing outwards on external stimuli. At the same time tell yourself that you will remain conscious....but that your body will drift off to sleep. This is known as the "Mind-Awake/Body-Asleep" state. It is the absolute basis of all mind power learning.

When doing this I use my mental picture screen to display a large BETA (B) symbol.

This reminds my mind that I want to stay consciously aware while dropping to lower brain frequency levels. This was hard for me to do initially as I found it difficult to picture a mental "movie" screen. It took weeks before I could reliably achieve this and I used to picture various fruits such as a lemon and orange on my screen. I then learnt to picture myself tasting these fruits to get the flavours. More about this below.

After you have practiced this 10-20 times your mind starts to accept that you require it to "let go" when you start the process. Something like the trained reaction with Pavlov's dogs. The process eventually becomes quicker and quicker....until you get to the point where you merely need to relax and "think" about your breathing....and you're in alpha.

These days it takes usually me less than 3 minutes to achieve the beta range.

Most of my mind power is done in the morning while I am fresh, so there is less chance of accidentally falling asleep.

Some of the professional RV courses tell you to imagine a ball of golden light centered in your stomach......and moving it around your muscle groups one by one to relax them. Apparently this is a highly successful technique for quick relaxation.

This is an ideal state to start your remote viewing practice.

It is generally considered that the lower state of theta is the best for remote viewing, but there are a number of professional remote viewers who use alpha.

This is where you will start. Eventually, you might even find that you can handle RVing in full awake beta, which is where you are at the moment.

The main thing at the start is to make yourself comfortable and let yourself relax naturally.

You can practice this in bed at might if you wish....and when you first wake up in the morning.

VISUALISATION EXERCISES

Once you are lying back relaxed in alpha, you start a series of simple visualisation exercises as listed below. These are designed to awaken your *input* channels. They appear to be simplistic and maybe even childish but it is amazing how many people there are who have *never* tried a visualisation practice before.

Some people are natural born visualisers while others (like myself) had extreme difficulty developing a mental picture in the "minds-eye".

What I did eventually was to visualise (imagine?) a movie screen in my mind...then imagine a ripe banana appearing on it.

Then I visualised peeling the banana, etc. I went on to practice visualising other fruit such as different coloured apples. Some people can automatically do this....I am one of the people who actually had to learn the process. Nowadays I can pull up any picture I want on my "mental screen", even while walking along the road!

If you are comfortable with your ability to bring up a mental picture then here are three exercises which you practice over and over until they become automatic:

1 FEELING EXERCISE
   Visualise a cat. "Feel" the soft fur. Feel its warmth. Feel the shape of its body as you stroke it.
   Practice this for several minutes.

2 TASTE EXERCISE
   Picture a lemon on your mental screen. Picture it being cut into pieces....and mentally place a piece in your mouth. Taste the acidic bitterness.
   Practice this for several minutes.

3 SMELL EXERCISE
   Picture a garden of flowers. See yourself walking among them until you are drawn to those with the nicest fragrance. Smell them. Enjoy this fragrance.
   Practice this for several minutes.

The reason for opening up your mind to the above sensations is that you will need these abilities when you start to remote view. Many of your RV impressions will arrive apart from your sense of sight. You might for example detect strong emotion at the RV target....or a sense of coldness (or warmth)....or in some cases it will trigger off the remembrance of a certain smell or odour.

As such the above exercises are part and parcel of learning remote viewing.

When I first started RVing I was somewhat intrigued by the emotional input I got. I was unaware that this would happen and I was pleasantly surprised. It added realism to the RV picture I was receiving. It basically let me know that I was on the right track....and actually receiving RV impressions, otherwise I might have assumed that it was all my imagination. When you first receive an RV image with an emotional component, you will probably find yourself somewhat awed.

The first dramatic experience I had along these lines was when I was doing a military style RVing course in Las Vegas. I was given a target and was sitting upright in a chair,

Suddenly I found myself "rocking" from side to side and had the immediate impression I was in a boat. This turned out to be correct.

YOUR FIRST STEP

Locate some old National Geographic magazines (or something similar) and cut out the pages which have simple-form pictures, such as a mountain, bridge or boat. Do not select pictures containing multiple different small objects. You need pictures with only one major gestalt.

Now place each picture inside an envelope face up. It is important to use a large envelope so the picture is inserted without a fold. The best idea is to colour-photocopy each picture so that there is nothing on the back of the actual target. The mind can get confused and try to RV the print or whatever on the back of the target. I suggest you prepare a pool of at least 18 such envelopes.

Take the 18 envelopes you have prepared and place them in a stack in front of you. Shuffle them each time you use them so that they are in a different order.

Select one envelope at random and place your hand on top of it. Relax into alpha. Let an impression float into your mind. Tell yourself that you want to become aware of the shape inside the envelope. After a while *impressions* of shapes may start to appear...nothing definite....just impressions.

You may for example, gain the impression of a *squarish* object. If, when you open the envelope the shape is of a square nature then you have had a fairly accurate "hit".

When you get really good at this you will be able to visualise the correct shape 40-50% of the time....without even putting your hand on the envelope.

Try it out various ways to see which gives you the most accurate response.

Initially I was taking around 5 minutes each envelope to achieve even mediocre results....but as time went by I could take a "snap guess" and still get acceptable results.

The first 2 or 3 times I tried this I got none right at all...and I wondered if in fact it was possible to RV this way.

Believe me...it is!!!!

It is a skill....and it takes practice.

Some readers will have immediate success with this exercise....while others won't. Don't be discouraged...there are plenty of different styles of exercises for you to chose from. One specific exercise will probably appeal to you above all others and give the best results.

When you score a "bullseye" for the first time, your heart might thump a little as you suddenly realise that it *can be done!*

The best time to practice the envelope exercise is when you're mentally fresh. Psi powers definitely work better with a fresh, clear mind. Tiredness and RVing don't appear to go together in the early stages.

The above exercise is designed to identify the shapes and forms of the picture inside the envelope.

The idea is to view the actual major gestalt shape in the picture. For example, if the picture is of a waterfall you might "sense" a vertical shiny bright reflective column or shape. This is your mind attempting to convey the image to you.

There are additional exercises listed below. Read through them and select the ones that appeal to you most. Try these out. There is no specific time frame involved.......simply carry on with an exercise until you become bored with it. Then try another.

You will probably find that if you are prepared to spend 30-60 minutes a day on RV practice then positive results will soon become evident.

Initially you may appear to have no success at all. Remember you are asking your mind to do something that it is inherently capable of....but has never been asked to do before. In actual fact you will be "setting up" your mental process for future success.

Like most skills it is sometimes the slowest learners who eventually achieve the best results.

It took me around a year of spasmodic "fiddling" before I started to acquire acceptable results. This was mainly because I didn't focus on it........I had serious doubts as to whether I could do it even though I was fully aware that I had some natural psychic abilities.

But with this RV course there is a definite protocol and plan of action. If you stick with the practice....you will achieve results.

If you have an Internet connection you will find a number of remote viewing sites that contain "target" pictures which you can practice on. You are given a group of numbers and basic detail of the target, such as whether it is manmade or natural. The idea is to use these number groups as the target identification for remote viewing. Amazingly enough this is all the information you require to do a successful remote view. After you've worked on this target you can click back onto that page and view the actual target picture. You can find these sites by searching for Remote-Viewing in the search engines.

FURTHER PRACTICE TECHNIQUES

REMOTE VIEWING TOMORROW'S NEWSPAPER

Here is an easy way to practice RVing into the future.

Relax into your meditative state and mentally picture the lead photo in tomorrow's newspaper. Try and visualise the main shape of the contents of that "future" photo. See if you can detect whether the picture represents a "motionless" scene or an "action" scene. See if you can detect emotion in it....and colour.

Next morning when you buy the paper check the lead picture on the front page and see how close you were. You might have mainly "misses" to start with but after a while you will get "partial hits'

For example, you might have received an impression of bushy, colourful shapes. The photo in the paper might be of flowers, so you had a partial hit. Occasionally you will find that you get a full on hit. This will be quite an exciting moment as your chances of guessing this correctly would be minimal.

Do not initially try to view the exact picture...merely the shape, colour, form and action/emotion.

The beauty of this style of RVing is that you are practicing to remote view the future and you might be able to refine the process to determine stock price *direction* twenty four hours ahead!

HISTORICAL ARTIFACTS

This is one of the first exercises given in some standard RV courses.

The idea here is to acquire an old artifact of some kind. Maybe a family heirloom or a postage stamp from a bygone era.

Or if you're feeling confident you might like to visit your local museum and try your RVing there.

The idea is to hold the object in your hand (if it is small) or merely place your hand on it if it is large.

Now drop into your meditative state and try to sense where the object came from. Was it a barren or tree covered area? Is there any emotion surrounding the object? Is there a feeling of isolation or of activity? Let these impressions build in your mind. If you feel that you're starting to add your own imagination to the picture, stop the exercise....clear your mind....and start again.

At the beginning, the main difficulty you will experience will be that your fertile mind will try to *overlay* detail that it thinks should be there. That is...it cheerfully fills in the gaps. Usually it's wrong!!

I keep instructing my mind ......"Give me the detail - do not overlay".

After a while your mind will faithfully start to follow these instructions. If I detect what I think is overlay coming in...I cease the exercise and start again fresh. I might have to do this 4-5 times.

When you start to receive an impression from your historical artifact you might like to ask your mind to supply input from a different perspective...maybe from a birds-eye view.

Professional RVers can swing their centre of consciousness all round the target subject, both from a geographical viewpoint and a temporal/time viewpoint.

ASSOCIATIVE REMOTE VIEWING

If you are looking for a yes/no answer for a specific problem....the Associative method appears to work reasonably accurately assuming you practice the process with determination.

For example.......let us suppose you wanted to RV two horses in the next Melbourne Cup. You would treat this as two entirely separate RV sessions.

You would attach a pair of objects to horse "A". Let us use the scissors and the orange again.

You would say to your mind that you wanted to know if horse "A" was going to be one of the first 3 winners. A pair of scissors would indicate a YES. An orange would indicate a NO.

Then do your RVing. See which object appears in your mental picture. If the answer is a YES, you may not actually receive an impression of a pair of scissors....you may merely receive the impression of a sharp object. This obviously relates to the scissors. But if you received the impression of a gentle rounded form ...maybe with pleasant emotion attached...you would treat this as the orange.

This is where your earlier practice of distinguishing shapes, forms, emotions, etc. come in to play.

Then you repeat the process for the second horse. Clearly tell your mind the name of the horse.....then you can use the same scissors and orange as associated objects.

Make sure you hold the name of the horse in your mind....so that you do not inadvertently RV the wrong animal. If you want to avoid confusion you could use two entirely different objects to represent the second horse.

There is no reason why you can't RV the whole field of horses in the race. As there is an emotive component to this form of RVing (i.e. you stand to win or lose money) then you may find that it works quite well, after a little practice.

Don't be too concerned if it doesn't work the first time. Pick a different race every day and keep practicing. You are asking your mind to do something it is fully capable of doing...but has never been asked to do before. After a while, you might really start impressing yourself.

Associative RVing in this manner can basically be used for any precognitive situation that requires a yes/no answer. Also the fact that you are using two dissimilar objects means that when you gain an impression of *sharp points* or *round object* you can more easily relate it to the correct object/outcome. It would be virtually impossible to *view* the actual winning horse.......but fairly easy to view the general shape of an object **associated with that horse.**

You may want to practice on a selected share/stock/commodity. You will be asking....."will this share go up or down in the next 24 hours?"

Because of the short time span .....24 hours....you are able to obtain fairly prompt feedback.

REMOTE VIEWING FOR MINERALS AND METALS

If you wanted to find, say, opal in a mine then the procedure is as follows:

Make yourself familiar with the layout of the mine then sit somewhere and enter your meditative state. Ask your mind to highlight pockets of opal as red colours on the walls of the mine. Try digging where impressions of red colour appear. Sit there, relax, and picture the walls of the mine. Sense for red colours. You might receive only a very vague impression....or you might get a full-on burst of brilliant red in one area of the mine.

This process can be applied to finding the location of any precious metal or mineral. By associating the mineral/metal with a colour, it makes it easier for your mind to produce results without erroneous overlay.

This process is really associative RVing using colours. Some people find it very easy to visualise colours...so this particular method may work well for them.

You can also use colours instead of discrete objects for racehorses, etc.

As with all RVing work you will need to experiment to see what methods give you the easiest and most reliable results.

REMOTE VIEWING BUSINESS/LIFESTYLE PROBLEMS

If you have a specific problem that you can reduce to a yes/no question, you can use the above described associated RVing.

OUTBOUNDER RVING (ALSO CALLED REMOTE TRACKING)

This will require the assistance of a friend.

You ask your friend to go for a 15-30 minute walk around the neighborhood. Give him or her a cassette recorder if possible. Every 2-3 minutes the friend stops in front of an object of interest (such as a spectacular tree, church, signboard, etc.) and describes it in detail for 60 seconds or so. He/she also notes the time on their watch. If they don't use a recorder the details...along with the time....can be noted down on a pad. (Recording the exact time is important).

The "viewer" back at home (probably you) relaxes into a meditative state and tries to capture the essence of what the viewer is doing and seeing. You may detect a shape, form, colour or emotion. You might even get a clear picture of what the outbounder is actually seeing.

During this exercise in the RV course I went to, there were an amazing number of direct "hits" that were stunningly accurate. This is probably because you are not being asked to view a discreet object directly....you are being asked to view that object via another person's mind. This seems to be a lot easier.

When the outbounder returns they read out their notes (or play the cassette) and a comparison of images plus precise times is made. The whole exercise is a lot easier than it sounds. Once you try it, you will find it very easy to do in the future.

COORDINATE RVING

This is an exercise where the viewer is given a set of latitude and longitude coordinates and is asked to view what is at that site. The viewer must not know in advance what the site is....or even have any form of clue.

REMOTE VIEWING LOTTO NUMBERS

Use the same process as used for racehorses. View each and every number and ask….."Will this number be among the winning six in Gold Lotto (or whatever) this Saturday night"?

(You must specify precisely which lotto and which night). Use associated items such as the scissors and the orange to give you yes/no answers.

This exercise was done by a small group of RVers in New Zealand some time ago. After each viewer spent countless hours on accessing the particular group of numbers provided...all the results were combined and tabulated. This was consensual RVing where an average from all the individual members was averaged and analysed. Unfortunately the exercise wasn't completed until just before the lotto closed and it was too late to enter.

To everyone's total astonishment....the group picked five of the six winning numbers. I lost touch with them at this point and have no idea what the final outcome was.

MOBILE RV PRACTICE

There are two simple ways you can improve your RV skills while on the move. The first is to buy a pack of cards and place them in front of you (after shuffling them thoroughly). Put your hand on the top card and ask.. *"What are the colours and shapes on this card?"*

Initially you might ask whether the card is a red or a black then progress on to shapes.

You can do this exercise anywhere. You may have a lot of success at this or you may not. Initially you may have to relax and spend several minutes on each card, but after a while you may be able to make "snap" judgments with reliable accuracy.

Another reliable practice method is when you are on a long boring drive and you have slipped into alpha and are driving "mechanically". Ask yourself...*"What will be the colour of the next car that appears on the road ahead of me?"*

You can do this exercise dozens of times during a long trip. It helps fill in the time and is highly effective practice. Alternatively you can ask what shape object you will see when you round the next corner.

I did a colour exercise at the local casino using the reds and blacks on the roulette table.

I tried this on and off for around a week in short bursts (I found the exercise boring as I did not bet). In the finish I figured I was "guessing" about 60% correct which would have been enough to make a small steady profit. Regrettably roulette bores me to tears as I can't get emotional about it. I guess this is because of the slow speed of play.

You also might like to gain an impression of who is ringing you before answering the phone. You start in a simple manner by asking...is the caller male or female. Try to get a mental impression of a male or female.... maybe by using associated objects.

I'm sure that once you start you will develop ideas of your own.

Please....do not be discouraged if you don't get immediate results. It took me at least a week to get a decent result initially...this was before I was aware of any of the above methods.

With these training methods you are likely to get early encouraging results with at least one of the methods.

Once you have developed a certain talent and gained confidence with the process then you can start to explore anything you want.

Probably the most fascinating is outer space.

There is no limit to how far you can "throw" your centre of consciousness. You might like to take a "look" at the alien mining ship floating in the Rings of Saturn.

As you continue looking at this your perceptions will be enhanced and you will be able to sense the bleakness and isolation of outer space, broken only by this enormous floating spacecraft.

Remember, once you become proficient at this skill....use it wisely.

LIKE ANY OTHER SKILL....YOU MUST PRACTICE....PRACTICE.....PRACTICE

8

PSYCHOKINETIC PROBLEM
SOLVING PROGRAM

This program involves making a special cassette tape. You can do this on any audio-cassette machine, Dictaphone stereo system or computer. It is easy to do.... instructions are given at the end.

The mind is a strange thing. In fact the human mind could almost be described as an ongoing non-physical event.

When we least expect it inspirations pop out!

Quite often soul shattering, awe-inspiring inspirations emerge, as if from nowhere.

And they are usually so obvious that we wonder why we didn't think of them before.

They were usually triggered by a special set of circumstances that created a necessity for some form of answer. That is, you might have chewed over some serious problem for days (or weeks) and because of the intensity of your thought and your utter absorption with the problem, it has been circulating in your subconscious mind for some time.

Suddenly when you least expect it the correct solution appears as an "inspirational flash".

This invariably happens when your conscious mind is relaxed and probably involved in some other activity. It may also occur during a dream that your conscious mind remembers after awakening.

The PSYCHOKINETIC PROBLEM SOLVING PROGRAM (PPS) you are currently reading will enable you to produce the "inspired" answers virtually at will. And once your mind becomes trained to the program format you will find that the process speeds up to the point where you can sit down at any time of the day, play the tape and get the answers you want. Eventually you will be able to do away with the tape altogether and produce inspirations on demand.

The whole process could be described as automatic lateral thinking!

Only 10% of our population have a naturally creative mind - the other 90% haven't, so this program helps to even out that imbalance somewhat.

Naturally creative people tend to use more of their right-brain which is where inspirations and hunches come from.

By using this program you will slowly train your right-brain to spring into action again, probably for the first time since you were 6-7 years old.

It will resist at first in the same manner that your body muscles would resist if you suddenly took up weightlifting after years of non-exercise, but before too long you will train it to do what you want.

The commercial mind-power courses show you how this is possible and teach you the very basics of the method. After that it takes constant practice to achieve the levels you want. That is, it takes constant effort and mental stamina to become proficient in right-brain creative problem solving.

This PPS program actually shortcuts all the effort.

It does the job for you while you are asleep which is normally wasted time as far as your everyday life is concerned. The program also awakens the right-hemisphere of the brain which in most of us has lain dormant since we were children.

When you were young you probably had no trouble "imagining" things. You might even have had "invisible playmates" which were very real to you but not so real to your parents. No doubt you were told to stop imagining things! After this was repeated to you several hundred times you became slowly aware that it was unacceptable in a grown up world to use your imagination like this. So you stopped doing it. If you had been encouraged to keep using this inborn mental faculty you would probably exhibit quite advanced intuitive and psychokinetic abilities by now. And life would be much more pleasant. It is an observable fact that the use of imagination by children is actively discouraged in most home and school environments.

Let's look at how dream inspired answers arrive:

For a start your left-hand beta brain (we're talking about the usual right-handed person here) which is the one you use while you are awake was never intended to supply inspirational answers. That is not its intended function.

It appears to have evolved as a *logical* analytical planning brain and when you go to sleep it stops working.

While you are asleep your right alpha/theta brain takes over.

During sleep your right brain electrical frequencies cycle periodically between 2-10 cycles per second approximately. That is, between deep sleep (delta) and the lighter dream type stage of alpha. It is during these alpha/theta cycles that your deep subconscious can be tapped to supply inspirational answers.

These often arrive in symbolic form (which is the language of the intuitive right-brain) where for example you might dream that you are having trouble steering a car on a winding road. This would usually indicate that you don't subconsciously feel in control of the course of action in life that you are currently taking.

The conscious mind appears to dislike messages from the subconscious and has to be "tricked" via symbols into accepting these creative or meaningful thoughts.

Our intuitive hunches come directly from the right brain subconscious mind but are usually *overruled* by the logical left brain.

People who train their right brain to work properly usually become very intuitive. Intuition is our *sixth sense*. It is something we were all born with but have lost the use of. Women tend to use their right intuitive brain more than their male counterparts and it was recently proven that given an identical test problem which required logical thought the women volunteers actually used both brain hemispheres ... the men used their left brain hemisphere only.

Intuition occurs naturally in most people but it appears that certain emotional states enhance it. In times of mortal danger, for example, some people experience a *sharpening* of their intuition. This is probably an inherent human characteristic which might explain why women are naturally more intuitive than men .... they have to intuitively protect their young.

Once you start getting into alpha/theta training - and thereby opening up your right-side brain - your intuition seems to improve .... sometimes quite dramatically. Strange, useful coincidences will appear in your life and synchronistic events will become quite noticeable.

Synchronicity can be described as a series of meaningful coincidences all apparently connected by some hidden agenda.

People who intentionally reactivate their right-brain invariably report a vast improvement in the quality of their life. The most frequent comment is that they *feel in control.* Petty annoyances don't trouble them and they are less stressed and much more relaxed. And once they have carried this a step further and learned how to handle subjective communication they can encourage people to whom they relate into their life and remove those that they find abrasive.

An earlier survey of the US FORTUNE 500 business executives revealed that most of them were highly intuitive and tended to follow their *hunches* or *gut feelings.* The executives who took part in the intuition tests generally scored very high marks.

As you use this PPS PROGRAM you will probably find yourself becoming more intuitive and it is highly likely that you will become increasingly aware of *synchronistic* events that you would otherwise not have noticed.

Once you start practicing alpha your awareness increases. You start noticing unusual *coincidental* events that would have escaped your attention before. And you start to feel that you were intended to notice these things. You get the impression that you are being *looked after* but you just can't quite put your finger on the source of the feeling. It is almost a sensation of knowing that things will average out in your favour.

Basically the program calls for the user to drop to alpha (daydream state) while considering his or her problem in a fairly specific manner.

He or she then drifts off to sleep while the program tape is running. The subconscious mind then works on the problem because it has been instructed to by the program on the tape. An inspired answer will usually arrive. This can happen almost immediately or over the next few days. The more you use this program the quicker the answers will come. On occasions you will wake up in the middle of the night with a crystal clear solution in your head. If you do write it down immediately. Do not wait until the morning. This action is necessary because your dream memories usually fade quickly...... sometimes they last only 7-10 seconds after waking up.

You can basically program your mind to do anything you want it to do.

For example...... if you tell yourself as you are dropping off to sleep (passing through the light hypnotic stage of alpha) that you will awaken at 5am in the morning your subconscious will faithfully awaken you at this time providing it absorbed your message clearly. This message is reinforced if you visualize a picture of your clock with 5am on its face.

On top of this your subconscious will automatically program your dream cycle so that you wake up naturally, fully refreshed and ready to go.

When an alarm clock wakens you it quite often catches you at the wrong part of your sleep cycle and you can feel quite lethargic for several hours.

This is why it is much better to use an alarm clock that plays music for 10 minutes or so before the alarm goes off. This way your subconscious has time to bring you up through the sleep cycle naturally.

You can actually program your subconscious to do quite an amazing number of things. The trick is to program while you are totally relaxed just before you fade off to sleep. If you program it in this alpha state (just before your mind starts wandering) you can give it any instruction you wish. Providing the instructions are given with sufficient conviction your subconscious will follow orders exactly.

You can, with enough practice develop your personal mental control to the point where you can cancel out pain in any specific part of your body that you wish. This ability can then be used to give yourself a "local anaesthetic". It is quite handy when visiting the dentist. The initial technique as taught by the personal mind-control courses is to mentally picture (visualize) one of your hands immersed in ice-water while the other is immersed in very hot water. You can quite easily achieve a temperature difference of 4-5 degrees with just a small amount of practice. You then visualize this "cold area" on your hand moving around your body until you center it in the place which is causing pain. If you "move" this cold area into your gums and visualize your teeth packed with ice you can do away with injections at the dentist. But I'd suggest you don't tell your dentist what you're doing ..... it unnerves them!

Your subconscious mind has total and complete control over your body functions. Once you learn to give your subconscious precise instructions it will modify your otherwise automatic body functions in any manner you wish.

Most people find this hard work unless they have taken a commercial mind course and have as a consequence developed control over their alpha state. Our PPS PROGRAM includes this alpha control factor on the cassette so you don't have to concentrate too much while falling asleep.

THE TAPE PROGRAM WORKS LIKE THIS:
(You make a cassette tape by following the instructions given later)
After you have retired for the night and are ready to turn out the light, you switch the tape on. Adjust the volume to play very softly. If you are using a small cassette tape you can place it under the edge of your pillow so you don't disturb your partner.

The pre-recorded voice gives you alpha relaxation suggestions for a couple of minutes. Then you will be asked by the voice on the tape to dwell on your specific problem .... in a special way.... for a couple of minutes. After that the voice cuts back in and feeds an instruction to your subconscious that it will solve the problem. It does not matter if you have fallen asleep at this point…..... your subconscious is still listening. After this various health and self-improvement suggestions are given.

You can also use the PPS PROGRAM at any time during the day. All you need to do is to sit in a comfortable chair, close your eyes and run the tape.

We strongly suggest that you run this tape through personal head-phones........ not your stereo system.

There are two reasons for this:

Firstly the padded surround of the headphones tends to reduce extraneous noises and secondly the message on the tape enters both your ears simultaneously and appears to originate in the center of your head. This sounds more realistic and tends to produce a better effect.

However if you're using the cassette in bed it is more convenient to place the headphones under the edge of your pillow and adjust the volume so that you can only just hear the words. Your subconscious mind will hear every word crystal clearly and this way you won't be disturbing your partner as the sound will appear through your pillow only.

Alternatively you might like to buy a pillow-phone which is a very flat compact loudspeaker. Either way the important thing is to keep the volume down to just above the threshold of hearing. If it is too loud, you may find the voice distracting. The message on the tape should ideally be a soft murmur in the background. Simply follow the instructions given - the voice fades out after 10 minutes or so and the rest of the tape is just a soft hissing sound.

If you wish you can voice your specific problems onto the tape itself. This will save you actually having to concentrate on the problem when you might rather be drifting off to sleep. (All this is explained later).

The tape you make has a 3 minute gap whereby you consider your problem. After this the tape will tell you to visualize a successful solution to your problem.

You simply visualize (or imagine) yourself going about your life with the problem solved!

You do not attempt to visualize a method of solving the problem - only the completed, finalized end result.

Your subconscious will supply the method and it may well be something totally unexpected but your "gut feeling" will tell you that it is exactly right.

It has been fairly well proven that psychokinetic effects are *goal seeking*. That is, all you have to do is to specify your goal - your PK abilities will determine how this goal is reached. If you try to specify a method you will probably restrict the abilities of your mind to achieve the required outcome.

Program yourself only for the destination ..... not the path leading to it!

There are basically 3 parts to the tape you will make:

Firstly there is a short relaxation message. Secondly there is a 3 minute gap for you to consider your problem and thirdly there is the instruction to your subconscious that it will solve the problem. This is done while you are visualizing or imagining a successful solution. Also there are overall health and self improvement affirmatives before the end of the tape.

Under no circumstances think of negatives while you are actually using this program!

In this semi-hypnotic state your subconscious mind will faithfully accept any suggestions you put to it ..... whether they be positive or negative!

Think of only a successful outcome as you drift off to sleep!

Picture yourself as you would be ..... with the problem successfully solved.

EXAMPLE

Let us suppose that you are in a job that is giving you no satisfaction.

You feel something is wrong somewhere but you just can't seem to pin down the problem. And you want to know exactly what it is that is causing you to feel uneasy.

You would break down this problem into 20 words or less as follows:

........*Something is wrong at work. I feel uneasy. I need to know why.*

This then, is the message you would repeat to yourself 10-20 times during the 3 minute gap in your tape.

And while you are drifting off to sleep and the tape is instructing your subconscious to give you an answer, you visualize yourself blissfully happy with your job!

See everything going your way! People work in well with you! (Visualize this). The boss is particularly happy with your work! You visualize him or her shaking your hand and congratulating you. (It doesn't matter what for - just mentally picture it!) And while you're at it..... you may as well visualize a pay rise!

The trick is to create a mental picture of total satisfaction with your job. If you do this properly there is no way it can fail to happen. Unless of course the job is totally and completely unsuited to your temperament and talents in which case your controlled dream should tell you this.

That is the way the programme works. But it may not happen over-night. It could be a gradual process so stick with it. After all it's your future and this is the only life you've got so you may as well devote a little time to making it a pleasant one.

The only type of person who cannot make this work is the dedicated loser. You will probably know a couple! This is a person who deep down does not feel they are worthy of any form of success. If they do happen to achieve even a modicum of success they will self-destruct and place themselves back at square one. This is an automatic subconscious pro-gramming on their part which they not only have no control over........ but don't want any control.

Do *not* under any circumstances tell this type of individual what you are doing in regard to this PPS system......they will automatically try to undermine your confidence. It is an unfortunate fact of life that you will probably have a number of these people among your family and friends, so keep this information to yourself.

I have met numerous individuals throughout my life who have a par-tial success then totally mess it up. They tend to carry on like this all their lives. It is <u>vitally</u> important that you refuse to associate with these types.

At some point after your programmed dream a solution will prob-ably arrive. (If it doesn't keep presenting the same problem until it does). The solution may present itself in the form of an increasing awareness of the problem area or it may arrive in the form of a symbolic dream. If so pay attention because this is your subconscious giving you what you have asked for. A dream inspired answer may be very direct and easy to interpret or it may be symbolic and vague. If so, you can always set a new problem for your mind that night....... to interpret the dream! Simply specify the contents of the dream and instruct your subconscious to clarify it. After a while your subconscious *gets the message* and provides dream answers that are clear and to the point.

Basically you *train* your subconscious in the same way that Pavlov trained his dogs to salivate at the sound of a bell, which they mentally connected with food. Your mind will accept this training if you keep practicing.

When you think about it this is probably the very first time in your life that you have set out to train the actual mechanism of your mind!

Quite often the results can be awe-inspiring ...... more so as you gradually realize that you can develop total control over yourself. The whole development of this process can leave one feeling quite stunned at the implications and simplicity of it all.

For the first time in your life you become aware of what is possible!

It can be quite a traumatic insight!

FIRST STEP

Read the tape-creation instructions right through so that you understand what the process is all about. It is actually quite simple and straightforward.

The next move is to work out your problem clearly on paper. Reduce it to 20 words or less.

ANOTHER EXAMPLE

Let us suppose that you feel you are not earning enough money to do what you want to do in life. The first thing is to identify exactly what it is you want to do. Forget all about what it is going to cost. You might for example wish to buy a new car but find that you can't finance it. You visit a car dealer and select exactly the car you want. Let us suppose it is a red Toyota Cruiser. Your wording would go like this:

........*I have a burning desire to own a new red Toyota Cruiser. I can see myself driving it. It is mine!*

As you go to sleep you see the salesman handing you the keys to this car. You see yourself driving it. You can smell the new upholstery. You see the neighbors peeking out of their windows as you drive your new car into the driveway.

Do you get the idea? You live and breathe the solution while the tape is running. Do not worry how it is going to be paid for. The countries top entrepreneurs always visualize the solution. The path to it is unimportant. This whole concept is based on the fact that thoughts have energy.

The results sometimes arrive in strange ways. Don't be surprised if on your next trip to the shopping center someone is selling raffle tickets in a red cruiser. And if you buy one there should be no surprise at all when you win it!

If enough concentrated energy is fed into your desire, you usually get what you want. Maybe not immediately (that is called a *miracle*) but sooner or later it will come. The PPS SYSTEM allows you to generate the necessary mental focus.

But if you confuse your subconscious with waffly *wishes* rather than a specific dedicated thought requirement, then you will get waffly results. Focus on one requirement at a time.

All you have to do is to follow the instructions on the tape. During the 3 minute gap on the tape you mentally voice your short 20 word (or less) message over and over again until the tape tells you to relax and picture the final outcome.

From that point on you just picture the end result until you fall asleep.

Do not even attempt to plan how to achieve your goal. Let your subconscious mind do this. It may well produce a course of action that you never would have thought of. Instead of repeating your short message over and over in the 3 minute gap you may elect to record this onto a tape as discussed earlier. But while this part of the tape is playing, concentrate on the sound of your own voice. Don't dream about something else during those critical 3 minutes.

Focus clearly!!!!

The final step while the mind-instruction and health suggestions are being played on the tape is to picture, in your minds eye, that your problem is solved. You do this by picturing yourself "patting yourself on the back" for having successfully solved the problem. That is..... see yourself free of that particular problem.

CRITICAL STEPS

Reduce your problem to no more than 20 words and verbalize these silently when asked to do so by the tape.

2 - Visualize that your problem is solved and see it solved in your minds-eye.

3 - Relax and drift off to sleep.

If the process does not appear to be working then check thoroughly to see that you have followed all the above steps. Some problems will be more difficult to solve than others so may take longer. If you are aiming for a major goal in life then you will have to allow a realistic amount of time for it to happen.

Some people will get a very rapid reaction - others will take considerably longer. But no matter what you ask for...... if it is realistic it will eventually happen. And..... don't be afraid to ask for a lot!!!

It will probably take a little while to get used to the process - it may feel strange at first but persevere...... it will be worthwhile in the end.

HERE IS ANOTHER EXAMPLE

Let us suppose that you have a business which has lots of potential but you just can't seem to generate that break-through concept that would make it "take off". You need a couple of top quality concepts to get the money rolling in!

Your abbreviated instructions to your subconscious would go something like this:

......*I desperately need business money-making ideas. I urgently require to double my present cash-flow.*

This is the message you would repeat over and over when asked to do so by the tape.

After this is done you mentally picture the cash rolling in and the staff working flat out to fill orders.

Don't worry how it is going to happen .... simply expect it to happen.

The ideas might come all at once or they might slowly materialize as an awareness of new openings. Some ideas will arrive as a sudden realization - others will creep up on you and you will probably wonder why you hadn't thought of them before, as they are so obvious.

After you have used this method for a while you can expect answers to arrive as a sudden burst of enlightenment. Usually one controlled "dream session" will do the job. The more you practice it, the quicker and more reliable it will become.

Initially at the start it might take a little time to get the process functioning the way you want it. Without the help of the special PPS program it could take several months (or even years) to achieve results. The PPS tape shortcuts the whole process.

When you first start using this program don't expect earth-shattering revelations - merely expect an expanded awareness of possible solutions.

You may have to repeat the same message several times before you notice results. On the other hand the answer may hit you immediately like a bolt out of the sky. It will all depend on how your mind works and the type of problem that needs to be solved. The answer you need may be in your head when you wake up or it may materialize when you are out shopping, gardening or whatever, several days later.

EMOTIONAL CONTENT OF MESSAGE:

When you are compiling your subconscious instruction of 20 words or less use fairly forceful unambiguous language.

Don't say "I want" or "I would like" or worse still "I wish".

Use terms such as "I need" or better still "I desperately need". This is because your right-brain deals in the language of emotions. Make your instructions to it emotional. The more emotional your words are the better it understands. Create the sort of language and phraseology you would use to give a misbehaving ten year old child a firm message.

Treat your subconscious mind as a 9-10 year old because this is around the age at which you were encouraged to suppress its 6th sense functions! True?

It has a lot of developing to do and is not yet very sophisticated. You are about to recommence its training program which stopped when you were encouraged as a child not to use it.

ANOTHER EXAMPLE

Let us suppose you have got yourself into a tricky financial situation and you just can't seem to find an easy way out. Creditors are chasing you and making life very stressful.

Your message to your subconscious would be as follows:

......*I am in debt. I desperately need an acceptable solution. I must quickly become debt and stress-free.*

This is repeated over and over during the 3 minute gap on the tape. Then you relax and clearly picture your circumstances after the problem

is solved. See yourself facing your creditors with ease and obtaining further credit from them (if required). See yourself walking around with
a smile on your face and planning the future with no worrisome debts
around your neck. Do not at any point picture yourself still in debt. See
only the successful outcome. Bear in mind that the problem will not go
away overnight. In fact it might take some time. But it will happen.

WHY VISUALIZATION IS SO IMPORTANT

Your mental processes contain an *information censor* that filters concepts
and thought-flow between conscious and subconscious mind. For this
reason you cannot give orders to the subconscious directly unless you
enter via its "back door".

This back-door entrance can be accessed under hypnosis ...... while
you are in the alpha/theta state .... or under special traumatic emotional conditions.

The subconscious mind belongs to a much earlier stage of human
evolution and was in place long before language was developed. We talk
to it in the same way we would talk to a foreigner who has little grasp of
English - we use sign language! The sign language that your subconscious
understands is pictures!!!

And the more graphic and emotional these pictures are, the better
they are understood.

So what we do is make a mental picture of what we want and feed it
into the subconscious while we are in an alpha or theta state. Alpha is the
dream state and theta is the light sleep state. We also back this message up
with simple, childish emotional words. If you persevere with the picture
and the words, your subconscious gets the message. So if, for example
you are badly overweight and you constantly "picture" yourself as "fat",
then that is the way you will stay. On the other hand if you intentionally
practice picturing yourself as you would really like to be, then that is what
you will eventually materialise, because that is the firm message you are
giving your subconscious.

Likewise if you constantly picture yourself as "broke" and a bit of a
loser, then that is what your subconscious will continue to give you. You
should, in this case, picture yourself already in possession of the things
and lifestyle you want.

This *picturing* is very slow to take hold if you do it in your ordinary wide-awake beta state because you are not entering via the *back door*.......
you are trying to enter your subconscious via the censorship of your conscious mind. The easiest way an individual can enter the subconscious via the back door is in the alpha or theta state.

This is what the **PPS PROGRAM** achieves.

Way back in time there was a well known positive affirmation that went like this:

Day by day in every way I will get better and better.......

Now if you repeated this 20-30 times a day for 6 months or more, you started to notice a difference. On the other hand if you had this fed into your mind once a day for a week by a hypnotist the same result would be achieved. This is because the hypnotist has temporarily removed your conscious "censor" and is putting the message directly into your subconscious. You can achieve the same effect yourself by using self hypnosis - alpha/theta techniques or our **PPS PROGRAM**. The easiest and most convenient way is the PPS method.

Our entire schooling system at the moment is based on feeding the information into the subconscious by the slowest method known to mankind...... repetition via the *front-door*.

When the educational authorities finally wake up to the alternative method of using alpha learning techniques the schooling time will probably be cut in half. There are some experimental forward thinking schools already trying this and the results are astounding!

SUGGESTIBILITY

As you go to sleep at night you drop down from your wide-awake left brain beta state through the highest of your right brain frequencies which is the alpha state. This is the relaxed state when you tend to start dreaming but are still basically semi-awake.

In this state your mind is highly suggestible and is similar to the early stages of self-hypnosis when the subconscious will accept anything repetitively told to it. When you drop to this alpha stage your critical left brain has stopped functioning. Your "censor" has finished its shift and clocked off. After you have practiced intentionally going into alpha for a period of time you are able to maintain this alpha state without "losing it" and dropping off to sleep. That is, you can maintain this "dream-state" indefinitely and give yourself positive suggestions and create positive mental pictures in your mind. There are some people who can drop to the lower frequency of theta/delta and still maintain conscious thinking. Obviously the big trick is to avoid negative thoughts or mental pictures while in either of these brain-wave states. When you daydream you do so in alpha. You temporarily disassociate yourself from the reality around you and create a new pictorial reality in your mind. After a period of alpha practice you get to the point where you can consciously control the content of these daydreams and produce the alternative reality you want in real life. It is important when using the PPS tape to avoid negative thoughts or images because these will be just as easily accepted by your subconscious mind.

Once again, if you clearly visualize all the bad things that could happen to you in this semi-awake/semi-asleep alpha state, they have a good chance of coming true.

On the other hand if you visualize a successful conclusion to your problem then this is very likely to happen.

TWO MAJOR DISCOVERIES

There have been two major discoveries this century which when taken together may explain why visualization works.

The first was Albert Einstein's discovery of the theory of relativity where he proved that mass and energy were interchangeable. His theory was proven in the atomic bomb, where a small amount of mass is suddenly converted into its energy equivalent.

The second discovery was made independently by several scientists about the middle of this century but it was not until the PEAR laboratory at Princeton University researched it in a well designed scientific program that it was confirmed. They found that the energy of thought-power under certain circumstances affected solid objects and electronic circuitry. (There is some suggestion now that this may happen via focussed information exchange).

That is the force of PK (psychokinetic) energy - in the form of a focused-intent thought which has been directly observed under repeatable conditions. Now if you combine these two discoveries together you might conclude that a dedicated focused thought produces measurable energy which is interchangeable with mass.

So if you clearly and intently visualize a new car the energy generated by this consistent thought pattern will eventually convert into its mass equivalent: ie. - a new car! Obviously this car is not going to be materialised by some instant alchemistry process, but over a period of time by the interaction of focused human yearning coupled with opportunistic forces....basically a consciousness propelled personal psychokinetic event which, as you will read in a later chapter, is basically the definition of *luck*.

This whole concept broaches the realm of Quantum Physics, which is attempting to explain why and how this actually happens. It may even evolve that the newer Superstring Theory eventually includes consciousness as another force.

WHAT DOES ALL THIS MEAN TO YOU?

Simply this: if you dwell on your problems while in the alpha state you are adding energy to them. The problems are likely to get worse.

On the other hand if you dwell on a successful result you will add the thought-energy required to produce a successful solution.

The **PPS PROGRAM** enables you to add positive creative energy to your problem, hence forming a solution.

When done properly, it works! And it works every time once you expect it to!

Even if you have no particular problem that you want to solve it is a good idea to run the tape occasionally as you go to sleep. The health and relaxation suggestions on the tape will keep you feeling good and free from stress. It is amazing the difference even one playing of the tape can make if you're feeling low or generally down in the dumps. Experiment with it and see what sort of results you get. In this case during the 3 minute gap in the tape merely *daydream* about how good you're going to feel tomorrow.

You could even dub the voice section of the tape onto your Dictaphone or Walkman and play it without the problem solving part. If you do this we suggest you record the health and relaxation message 2-3 times so you get a continuous message. Don't worry about tape clicks or discontinuity - you will be playing the tape softly so you probably won't notice them. In fact you can play it just below the threshold of hearing - something like a subliminal tape. Your subconscious will hear it perfectly clearly even if you can't consciously notice it at all! Experiment for best results.

INSTEAD OF PASSIVELY SOLVING PROBLEMS BY WAITING AND HOPING FOR ANSWERS...... THE PPS SYSTEM ENABLES YOU TO *ACTIVELY* SOLVE PROBLEMS BY ENCOURAGING YOUR SUBCONSCIOUS TO SUPPLY ANSWERS.

If you use the PPS SYSTEM constantly and regularly it will eventually become an automatic process - you will not need to use the tape. Your subconscious will know what is expected of it and you will be in control.

INSTRUCTIONS FOR USING THE PPS TAPE

After you have made the PPS tape place it in your cassette machine and start running it as you turn out the lights at night. Run it at low volume but at a level whereby the words on the tape are clear. Let your body relax and simply follow the instructions on the tape. If you wake up during the night with a very clear solution to your problem turn on the light and write it down immediately. Keep a pen and notepad handy.

THE METHOD:

Prepare your body for sleep by showering and having a warm glass of milk or something similar. If you feel uptight at all do 5 minutes simple exercise such as squats before having a shower. But if you're really tired you could ignore all the above and simply go to bed.

You will notice that on this tape we have provided a "trigger" suggestion that every time you relax and twitch your toes you will feel a wave of relaxation wash over you. After a few weeks of using the tape this "trigger" can be used anytime you feel uptight or stressed. Simply twitch your toes and draw a slow deep breath to activate this trained "trigger" reaction. It can also be used to induce sleep. This is known as a post-hypnotic suggestion.

Follow the relaxation message on the tape. When asked, recite your 20 word message over and over until told to stop.

Then merely picture in your minds eye the finalized result you want until you drop off to sleep.

If playing this tape during the day simply visualize your required result until the voice on the tape stops or until the tape runs out. It will be a good idea to stop the tape prior to the final sleep suggestions.

If you feel the urge the next day to take a certain..... maybe unusual..... course of action then seriously consider following this "hunch". It will probably be your subconscious giving you directions.

If for any reason you can't interpret a dream feed details of the dream into your mind during the 3 minute gap the next night and insist on a clearer solution. Keep doing this until you are clear about what the dream actually means.

Now purchase a blank cassette (30 minutes will be ample) and prepare to make your PPS tape.

THE MESSAGE ON THE TAPE

Here is the basic message you record on the tape. Speak slowly and evenly at about <u>one quarter</u> of your usual talking speed. Leave a 2-3 second gap between every sentence. The more you *drag out* this message...the more effective it is likely to be.

Press **record** and start:

Relax.....relax.....relax ..... let every muscle relax.

Relax....relax......you can slowly feel the tension leaving every muscle.

Focus on your breathing and notice it becoming slower and steadier.

Your scalp is relaxed .....your scalp is relaxed.

Your forehead is relaxed ....your forehead is relaxed.

Your eyelids are relaxed ....your eyelids are relaxed.

Your eye muscles are relaxed.......your eye muscles are relaxed.

Your face is totally relaxed....every muscle in your face is relaxed.

Your neck and shoulders are relaxing....... your body is relaxing...... your arms are relaxing......your hands are relaxing......your fingers are relaxing.

Your thighs are relaxing.......your legs are relaxing........your feet are relaxing...... your toes are relaxing.

Now twitch your toes and take a deep slow breath.

Feel the tension in your body ease away. Feel all tension in your body ease away. You feel waves of relaxation wash over your body when you twitch your toes.

You are now feeling totally relaxed and peaceful.

(At this point leave your recorder running while remaining silent....for 3 minutes. This 3 minute gap is where you repeat your "special problem" message over and over in your mind later on. Alternatively you can keep talking and record your problem message over and over in this 3 minute space).

(Now - start recording again and speak the following onto the remainder of your tape.....)

Relax..... relax..... relax.....relax....... relax..... relax.

Picture as clearly as you can what life will be like with your problem solved.

Keep picturing this while I am giving you subconscious instructions. I will do this very softly so that my voice will not distract you. Your subconscious mind is hearing my instructions clearly and is acting on them.

Your subconscious mind will provide a solution to your problem. If this is in the form of a dream, the dream will be easy for you to understand. Your subconscious will transfer the memory of this dream to your conscious mind so that when you awake you will have full memory of the dream.

If the answer to this problem is not provided in a dream it will appear in your conscious mind as soon as your subconscious has solved the problem. Your subconscious will supply the answer you require either as a dream, a flash of insight, or a slow dawning of realization.

You seriously desire to solve this problem and it will be solved. Your subconscious mind will easily solve it.

You can clearly see in your minds eye how life will be after the problem is solved and you can easily look back in hindsight and remember how it was solved.

After you finish listening to this message you will drift off to sleep.

You will wake up in the morning feeling totally refreshed and inspired.

As the days progress you will feel better and better. You are relaxed and cheerful all day and are free from stress at all times. Your health is improving daily and you wake up every morning ready to face the world.

Nothing worries you. You know that you can easily solve any problem that arises.

This knowledge gives you total confidence in yourself. You exude self-confidence and people look up to you.

You feel great during the day and sleep soundly at night and each time you play the tape this program reinforces itself.

(Stop talking and turn off your recorder)

The idea of leaving the 3 minute gap in your message is to allow you to insert a new problem at frequent intervals. However if you have only one current major problem you can "read" this on to the tape instead of leaving the 3 minute gap.

Simply repeat your chosen 20 words (approximately) over and over for about 3 minutes.

If you follow this process exactly as described above, you will find that with a little practice problems will be easy to solve. And all you need to do is solve ONE serious problem in life....and you've paid for this book a thousand times over!

9

HOW TO REMEMBER
YOUR DREAMS ...
... AND GENERATE THE
DREAM YOU WANT!!!!

This sounds difficult, doesn't it?

But in reality, it is a lot easier than you might think.

The simple trick is to *convince* your subconscious mind that it is to perform this task for you.

And how is this achieved? The easiest way is to give your subconscious precise instructions while you are in a "dream state" just before you go you sleep at night.

And the most effective way to do this is to go to bed an hour or so earlier than usual so that you are still fresh enough to effectively do this "programming" without drifting off from over-tiredness.

You simply instruct your subconscious as follows:

........*"I will wake up when I have a really important dream and I will remember it consciously"*......

Alternatively you might say........

.......*"I will have a dream about (whatever) and I will wake up and remember it consciously".*

This message must be repeated over and over as you go to sleep.........
either mentally or softly to yourself. This can sometimes be quite hard to
do as you may drift off half way through your self-programming.

The easiest way to overcome this problem is to pre-record a simple
cassette/Dictaphone message to yourself and let it play as you drift off.

But instead of using the word "I" in your tape message, you should
use the word "you".

For example: *"**You** will wake up when you have a really important dream,
etc. "*

Even after years of practice I still occasionally find that I drop off
to sleep before completing this subconscious programming so I quickly
repeat my message a dozen times or so on a Dictaphone I keep at my
bedside. This only takes 3-4 minutes. Then I go to bed and place the
Dictaphone beside me (set at just audible volume) with my fingers ready
to press the start button. As I feel myself starting to drift off I trigger the
machine by pressing the start button. It seldom fails to work.........and
generally only fails if I am too mentally exhausted from recent activities.

By doing this you are telling your subconscious exactly what you
expect it to do.

A lot of people don't realize that this is possible.........but it is the basis
of self hypnosis.

The remote viewers have discovered that the mind will follow instructions precisely, providing these instructions are given with serious intent.

One of the most interesting discoveries to emerge from the United
States military remote viewing program was the factor of **intent**. We also
found that it applied to psychokinetic activities.

When a person develops a serious intent......and lives, breathes and
visualises that intent....then in many instances the mind will supply the results required. The other factor is the emotional input behind the intent.
Our inherent ability to become emotional about a given subject appears
to trigger a focussed mental energy state which causes the desired result
to manifest itself.

**The research we have done to date indicates that a deep emo-
tional yearning coupled with focused intent are the two factors**

that cause an individual to evoke the circumstances and events that are required to manifest their desire.

You may have noticed this in your own life. When things have come to the stage of literally falling apart for you and you are living and breathing this situation you may recall that quite often the problem has suddenly solved itself........leaving you totally free.

This has happened so often in my life that I have forgotten how many times this "magical" event has occurred. Unfortunately it has always happened at the last moment before disaster. On one occasion I was 3 days off bankruptcy and all of a sudden I acquired S40,000 into my bank account from a totally unexpected source. For years I have been trying to train my mind to make this happen long prior to the onset of the potential disaster. What happens of course is that just prior to this unwelcome event your emotions are so high that they affect the universe around you.....and positive results happen, <u>providing you are programming for success, not failure.</u>

Positive thinking and visualisation by themselves are not enough..... absolute intent and emotional yearning must be added.

Which is why people who merely "wish" for nice things normally don't get them. But the individual who develops a burning emotional desire coupled with absolute intent usually ends up with what they want.

So it is with dream control. If it is your intent and focused desire to achieve a level of dream control for yourself......then so you shall.

You may achieve results the first time you try it but usually it takes weeks or even months of practice. One helpful aid is to have your pen and paper ready by your bedside so that when you suddenly awaken with full memory of a dream you can quickly jot down the main details.

This process tells your mind that you are serious about dream control and that your intent is to capture these dreams. That is, you are *proving* your intent.

Your subconscious will soon wake up to the fact that you are very serious indeed about the process and eventually supply results that may sometimes leave you breathless.

If you don't get it right the first time keep practicing it.

Your subconscious will soon "get the message" and do things your way.

If you want to have a dream about a specific subject.....then instruct your subconscious accordingly. This is only slightly harder to achieve than remembering random dreams.

After you practice this procedure for a week or two you may be quite pleasantly surprised to find that you can not only trigger dreams at will.......but actually remember the main details.

When you get to the point when you can program up a dream that you want you will find that it is presented to you in "coded" format. That is... it is not usually straightforward. The trick then is to analyze it correctly.... and this is actually the hardest part.

You can buy a multitude of books on dreams but as every dream is an individual experience it is most likely that your particular dream will not be explained in any detail.

This is where the Mental Pendulum can be extraordinarily useful. It can help you "decode" your dream there and then....while you are lying in bed with full recall of the dream.

Once you learn to generate and recall dreams....then decode them with the Mental Pendulum you are in a very powerful personal position. You can basically get an accurate "sense of direction" in life that others are unable to figure out.

This gives a person a strong feeling of self-confidence...maybe for the first time in their life.

Your biggest aid initially is the simple cassette recorder. I bought a cheap Dictaphone which I have used for a couple of years. I can easily change the message on it every night if I wish and because the unit is so small and flat I place it under the corner of my pillow so the sound filters through the pillow. I hear it.....but my spouse does not.

The other advantage of a Dictaphone (or any small player) is that you can drift off to sleep with you hand on the machine and your finger on the **play** button. As you feel yourself losing consciousness you simply press the play button.

Another idea is to record 5-10 minutes of background music.....or even record 5-10 minutes of silence *before* you record your message. Then when you press the play button on your recorder you will have some minutes of either silence or background music before the actual message starts. By this time you will probably be totally relaxed and on the verge of sleep.

The message will impinge upon your subconscious mind, even if you are asleep. The 5-10 minutes of silence or light background music gives you a chance to relax. If your recorded message were to start immediately your subconscious mind might not be ready for it.

EXAMPLE:

Let us suppose that you wake up with the full memory of a dream where you were flying unaided through the air.

You would ask the following questions of your mental pendulum:

** *Is this dream significant to my wellbeing. Yes or No?*

** *Does this flying represent a positive outcome for me. Yes or No?*

** *Does this indicate that I will soon be as free as a bird. Yes or No?*

** *Does this dream represent my future in some way. Yes or No?*

** *Does this dream represent my personal life. Yes or No?*

** *Does this dream represent my business life. Yes or No?*

** *Does this dream represent my emotional life. Yes or No?*

** *Is this dream telling me to follow any particular path of action. Yes or No?*

** *Overall, is this dream good news for me. Yes or No?*

Obviously you could ask dozens of related questions such as *"is this dream representative of my current state of affairs?"*

As the pendulum can basically only give digital *Yes/No/Maybe* responses then it cannot voluntarily feed you information, unless you ask specific questions that it can answer with a *Yes* or *No*.

Do not be afraid to ask *off-beat* questions, because sometimes the answers will not be what you expect and may guide you to start a different line of questioning.

The more you use the Mental Pendulum for dream decoding.....the more accurate it will become. After a while you will develop a pattern of questioning which will give you accurate answers fairly rapidly.

You can also use a conventional dowsing mechanism such as a pendulum or L-Rods to achieve the same answers. The advantage of the mental pendulum however is that you can start the decoding process while you are lying in bed....immediately after you have woken from the dream.

Recently I developed a feeling that something was not right somewhere. It was a feeling of uneasiness or apprehension. I decided to program up a dream to determine if there was a real problem or whether it was just my imagination.

That night I stated the problem clearly as I was going to sleep. I asked that if there was a real problem that I be given a dream that would identify it.

Early the next morning I woke up with full memory of a very frustrating dream. I had dreamt that I could not locate a car I had parked earlier. I walked around the area looking for this car but it was nowhere to be found.

The first thing I asked my mental pendulum was whether this dream was relevant to me. The answer was yes. I then asked if it was anything to do with frustration...the answer was yes. I then queried the pendulum to determine whether this frustration was connected to my business, personal or emotional life. The answer indicated it was related to business.

I next asked if it was connected with my overall business life or a specific aspect of it. The answer indicated frustration with a specific project. I then listed out all the projects I was currently involved in and a particular one was identified.

I then used the mental pendulum to confirm that this project was the one that the dream referred to. The answer was a definite yes.

At this point I thought long and hard about this particular project as I was not consciously aware of any actual frustration. In a sudden burst of inspiration I asked if this frustration referred to the current state of the project or the future state. To my surprise it gave a very strong yes response for the future state. That certainly got me thinking as the whole project seemed quite straightforward. But the more I thought about it the more uneasy I became. Something didn't add up with one of the participants in the deal. To save time I then decided to remote view this participant and acquired a "bad news" impression. I then used the pendulum to check this out and came up with the same results.

I decided to make some serious enquiries about the individual concerned and to my dismay discovered that he was in no financial position to complete his end of the deal. In fact one of the contactees referred to him as a "bit of a con artist".

Later that morning I contacted this person and confronted him with my remote viewing of his situation. After a little verbal pressure (dedicated intent on my part?) he admitted that he couldn't keep his end of the bargain financially but that he had "hoped" things would get better before the deal was to be concluded.

Obviously he would have failed to complete his end of the transaction which would have thrown the project into chaos causing me some financial loss and considerable frustration.

I bailed out of it then and there.

Without the dream control warning I would have been headed toward some serious frustration and annoyance, not to mention the financial loss.

The interesting thing is that this type of dream scenario has happened probably a dozen times over the past few years, giving me warning in advance of impending problems.

I honestly don't know how I made it through my business life prior to developing this dream control/pendulum mechanism.

The ability to use these intuitive mechanisms has made the passage of life much smoother.

The small group of Australians and New Zealanders who have followed our research have also reported benefits.....in some cases, quite spectacular ones.

The bottom line is that these intuitive procedures are of definite benefit in daily activities.

Dream control and interpretation is an extraordinarily useful process for determining your future track through life.

If you have a serious intent about learning the process then your mind will oblige. Like any other skill that has to be learnt you need to keep practicing until you get results.

If you were learning to play the piano you would recognise that you needed to keep practicing to gain any degree of expertise. Strangely enough individuals who start learning these personal mind techniques quite often give up after a few sessions. This appears to be something to do with the ego becoming worried about loss of control. While piano practice is an acceptable activity as far as the ego is concerned, deep down personal mind control *is not* and your subconscious may throw up negative messages about it all. For example you may rapidly develop the feeling that it is all a waste of time while prior to that you thought it was a vital process to learn. You recognise that it will be of major benefit to you but for some reason you lose interest in doing anything about it.

If this happens be aware that it may be an ego-control thing and if you override your ego by setting aside a specific time each day or night for practice then your ego will slowly accept that you are serious about learning this process. You may find that your interest in this new process rapidly increases as your successes add up.

When it gets to the point where you are reliably calling up dream answers then your ego is basically out of the picture and has accepted your interest in this new discipline.

I am always amazed at the number of people I have met who have had an absolutely stunning success with their first controlled intuition experience....then <u>totally lost interest</u> in doing a follow-up. When I query them about this they always agree that the results were breathtaking and they must try it out again. But they seldom ever do.

Beyond belief.....isn't it?

10

THE EXTRAORDINARY WORLD OF PSYCHOKINETICS AND LUCK

NEW MIND TECHNOLOGY DISCOVERY ENABLES YOU TO PSYCHOKINETICALLY RESONATE WITH YOUR ENVIRON-MENT... **AND CONTROL YOUR OWN NATURAL LUCK !!!**

One of the more extraordinary discoveries our research efforts made was in the field of **luck**!

After many years of research we have concluded that luck is a *personal psychokinetic event.*

In effect it is a "personal tuning in", or *resonance* between the mind and the environment.....a sort of natural resonant state where information is shared.

It is equivalent to the "zone" that top athletes get themselves into.

For many years I had suspected that the mind could influence electronic circuitry and I was also puzzled as to why some people were naturally lucky while others were definitely unlucky.

Let me start at the beginning and explain exactly what sparked my interest in the field of psychokinetics and luck.

I became aware of mind/machine interaction many years ago when I owned an electronics design company.

During my years as chief designer in developing micro-chip based products I noticed a very strange thing. Occasionally a chip appeared to be affected by my thoughts, something that a lot of electronics people have reported. Occasionally I could apparently "will" a circuit to work yet the other designers in the place would have no luck with it. This happened often enough to mention it at a staff meeting and somebody commented that I was obviously affecting it with my mind. We all laughed!

But if I had known then what I know now, I definitely would not have laughed!

I had been fascinated with "radio" since I was a kid but in those days needed quite a lot of money to finance my training, so I took up something I was really good at to pay for it all....Hypnosis. I became a stage hypnotist for several years until the electronics career blossomed. This knowledge of mind power techniques enabled me to develop the programme you're about to read. Eventually I lost interest in electronics and became involved in lateral thinking, which can best be described as inspirational thinking and created the Australian Lateral Thinking Newsletter.

This was distributed to business orientated people but about 7 years after this a strange thing happened which changed the course of my life and has affected many others as well.

During one of our regular Monday morning staff meetings somebody produced a copy of a book called MARGINS OF REALITY authored by Jahn and Dunne from Princeton University in the US.

This book detailed their experiments in psychokinetics and they appear to have accumulated considerable proof that mind indeed affects matter.

This got my staff thinking and we decided to run some experiments in PK but instead of using laboratory style random-number generators, we elected to use real-life random devices ….....the infamous *slot machines*.

This might sound like a strange thing for a business newsletter to become involved with but some compulsion drove us along.

And we made an extraordinary discovery. Firstly we found that "luck" appears to run in cycles (and we suspect that this might be a 5th biorhythm) and secondly we found a way to *enhance* this natural cyclic luck *window*.

I had never been personally 'lucky" with slots. Usually the person sitting next to me wins the money.

We produced a research report on our findings and sold several hundred copies to our private client list in Australia and New Zealand. Within a couple of weeks the mail had produced some fascinating comments from purchasers who had applied the methods outlined in this report. In many cases they confirmed our findings and were able to use the knowledge not only to predict their personal "PK Luck" peaks, but also to enhance their natural luck by using the method we had evolved. This raised a few eyebrows among members of the gambling fraternity, particularly from the casino managers.

It appears that during certain predictable cycles every individual has a period when he or she is more "resonant" with the environment. If the person considers themself to be naturally unlucky then it is during this period that bad luck is likely to manifest itself. On the other hand, if the person deep down knows they are naturally lucky then during this period of "high Q" resonance they will experience good luck runs.

What we have found is that by changing a person's mental programming in a unique way, then the PK luck runs can be enhanced in a very positive, and occasionally spectacular manner.

So far it appears to be working quite well, but it is still highly experimental. The exact results appear to depend on the mind-set of the user.

However nearly everyone who has contacted us has confirmed that they have been able to identify their own personal luck cycles which they all agree is a useful piece of permanent knowledge to have.

The actual process involves recording a simple cassette from wording supplied later in this book.

I realise that this sounds too simplistic to be true but dozens of clients have confirmed its effectiveness and I've got the jackpot cheques to prove it!

All you have to do is read the message on to your cassette recorder. This is played back as you drift off to sleep at night. The message also contains health/sleep suggestions and as it is in your own voice, your subconscious not only trusts it, but will also react to it.

We found a strange thing in our earlier tapes. The mind appears to see the future as moving from the right to the left....this was more or less proven by the Silva-Mind people. So when we instructed the mind to produce 5 identical symbols in a payline on the slots, it quite often faithfully produced them.....starting from the right hand side, which in many slot machines will not produce a payout if only 4 symbols appear.

(Australian and New Zealand usually have 5 reels so 5 identical icons are required to win a major prize).

When we discovered the error, we were able to make a correction to the tape message so that the PK mind-control caused the winning runs to start from the left hand side of the machine.

The wording on the tape is quite unusual and appears to have quite a profound affect on the mind during high PK periods. However it appears to have no effect at all during low PK cycles.

A number of our earlier clients reported the results as being "uncanny". During the earlier experiments I played the tapes non-stop all night, every night and started to notice minor side-effects. I became slightly disorientated and unusually tired so had to give the tapes a rest for several days. From this I concluded that the unusual message on the tape gets right down into the deep subconscious - more so than any other sleep learning tape I've used. As a former mind-control practitioner I've been able to develop the precise wording used on the tape as a non-hypnotic alpha/theta programme. However I would suggest that you use it sensibly and in moderation.

Give it a try for a few days and see what happens.

Basically what we are dealing with here is innovative personal mind control which will make a lot of people uncomfortable. It is rather akin to the discovery of magnetic fields and electricity back in the 19th century. Neither of these discoveries was understood because they were the science of the 20th century, but that didn't stop entrepreneurs from using the concepts to make money. With this new mind control business we are dealing with the science of the 21st century and it will probably be 40 years or so before the mechanism is fully understood.

But in the meantime, that does not stop you using the knowledge to your advantage.

DETERMINING YOUR LUCK CYCLE!

Is it possible to make money from Psychokinesis by manipulating your mind to produce positive PK effects in a financial environment? Is there a 5th "PK" biorhythm ?

We searched long and hard for answers and eventually concluded that there may well be a 5th biorhythm centred around an individuals natural psychokinetic ability. This was one of the many observations we made during our years of research.

After 7 years of experimenting with psychokinetic interaction with the environment (commonly known as luck) a number of quite startling observations have been made. It had been decided to extend our lateral thinking operation by the inclusion of mind-power techniques, based on the observation that lateral thinking is basically the intentional induction of creative alpha/theta bursts. However the field extended somewhat and we became absorbed with the science of psychokinetics.

We decided to build a random number generator for the purpose of controlled experimentation but wondered about the "boredom" aspect involved in the consistent use of one of these machines. As we did not feel the need for laboratory precision in a general purpose experiment it was decided to use a commercially available random event device which supplied a consistently fresh emotive content in the form of a financial gain or loss. That is, we elected to base our experiments around the commonly used poker (slot) gaming machine. We found that we could get quite emotive about losses (terminally depressed?) and quite ecstatic about wins.

The overall results have been somewhat astounding, almost to the point at times of being hard to believe.

Up to now it has been common knowledge that some people are just naturally "lucky". Everything they touch turns to good fortune. What is not so commonly known (in fact it is generally not known at all) is that an individual's "luck factor" can be changed.

This is what our extended research program has been all about.

Firstly our experiments have got to the stage where we deeply suspect that some kinds of luck appear to be cyclic. That is psychokinetic interaction appears to run in cycles. The problem we have had is determining what these cycles are and how to predict them.

It is clear that we have a long way to go yet but some definite patterns have emerged which enable us to roughly predict when we will have the greatest winning chances in a gaming (gambling) environment.

For a start it seems that there are two kinds of luck. The first is what we consider to be a "random event" which happens unexpectedly. This may well be part of an individual's **personal synchronistic event-train** which in *real time* appears to happen for no discernible reason. However future hindsight may indicate that this event-train was part of an overall pattern.

The second kind is the most important. It is created by your own personal ability to interact with your environment in a positive creative way.

Before we go into detail about how this can be achieved let us look at the current state of knowledge about psychokinetic (PK) effects:

Brain wave measurements on Russian PK subjects indicate that there is usually pronounced theta wave activity during the PK events. Theta wave activity also occurs in emotionally unstable adolescents and in normally adjusted adults when they are containing suppressed anger or frustration. We have noticed consistently when playing poker (slot) machines that they tend to pay out on the final spin after we have given up in disgust and are about to walk away in frustration.

This has become a regular occurrence and we can rely on it 20-30% of the time.

However this effect appears to depend on whether we have "resonated and bonded" with the machine being played. In this case we may achieve positive **PK effects** or alternatively PK missing effects. It is in the latter case that the machine will usually pay out at the instant of "letting go". If it becomes apparent that the machine is operating in this **PK-missing** mode we move on to another machine. In this case we usually observe the device to present fabulous winning combinations ....on the wrong payline or alternatively display a jackpot combination with one of the vital symbols displaced by one payline. Another observed fact about PK effects is that they tend to happen when you are not looking. That is they tend to occur while your attention is elsewhere.

It is for this reason that I tend to play two machines side by side so that I am alternately focusing on each individual machine.

I should stress here that these are our *own personal experiences* and may or may not apply to other people.

Most of my own major jackpots "just appeared" on the poker machine. In fact the $65,000+ jackpot did not register consciously at all until after the jackpot bells started ringing. Yet the 5 jackpot symbols were clearly visible on the screen. It has been noticed that this PK effect almost seems to *block out the conscious mind*. When the machines are being played normally the more intently one stares at them the slower they seem to spin. But the PK effect does the reverse. It is almost as if there is a time-free zone operating in conjunction with PK.

The overall impression gained is that the mind "stands still" - almost like that strange feeling of "lost time"!

When one slips into that altered state of consciousness which causes the machines to pay out spin after spin, the actual spins themselves sometimes appear to be instantaneous.

It should be noted that my personal major wins have occurred on both electronic machines and mechanical/electronic machines. The mechanical machines are controlled by a computer which determines absolutely the spin of the 5 mechanical drums.

Another observable fact about PK is that it tends to appear when the mind is in some form of altered consciousness state.

This may be in the form of a relaxed focus state or in some deep conscious or subconscious emotional state. The feeling observed when having an excellent run on the poker machines is of being *larger than life* or an awareness of a relaxed focus and *"oneness"* with the equipment. However it is very easy to slip out of this state if one becomes "too aware" of it. The exact state is transient, nebulous and requires defocusing. It is rather like looking up at the night sky and becoming aware of faint stars out of the corner of your eye. If you try to focus on them they disappear because of the way the rods and cones of the eye are structured.

The required mind-state for these slot machine/PK effects is similar. It is actually quite hard to describe but one sometimes becomes aware of this altered consciousness feeling prior to visiting the gaming establishment

The feeling could best be described as a "knowing" that the trip to the gaming establishment will not be wasted. Also in this mind-state normal body discomforts such as aching feet are simply not apparent. The mind-state seems to over-ride physical sensations and enhances non-physical sensations.

THE "LETTING GO" FACTOR

A widely held belief among gamblers, particularly those who roll dice is that once you have literally "prayed" for sixes, you *let go the thought.*

You attempt to dismiss it completely from your mind. Our observations indicate that this factor is fairly important. Once we have mentally expressed "disgust" with a machine and have formed the intent to walk away from it, we have "let go". Often the machine will pay out - even after a long run of virtually no wins at all. Also there is some evidence that a person may generate a PK field around the machine which tends to linger for at least several minutes. We have consistently noticed that a gambler having an extraordinarily good run on a slot machine will sometimes affect the machines on either side, which also start to generate good runs. This has happened often enough to make us wonder about the possibility of such a field.

On one specific occasion a lady who was known for her extreme runs of "luck" had achieved a jackpot on a five cent machine and continued to play because the machine "refused to back off". But the machines on either side of her were also paying out extraordinarily well. We tend to think there may be some basis in reality for the concept of a PK field, but from our observations it would appear to be a geographically restricted field. But having said that one of our team has on several occasions influenced a "spinning Jenny" type prize wheel at a distance of 40 feet. In one particular club we attend this wheel is spun at predetermined times during the day. It contains a series of numbers around the circular perimeter. If the number of your particular slot machine is called you win $20 worth of coins.

Our member influenced the wheel on 3 separate occasions over 2 hours, to select his particular machine from the other 80 machines in this small club. That is somewhat beyond the laws of chance, particularly so as he focused his mind on the required result. It might be added that he is an accomplished alpha/theta practitioner.

PK effects are generally thought of as being associated with theta brain waves but a lot of the effects we are noticing are happening in an altered state of consciousness which may or may not have anything to do with theta. According to the literature we have studied a hypnotised subject is in an altered consciousness state but their brainwaves don't appear to vary from the norm. Until more precise data comes to hand we are unable to draw any definite conclusions on theta/PK interaction. No doubt time and reader feedback will educate us.

THE EMERGING FIELD OF MIND INFLUENCE

What used to be known as mental telepathy and ESP slowly evolved into the field of parapsychology and has more recently impinged upon the world of higher physics. The fact that some of the world's most eminent physicists are actively trying to link consciousness as a force in a universal equation adds credence to the suspicion that mind-power technology might be the next natural human evolution after computer technology.

Quantum Physics, which deals with the world of sub-atomic particles is now developing an increasing respect for the effect of the experimenters consciousness on the actual outcome of the experiment.

Mind-power technology is basically the science of the **21st century** - it is alien to everything we currently understand about the laws of physical reality and it is viewed with suspicion in certain quarters because it threatens to provide a mechanism whereby reality as we know it ...can be modified at will!

Having given you a little background on PK let us get on with the concept of **luck cycles**. That is, the cyclic periods when your natural PK abilities appear to be at their strongest. However bear in mind that PK luck, positive thinking and all the creative affirmations in the world will be of no use to you unless you are in the market place to receive the benefits. That is, if you sit at home and lock the doors it is totally unlikely that bags of money will materialize out of thin air. You need to be out and about and interfacing with people, things and realities about you. On this basis any inherent PK abilities you may have or eventually acquire will be given the best chance to manifest themselves in a *positive constructive* manner to enhance your lifestyle.

THE FASCINATING WORLD OF LUCK CYCLES!

When we decided to experiment with slot machines in a real-life situation rather than random number generators in a non-commercial non-emotive environment, we gained the impression that if we played the machines while in alpha, we might release our natural PK abilities. This worked well for about a week then stopped dead. We tentatively concluded that alpha had little to do with it. At this early point in the experiment we were visiting the local slot machine clubs at irregular intervals - mainly when we had some spare time (and the petty cash tin had accumulated a few dollars).

During extended periods of playing we became aware of two strange things:

Firstly we quite often got a payout on a final spin as we were giving up in disgust and secondly a rather unusual trend emerged which caused us to start to wonder about "luck cycles".

What was happening was this: we would be cycling through the various machines giving each 3 or 4 spins and generally getting nowhere. Then, quite suddenly, our "luck" would change. Literally out of the blue all those machines which had not paid out before would start paying us. Sometimes quite generously! This would last for 30-60 minutes then appear to revert to the non-payout mode (for which they are internationally famous!)

We also found an intriguing "PK Missing" effect: Most of the machines we play in Australia have 5 paylines.

We have noticed consistently that if we play 4 lines instead of the maximum of 5 lines, a significant payout will often occur on the 5th line - that is the line we have not covered. In fact we missed a $680 jackpot on this basis. This might be due to the computer chip programming but we have reason to believe it is more to do with PK minus effects.

After some months of frustrating experimenting this "luck window" reared up consistently and we started to search for a pattern. Initially we started playing at the same time each day but quite by accident found that these "windows of PK" appeared to retard each day by several hours. That is, if we caught a window at 10pm one night we seemed to be able to catch a similar window 2-3 hours earlier the next night. We followed this theory for a couple of months and eventually found it non-valid.

Then one of our players had a strong luck run over 10 days and kept precise notes of his peak runs. The mathematical analysis indicated that these windows regressed an average of 1.25 hours each day. So we worked on this theory for a while and found it reasonably accurate except that it tended to phase in and out over a month or so.

Now earlier on we had scored 3 jackpots all around full moon, so we wondered if the high human-emotion period of full moon was having an effect on PK.

This line was pursued fairly enthusiastically for 3-4 months but these so called monthly peaks jumped right out of phase with the moon and put us back to square one.

At this point I decided to do some serious night-time alpha work to see if I could solve these puzzles. With the help of the mental-pendulum techniques I had developed I asked specific questions as to the manner in which I should use dream-control programming to obtain some sort of clue. I then used standard alpha programming just prior to sleep and fed the problem into my subconscious with specific instructions to awaken me with a full conscious memory of the dream-solution. As usual the process worked fairly well but in this case the results were quite extraordinary. I got one very definite dream about bio-rhythms.....another (which occurred twice) giving me a very clear graph pattern and the final one was some vague equation which was somehow connected with moon cycles and daily luck peaks.

It took about a month to complete the deciphering and it changed everything!

The analysis formed the basis of a luck cycle theory which may well be full of holes, but it is connecting with financial reality sufficiently well at this point to produce results which are way above our initial expectations. But we were well aware that there may be a longer term cycle which would cause peaks and troughs in this basic pattern.

The first thing we did was get hold of a bio-rhythm program and try and find a connection between all our major wins and the bio-rhythm chart. And strangely enough a strong connection was found with the critical days on the emotional chart. Most of the wins occurred within 2-3 days of the critical emotional crossover point.

Two of the major wins (or runs) occurred on the critical day and most of the others within plus or minus 2 days.

My first big jackpot of $65,700 occurred 3 days before a triple critical biorhythm but at a point when the intuitional rhythm was at a peak. Which figures, because I went into a daydream and stayed on a machine far longer than I normally would have - next thing I knew - the jackpot bells were ringing!

We had a lot of trouble with the vague equation I dreamed up. Finally we got it! It is a well known fact that full moon affects the human emotions in a strange manner and we had also suspected that the emotional biorhythm had something to do with our cycles. So, working on a 28 day emotional bio-rhythm we expanded this to the number of hours in the 28 day month - 672 hours. We then looked at the lunar cycle which is approximately 29.5 days and divided the hours by the days. Result approximately 22.75 hours.

As our luck peaks seem to drop back by 1.25 hours each day this tied in with the amount our daily luck cycles seemed to retard.

The final aspect of all this is the graph, which appeared clearly in the dreams. But before this is presented another strange observation has been noticed which ties in extremely well with the graph.

It is this: It has been observed consistently that just prior to the onset of a "luck window" the payouts go "flat". That is wins are few and far between. But within several minutes virtually every machine we touch can be induced to provide some form of win, occasionally quite spectacular.

This used to frustrate us no end as we assumed that the predicted luck peak was not valid. It took some time to notice that immediately after this dead period we usually had extraordinarily good runs.

It is interesting to note that in observing other players the same pattern often emerges.

The graph that materialised in my programmed dream looked like this:

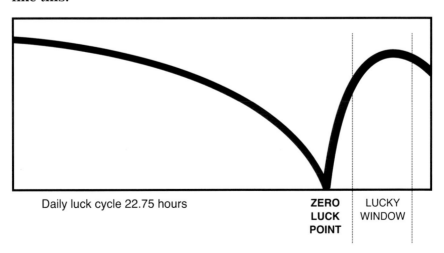

Daily luck cycle 22.75 hours   **ZERO LUCK POINT**   LUCKY WINDOW

This concept of a "luck window" ties in with the financial reality of our experiments. The window appears to be the point of highest PK. All natural luck seems to disappear just prior to the onset of the "window".

Until recently the method of determining our daily peaks was to play the machines on and off over several days until we struck a "window" then base our playing around this. We tried rolling dice to try and affect the number of sixes that appeared, as a method of determining the window.

That wasn't reliable.

We tried using the mental pendulum but it is a fact that the pendulum has two modes of operation: either it is extraordinarily accurate or alternatively it goes to considerable lengths to convince the user that it has conscientiously acquired a doctorate in the noble science of pathological lying! We don't find it reliable as a predicting device (at this point anyway) but quite usable as a mechanism to confirm what we already know.

We then developed a software program called a **PK TESTER** which tends to indicate when the user is experiencing high psychokinetic abilities.

SUMMARY

The idea of the whole experiment was to determine if personal alpha techniques enhanced ones ability to influence the environment. It progressed on from there quite by accident to encompass the possibility of luck cycles.

It has become obvious over the past two years that the practice of alpha causes a spatial expansion in consciousness which appears to act holographically.

PK abilities appear to be part and parcel of this expanded consciousness. Nobody knows exactly how they work but our PK tape certainly had a pronounced affect on some of our clients. One client even reported poltergeist effects in that electrical devices switched themselves on and off in his presence. This was after using our tape programme for several months.

We feel that the same PK luck cycles might be used for virtually any form of random event gambling. No doubt after reading this a number of our clients will experiment in this direction. There have been a number of well publicised lotto wins in Australia recently whereby the winner felt the urge to take a "QuickPick" ticket rather than enter their own regular numbers. In other words, instead of trying to pick the winners, they let the **winners pick them**! If they had a strong intuition cycle at this point, coupled to a strong PK cycle at the time of having their ticket computer selected, then from what our experiments have indicated this spectacular result might not be entirely unexpected.

One important observation has been made in the past 12 months which has become quite important.

It is this: If the mood, feeling, vibes or general interaction with the specific gaming environment does not feel right we do not waste our time playing! Our personal "feeling" about the gaming establishment and the people in it is extremely important.

Likewise with the slot machines themselves. If a machine has a "warm friendly feel" about it, we give it a few spins. If it appears to be "aloof" or "detached" we give it a miss.

I realise this phraseology is a little strange but the words used above actually convey the meaning quite well. Any experienced slot machine player will probably echo these comments.

From a personal point of view one thing has become very apparent and that is as follows:

My emotional state can overcome all other considerations when it comes to triggering a slot machine to pay out. A burst of intense emotion on my part can (and does) trigger a machine irrespective of where I am in my luck cycle. The emotional states I have noticed are - anger, disgust, extreme frustration and that special state of altered consciousness which I can't easily define but invariably always recognise in advance.

For the past 5 years I have won a jackpot on my birthday. Last birthday I won two jackpots on the same day!

Possibly this is caused by my mind-set regarding my feelings toward growing older....and being reminded of it at the end of June each year!

The next chapter explains how to create and use this luck program for yourself.

11

MAKING YOUR
PK LUCK TAPE

For a start, it is vitally important that you follow
the procedure outlined ahead - to the letter!
And deviation will produce uncertain results.

Here is what I suggest you do:
Read through this instructional chapter once to get an idea of the procedure then transfer the pre-prepared "script" onto a blank cassette tape
as instructed.

THIS IS YOUR PSYCHOKINETIC PROGRAMME.

This chapter explains how to make your PK tape which will instruct your
subconscious to make you **consciously aware** of your luck cycles.

And it will do so because it has been TOLD to do so. Any clear, concise, precise instruction that you give your subconscious will be followed faithfully, including the enhancement of your psychokinetic and intuitive abilities.

It is a fact that people who are "naturally" lucky **expect** to be lucky because that is the way they have instructed their subconscious to interact with the environment!

Instructions for the actual making of this tape will come later on. They are simple and easy to follow.

WARNING!

I would seriously suggest that you tell **nobody** what you are doing. Especially your closest trusted friends, because any negative input during this critical period may work to negate the effect of the procedure. Remember, you are about to change something you have believed in all your life - **mediocre luck!**

You are dealing with a very sensitive mind-state here and you are about to re-programme certain basic subconscious beliefs that you have held since a child. Any outside comment, influence or negativity will most certainly affect the outcome you are dedicated to achieving. Apart from that *you are paying to gain knowledge that others do not have - why give this advantage away!*

By all means, when your first major "win" is in hand, show the cheque to your friends, but, it will be to your disadvantage to let them know **how** you did it! Let them think that you are merely having a "run of luck"!

THERE ARE TWO PARTS TO THIS PROGRAM:

The first is the actual making of the tape and the second is to determine the best times of the month to "gamble". i.e. to take lotto tickets, etc. We could easily have supplied a completed finished cassette where all you had to do is listen to it. But for psychological reasons, it is vitally important that you put some emotional energy into actually making the tape yourself (a very easy task) in your own voice!

The reason is that your subconscious mind will trust your own voice - it may not totally trust the voice of a stranger.

Also you know exactly what is on the tape - there can be no hidden subliminals which tends to worry some purchasers of commercial tapes. We suspect that by recording in your own voice the resultant effect will be 2-3 times stronger and quicker.

Initially you will be asked to play the tape for 3-4 nights in a row - then have a break for a day and do the same thing again.

This is to avoid any possible side-effects such as tiredness which can happen if you play a re-programming tape week in, week out, without a break. Basically if you limit it to 3-4 nights per week you will not experience any problems. However if you have a history of any form of psychological disorder, it would be advisable to consult a Doctor or Psychologist before using any consciousness-altering program

You can play the finished tape through the cassette loudspeaker if you wish but if you are in a situation where you don't wish to disturb your partner then you might prefer headphones. But it is *not actually necessary* to wear them. I'd suggest you do what I do - place them under the edge of your pillow so that the sound filters up *through* the pillow and your partner doesn't hear it.

The volume can be turned down to a level where you can barely make out the words. The message will be heard clearly by your subconscious mind - something like a subliminal tape. I put mine under the edge of my pillow with the recorder in a convenient position by my hand, so that I do not have to open my eyes and fumble for the switch when I am almost asleep.

Alternatively you can play the tape during one of your daily alpha sessions - the effect will be about the same.

Apart from the *psychokinetic enhancement* message, there is a space in the script for you to include a habit-transforming message of your own. For example, if you want to improve your self-confidence then you merely include that particular message in the script space provided.

You may elect to ignore the habit-transforming messages and focus on the PK message. The choice is yours.

PART 1

MAKING THE TAPE

Purchase a blank tape cassette on which you record the message repeatedly 8-10 times or more, or alternatively until one side of the tape is full. It does not matter if the tape finishes half way through a message, but if you make a mistake, **do not** stop the tape - just carry on. The reason is that when you stop a tape during a recording process there is normally a loud click evident on replay which tends to startle the subconscious mind. The odd mistake is acceptable and does not jar your subconscious if it is not too obvious.

The message is divided into 3 sections

1. **The countdown which prepares your mind for the message and relaxes you. It doesn't matter if you go to sleep during the countdown - your subconscious will hear the message.**
2. **The psychokinetic message itself.**
3. **Your habit-transforming message (if required). If you don't wish to include one of these messages then simply leave it out.**

When making the tape, section 1 (the countdown) is read slowly onto the cassette - <u>once only.</u>

But sections 2 and 3 are repeated over and over again until the tape is full.

Alternatively, if you don't wish to fill the entire side of the tape up, at least make sure the message is repeated 8-10 times.

CAUTION: Some people like to put these hypnotic tapes into an automatic machine which repeat-plays all night. Due to the nature of this programme we do not advise doing this!

When making this tape, it is helpful to have a "white-noise" background such as the sound of rain-on-the-roof, or seashore sounds.

The easiest way to achieve this is to make the recording in your bathroom with the cold shower running. This provides a "masking" effect that is very soothing to the conscious mind, but it is not strictly necessary if the process is inconvenient.

I place an old cardboard carton upside down under the stream of water as this tends to give a better rain-on-the-roof effect.

What happens is that this white noise makes the relaxation exercise easier and masks against outside noises, which may otherwise distract you.

I suggest you read the following through before recording it so that you understand it clearly.

Do a practice run with the following message - section 1.

It should occupy approximately 3-4 minutes on the tape. If you are recording your message any faster than this, I'd suggest you slow it down. Also leave 3-4 seconds of space between each countdown. For example, you are starting the countdown with: *"Twenty"* ....*you are feeling sleepy etc.* Leave a 3-4 second gap before you start on countdown *"nineteen"*. There is no hurry.

Do it all slowly and clearly. Sit about 2 feet away from your tape machine (with your cold shower running if desired) and speak in a quiet but very slow voice. Keep your voice low and "friendly" without any overly loud words.

Start your practice run by pressing the record button and speaking clearly. Time yourself.

SECTION 1

Say the following slowly into the microphone:
(allow a 3-4 second gap between each countdown line)

> ....*You are relaxed. Your eyes are closed ... You are taking deep slow breaths.. Each time you exhale - you relax more.*

> **Twenty**......*you are feeling sleepy and drowsy - you are feeling sleepy and drowsy.*

(3-4 seconds pause between each line from now on)

> **Nineteen**....*all your limbs are relaxing - all your limbs are relaxing.*

> **Eighteen**....*your breathing is becoming slow and even - your breathing is becoming slow and even.*

> **Seventeen** .*you are feeling sleepier and more tired - you are feeling sleepier and more tired.*

> **Sixteen** ......*your eyelids are feeling heavier and heavier - your eyelids are feeling heavier and heavier.*

Fifteen .... *every muscle in your body is relaxing - every muscle in your body is relaxing.*

Fourteen ... *your head and shoulders are relaxing - your head and shoulders are relaxing.*

Thirteen .... *your arms are relaxing - your arms are relaxing.*

Twelve ...... *your chest is relaxing - your chest is relaxing.*

Eleven .... *your thighs and legs are relaxing - your thighs and legs are relaxing.*

Ten .... *your feet and toes are relaxing - your feet and toes are relaxing.*

Nine .... *with every breath you take, you go deeper and deeper - with every breath you take, you go deeper and deeper.*

Eight .... *you are feeling pleasant and relaxed - you are feeling pleasant and relaxed.*

Seven .... *deeper and deeper, nothing disturbs you - deeper and deeper, nothing disturbs you.*

Six .... *listening only to my voice - listening only to my voice.*

Five .... *everything I say will be heard by your subconscious mind - everything I say will be heard by your subconscious mind.*

Four .... *deeper and deeper, sleepier and sleepier - deeper and deeper, sleepier and sleepier.*

Three .... *totally relaxed, listening only to my voice - totally relaxed, listening only to my voice.*

Two .... *with every breath you take, you go deeper and deeper - with every breath you take, you go deeper and deeper.*

One .... *down, down, down, deeper and deeper - down, down, down, deeper and deeper.*

Now _**press the pause button**_
(So far, you will have used up 3-4 minutes of tape)

Have a listen to the tape. Are you reasonably happy with it? Did it flow satisfactorily? Do you need to slow down your delivery a little?

If you are happy so far then proceed with the next step.

If not then redo the tape and press **pause** when you finish.......ready for the main message below.

Take a breather before you start on the main message.
But before you start again, make sure you are sitting in the same position and speaking at the same volume. This is important to prevent subconscious "jarring".

The following message is preferably repeated over and over, until you run out of tape. (Record one side of the tape only). If you have a computer with a sound card you can record this message once then play it back on *repeat* so that you can feed a continuous message from the computer to your tape recorder. It is a good idea to add a medium amount of echo if your software allows this.
Leave a 10 second gap between each repeat.

SECTION 2

Repeat the following psychokinetic message over and over:

(RELEASE THE PAUSE BUTTON & START - - S L O W L Y)

....You are becoming aware of your natural luck cycle and you are noticing increasing runs of good luck. When you enter a gaming establishment of any form you will slip into that mental state required to affect your environment and you will automatically evoke the same mental state which was present during previous successes.

When you play slot machines you will search for one that you resonate with and you will remain bonded with it, as it pays winning combinations continuously. You will tend to drop into alpha as you play and remain relaxed and casual. Three, four and five winning sequences will occur frequently, starting from the left-hand side of one of the pay-lines you are playing. Jackpot combinations and 5 of-a-kind will occur regularly. When you place a bet, play lotto or enter games-of-chance, you will let your intuition guide you. Increasingly you can trust this, as it becomes more accurate.

You feel good about yourself and appreciate the nice things that now happen to you. Your positive outlook and health are improving daily and your intuition is becoming quite remarkable. You are sleeping well at night and wake up refreshed and enthusiastic about the day ahead.

You remain relaxed and stress-free at all times and you find problems easy to handle. As you play this program you feel increasingly better about yourself and life has taken on a new positive meaning.

Every time you take a drink of liquid, this programme will reinforce itself.

(Insert your habit-transforming message here if required) - (Section 3)

Now repeat the psychokinetic message and your habit-transforming message over and over. That is, repeat Section 2 & 3 over and over.

After you finish your recording listen to the tape right through to make sure it flows reasonably smoothly. It is now ready for use.

Following are 5 of the most useful habit-transforming messages.
They are:

1 Weight loss

2 Disease recovery

3 Concentration and memory

4 Self-confidence

5 Goal setting

Select <u>ONE ONLY</u> of the following messages and add it in directly after the psychokinetic message. It is repeated over and over along with the psychokinetic message.

If, after several weeks, you want to use a new habit-transforming message, simply re-make the habit-forming part of your tape again tape again.

SECTION 3

1 - WEIGHT LOSS:

If you have any medical problems associated with your weight condition, consult your doctor before including this message on your tape.

Read the following message onto your tape -

..... You desire a healthier and happier body. When you achieve this, people will look at you with admiration. You are now aware of the fat, salt and calorie content of the food you eat. You search out foods that are low in these items. Your body is now storing less fat and when you feel hungry between meals, you will drink a glass of water or chew on a carrot or something else non-fattening.

When you do this, the hunger pangs quickly disappear and you enjoy your low calorie, low fat meals. You find yourself filling up quickly at meal times and you always leave food on your plate. You find the taste of desserts nauseating and sickly and realize your body does not need them. You feel more active and energetic and do more natural exercise. You realize that this extra activity will quickly burn off excess weight. You eat more slowly than you did before.

You are looking better and feeling better. Your clothes are now fitting loosely. People are commenting on your improving appearance.....

2 - DISEASE RECOVERY:

(Read the following message onto your tape)

......Your body produces healthy cells and antibodies that now fight and destroy the harmful cells and bacteria. Your system is now producing large quantities of these disease-destroying antibodies and your bloodstream is transporting them to where they are needed the most.

They are killing the unwelcome invaders and you can feel your health improving daily. Your mind and body are now working together to bring your system back to its normal healthy state. You notice this improvement daily and you know you will be back to normal health quickly. You feel more energetic and alert and as each day passes you feel better. You have total confidence in your ability to heal yourself......

3 - CONCENTRATION AND MEMORY

(Read the following message onto your tape)

........Your memory and concentration are improving daily. Every impression you have ever had is stored in your subconscious mind so you recall details of specific events easily. You remember things easily and your concentration is improving rapidly. You remember names, faces, dates and places and when you study you concentrate deeply on the subject matter and remember the details clearly. You are becoming proud of your excellent memory. You now have total confidence in your ability to remember things......

4 - SELF - CONFIDENCE

(Read the following message onto your tape)

......You now find it easy to think clearly about your concerns and you make positive decisions promptly and effortlessly. Your confidence in your ability is growing rapidly and you find that your daily activities are easy to handle and stress-free. When you retire at night and reflect back upon the day's happenings, you will be happy with the

decisions you made and the confidence with which you handled yourself. You now know that YOU are in control. Your confidence in yourself is very high and your self-esteem is rising rapidly. You notice others showing you more respect and you realise that this is because of your increased confidence ....

5 - GOAL SETTING

(Figure out precisely what your goal is then read the following message onto the tape)

..... Your goal is to _____
(specify what it is in as few words as possible)

It is your ambition to achieve this goal because you know life will be much better when you do. You concentrate on your goal intensively and you know that it is coming to fruition. You easily overcome all obstacles and find that others help you in your efforts due to your concentrated dedication. You are totally confident in achieving it and brush aside anything that is not orientated toward achieving your end result.

You feel good about your goal and know that it is the right thing to aim for. You are succeeding - you can feel it. Your sense of expectancy toward the desired result increases daily. You can easily visualise your goal having been achieved ......

NOTES ON PLAYING THE TAPE

How to use the tape:

You might find it more effective to play the tape - softly - while you're lying in bed reading, before you turn out the light. When you are reading you tend to drop into alpha (focused concentration) and some readers have reported a faster and deeper effect when they play the tape at this time. You can play it slightly below the annoyance level.

That is, softly enough so that it doesn't disturb you. Your subconscious will hear it, even if you can hardly detect it consciously. (This is how subliminal tapes work). If the message is entering your subconscious properly you should wake up feeling quite refreshed and enthusiastic the next morning. This feeling will improve over the weeks. This program will work better at some times than at others - it varies from person to person. You might like to try playing it as you're reading in bed and again as you're going to sleep.

You will not overload your mind initially if you play it 2-3 times per day, but don't use the tape like this week after week. Take a break between bursts of mental input. You can also play it while you're watching TV, reading in your lounge chair, in fact anytime your conscious mind is "switched off".

If you're not specifically interested in poker (slot) machines you can re-record your PK tape and leave the paragraph about the poker machines out. That is, paragraph 2 (starting with - "when you play poker machines ....") can be left out. This will convert the message into a highly effective luck/health/positive thinking format. Even after you stop playing this tape it will keep reinforcing itself because your subconscious has been told that every time you take a drink of liquid the program will be recalled subconsciously. So for a week or so after you cease using the tape the mere act of drinking a liquid will cause the program to reinforce itself in your mind. After this period of time the post-hypnotic message will have lost its effect.

Once you have played the PK message for 3-4 nights it would pay to give it a break for a day or two.

You are actually changing a lifelong belief in your luck so if you overdo it there may be negative side-effects. There is no hurry - you have the rest of your new "lucky" life ahead of you.

You will have noticed the strange phraseology in these messages - they are worded this way because the subconscious mind recognizes the "here and now" rather than the future. The way these messages are worded will break through to your subconscious, which is what this programme is all about.
Do not change any of the wording.

PART 2

LUCK CYCLES

Everyone has a natural luck cycle. This is the time when good things just seem to happen unexpectedly.

It is well known that professional gamblers have "hot runs" when for days on end everything goes the way they want. It is not so well known that this state is actually caused by a combination of their natural luck cycle PLUS their emotive interaction with the environment.

In other words they are *psyckokinetically driving* toward the results they want. They have added an emotive **psychokinetic plus** factor to their natural luck cycle peak. This type of event is an observable fact and it is quite likely that at some point in your life it has happened to you or to someone you know.

It is suspected that luck runs in monthly cycles and there are times when everything appears to go wrong. This happens to me on a regular monthly basis and during those times I leave all forms of gaming alone. There are also much longer luck cycles but these are not relevant to the PK LUCK program.

I strongly suggest that you buy a cheap diary and keep notes of your lucky - and unlucky - streaks every month.

You will become aware (due to the programming on the tape) of when these cycles appear and after several months you may notice a pattern emerge.

Probably the easiest way to determine your luck period is to visit a slot machine establishment 2-3 times per week and purchase a small amount of coin. Play one machine after another, giving each one 3-4 spins.

The idea is to note how long your container of coins last.

During your natural good-luck period you will probably run at a slight profit or break-even for some period of time. During bad luck periods your money will disappear rapidly.

Once you establish the psychokinetic tape programme in your subconscious mind, you will achieve some quite spectacular "runs" of extraordinary luck during the good-luck part of your cycles.

At one point I was in an Australian casino and over 2 hours scored 5 small jackpots.

In each case the attendant was called over to reset the machine and pay me out.

She was quite impressed by the number of jackpots I had scored and stated that she had never seen anybody have such a good run before.

You can see that it is fairly important to determine where your luck periods actually lie. It is obviously pointless trying

to manipulate your environment psychokinetically when your natural cycles are against you.

However, if the idea of visiting a gambling establishment does not appeal to you, it is still relatively easy to determine your luck cycles by simply **being aware** of when good things happen. Due to the programme suggestions on your cassette tape you will start to *notice* events and trends that were not apparent before.

To clarify what I mean by becoming *aware* of events I'll give you a personal example of a series of incidents that happened to me recently. These happened during an obviously very low PK *unlucky* day.

Five different, but **synchronistically related** events happened on one day. Normally I would have made no conscious connection between them but due to my increased awareness, the message was obvious. It was the unluckiest day of the month for me!

Firstly I was driving along a main highway and decided to take a shortcut via a toll road which required a payment of 60c at the toll booth. I threw a 50c and a 10c coin into the coin basket and waited for the boom gate to lift. It didn't!

I called the attendant over and when he checked the machine the 10c piece was nowhere to be seen. He commented that the machine hadn't played up like that for a long time. That was event number one.

Later in the afternoon I walked into a Chinese Restaurant for a take-away meal. It cost $9.80. I gave the attendant $20 and she gave me 20c change. For some strange reason, I didn't wake up to the fact that I was $10 short until 20-30 seconds later.

However when I pointed out her error, she readily acknowledged her mistake and apologized. (I was psychokinetically affecting my environment negatively). That was event number two!

Event number 3!

I drove down to my favourite club in the early evening and had difficulty finding a park, which is unusual for me. I finally found a spot, several hundred metres up the road. I had run out of parking change so I dashed inside the club to get some 10c pieces. When I came out there were *two* empty spaces right outside the front door and *both* had time left on their meters. Normally during my luck period I "score" a car park with money left on the meter.

Now for event number four!

You guessed it! Not a single poker/slot machine wanted to know me!!

After spending around $30 in 10c pieces I couldn't persuade a single machine to do much more than "twitch"!

It was one of the worst runs on slot machines that I had experienced.

At that point, I knew it was time to drive home.....carefully!!

Event number five had me shaking my head!

I left the club to drive the 3kms home around 11pm. As I neared my residence there was a siren behind me and rotating police lights. I pulled over and climbed out of the car. The police officer walked up and asked if I was aware that I was driving without my headlights on. As the whole road was illuminated by overhead street lights I hadn't noticed. He was quite good about it and let me go.

I had totally forgotten to turn my headlights on.

It was an absolute disaster of a day and was one of those rare, intense "PK negative" situations.

Oh yes, and when I got home, the carport bulb had burnt out. It had been working perfectly for the past 12 months!

Now normally, all these items would not connect together in my mind, I would have put them down to a "bad day". I would not have been aware that they were the result of my psychokinetic manipulation of my immediate environment. And when I looked at my diary I noticed similar things had happened about the same time the month before. And also the month before that!

So I now know when my psychokinetic negative period is. I add about 2 weeks to that date and expect reasonably good luck. And so far it is happening according to plan!

So from the above, you can see how to evolve your own natural luck chart. However due to the *luck awareness* message on your cassette tape you should become aware of bad luck things that happen. This may cause you to think that the tape program is not working.

Wrong! What has happened is that you are *now aware of these events* which you weren't consciously aware of before. You simply didn't tie them into a pattern. They were happening to you but you didn't notice them! This heightened awareness is good news - it means that the program is working! You can now use the knowledge of your luck cycles to work around your bad luck periods.

In fact you will become aware of quite a number of things that you never noticed before and some of them may surprise you. Just remember it is all part of the process of modifying your long-held subconscious beliefs.

In time, you will become intrigued and gratified by the results of your new awareness. I can assure you it is a fascinating process!!!

NOTES ON USING THE HABIT- TRANSFORMING MESSAGES

Once you determine your luck cycles, you may decide *not* to play your cassette tape during your negative psychotronic periods (bad luck periods), so there is nothing wrong whatsoever in making a second tape with one or two of the habit-transforming messages and playing it during this "off" period.

You would start your new tape with the same 20 to1 countdown, then leave Section 2, the PK message out. In its place, you insert **no more than two** of the habit messages.

For example, you might want to couple the non-smoking message (detailed elsewhere in this manual) with the weight loss message. Simply read these two messages (in any order) on to your second tape, directly after the 20 to1 countdown message. Your two habit messages are repeated over and over as before.

You could also play both tapes alternatively. One tape one night and the second tape the next night. However, after 3-4 nights of programming take a break for 2-3 nights then start again. Do not overdo it!

But *do not* put more than two messages on any one tape. If you do they will not work as well as they simply cause confusion. Each individual will react differently to the programming on the tape. One person may experience a vast change after only one night of playing while another may notice nothing much for the first two weeks.

But one thing is for certain, if you play them regularly as instructed they will have an increasingly noticeable effect which some users will notice more than others.

Do NOT give up! Keep at it. The results you want WILL happen.

But only your subconscious knows the timing and it is not about to let you know! Remember you are changing your basic belief system and there will be a certain amount of subconscious resistance to this. I must stress here that if you experience any unusual side-effects then stop playing the tape until they disappear. Like any other hypnotic program the program effects your subconscious mind.

HOW POWERFUL ARE THESE SELF-HYPNOTIC PROGRAMS?

I will give you an example of a personal event which demonstrates graphically just how powerful self-hypnosis is!

It goes back to my teenage years. At the age of sixteen I was the shyest guy in school. One particular girl fancied me but each time she spoke to me I turned bright red and sidled away. I was shockingly shy and even though I fantasized about dating her the thought of actually speaking to this appealing young lady made me very nervous.

This was before I discovered the power of self-hypnosis. And almost exactly 2 years later, at the age of 18, I was an extremely professional well-known stage hypnotist!

Wouldn't you consider that to be a major turn-around!

My parents were amazed! So was I. But it just happened.

And I took it all in my stride. The beauty about self-hypnosis is that after you program for all these magical things to happen......and they actually **do**, it is really a non-event. I knew it was going to happen so I was not exactly overcome with awe....but my friends and acquaintances were!

And THAT - is the power of self-hypnosis !!!

After spending my entire life in mind-power, electronics and business in general I have come to totally believe that we become, not so much as what we think about all day long, but what we **psychokinetically manipulate our environment to provide.**

It is a fact that some people think positive thoughts all day long and get nowhere in life.

But others just seem to have it all fall into place for them. They are the ones who adjust the environment to suit themselves. This is what you will be able to do from now on

This programme is all about changing your basic belief system, so that you not only feel good about life, but life **feels good about you**..... *and proves it !!!!*

WARNING:

If you find that you get half way through this programme and for no logical reason at all, start to wonder why you are doing it at all then this is probably your subconscious belief system suddenly waking up to what is happening.

It will be saying to itself .....*"Hey, hang on - if my program is changed I won't be able to carry on in the same moronic stupid way anymore. This stuff is dangerous to my status-quo so I'd better stop it now!"*

And it does! So if you suddenly develop negative feelings about this program then this is probably the reason!

THE POWER OF SUGGESTION

The incredible power of hypnosis does **not** come from a hypnotist, contrary to popular belief. It comes from **your** subconscious mind!!

And if you don't control it then **it controls you!**

Every sane living individual on this planet is under the control of their own subconscious mind but only a few of us have learnt how to turn the tables *and take charge*!

Each and every one of us are the product of our lifetime of indoctrination.

So if you feel that you are in a mess it is probably because your basic subconscious belief system is happy that way.

And the same applies to luck. If you consider yourself unlucky it is because your belief system has "trained" you that way.

This single cassette tape, created by the best personal hypnotist in the world ......

Y O U ....may change your life .....forever .....if used properly.

THE NOVICE EFFECT

This is also known as beginner's luck and is a frequent occurrence among those who try psychokinetics (PK) for the first time. You may have a phenomenal run of luck initially and then it might die right off. This is quite often bought about by boredom with the process. If this happens don't become discouraged because it is a fairly common occurrence. All you have to do is to persevere until it settles down.

Also if you push too hard for too long the PK effect seems to die away. I have found that it takes 48 hours or more to recover after an extended slot machine session. This will probably vary from person to person depending upon their own initial belief system. Tiredness or a low emotional state can also negate positive PK. I have found that if I travel directly from New Zealand to Las Vegas the resultant jetlag totally destroys my PK abilities for several days.

Some of the runs I have had have left me feeling quite astounded and totally astonished the onlookers. Several of our clients have found that the effect works just as well when rolling dice but I have no personal experience of this.

All my PK experiments have been done on slot machines because the results are virtually instantaneous and I can play them at my convenience and at my own speed. Also they are very similar in concept to the random-number generators used by the original mind-matter researchers in the PEAR laboratory at Princeton University. The only difference is that instead of playing a "computer game" I am using a real life device with an associated emotional component. ie. I can lose money if I am not careful.

Once you have figured out your approximate luck cycles then it would pay to do any form of gambling - such as taking lotto tickets - during your luck peaks. The whole idea of this PK program is to enhance your natural luck peak.

If you happen to have an internet connection you can visit one of the many gambling sites and play slot machines, sometimes for free. This way you can potentially determine your luck cycles without leaving home as there seems to be no geographic distance limits to PK effects.

LETTING GO

There is an extremely important aspect to manipulating events with your mind (PK).

This is as follows: after you have formed the desire for the dice to roll up sixes or for the slot machines to produce 5 of a kind in a row then you must **dismiss the desire totally.**

It appears to be this letting go that makes the process work!

How many times have you played a slot machine for a length of time with negative winnings and decided to give up in disgust and walk away? You form the intention to walk away and give the machine one last spin and much to your surprise you often capture a decent payout. It was your **intention of dismissal** that triggered your PK !

After you have re-programmed your belief system with this PK program it may work against you if you consciously and consistently desire a win.

But if the machine doesn't look like paying in the first half dozen spins I walk away to try another one. Many players tend to play two machines at once by giving two side-by-side slot machines alternate spins fairly rapidly. They insert their coins in one machine, press the play button and then *promptly* flick their attention to putting coins in the other machine. That is, their concentration is taken off the spinning machine.

In fact I was unaware of my first major jackpot as I was focusing on the second machine when the player next to me became all excited and said - "Look, you've got a jackpot". It simply did not register with me. My mind was elsewhere. Several seconds later the jackpot hooter went off and I had won $67,000 !!!

In fact it seems to go blank when I get these larger wins - a state which I've noticed quite often. These wins always seem to *just occur*. I have the impression that the burst of PK energy needed to trigger the machine temporarily blocks conscious awareness. I can not prove this but it has had me puzzled for some time.

Maybe some of my readers will have noticed the same effect. If so keep a note of the mind-state you were in during the winning spin and try to re-create it in the future. Once you find a machine you appear to resonate with (develop an affinity with) express the desire strongly to yourself for winning combinations .... then LET GO!

LOTTO AND POOLS

Many players have favourite numbers which they enter each week. If you play these numbers during your lucky period you are not allowing PK forces to help you select the numbers. You might like to let these forces work for you by taking Quik-Picks - that is, you let the computer select the numbers. In this case you are not selecting the numbers.....*the numbers are selecting you!*

Do this only during your luck peaks.

FINAL NOTES ON THIS PK PROCESS

I had an interesting letter from a client earlier in the research program which is worth mentioning. She had used the PK tape for 6 weeks and hadn't noticed any results, apart from becoming aware of her luck cycles (This is a major result). So she stopped playing the tape.

Three weeks later she felt the urge to start the program again and apparently the results were immediate and spectacular. She said that luck-wise, everything was starting to fall into place.

The point is most of us have had our "luck level" for all of our lives. It takes a major shift in psyche to change it. In most cases this will not happen overnight. It is like losing weight ....it may have taken many years to slowly stack on excess weight so a person cannot expect to lose it quickly. A consistent low calorie diet and moderate exercise will cause the excess to disappear slowly.

In the same way it may take a little time and effort for your personal luck levels to modify themselves.

The PK tape you have made contains the message - *"every time you take a drink of liquid, this program will reinforce itself"*.

This message will work for a week or so after you stop playing the tape, so the positive message on the tape keeps reinforcing itself....for a while!

As the effect fades you will probably feel the urge to re-start the program. This is your subconscious mind telling you that it is now tuned to your new positive health/luck belief system. If this happens then re-start the program - the results may astound you.

The first thing that you should gain from this program is a knowledge of your luck cycles. And this knowledge is yours for the rest of your life! The next thing you might notice is that you develop a more easy-going attitude to life depending on how effectively you are playing the tape. If you are not noticing much improvement try playing the tape in the mornings just after you wake up. (Re-set your alarm if necessary). But whatever you do don't give up!

The tape <u>will</u> be working on you.

One of our clients says he didn't notice much improvement until he started playing it 3 times a day - once in the morning - once just after he goes to bed (while he is reading) - and finally as he turns off the light and goes to sleep. He says that the main thing he notices is increased energy level and the ability to handle problems more easily. However if you decide to do this make sure you do not overdo it. Give it a rest by leaving the program alone for several days.

But whatever you do don't go overboard and spend large sums of money on gambling to determine your luck cycles - let intuition guide you, not greed!

One special note – one of my clients who was naturally extremely lucky found that the programme actually diminished his luck instead of improving it. I told him not to use the programme at all and it took several weeks for his natural luck cycle to return.

I have no explanation for this but might suggest that "if it isn't broken then don't fix it."

USING A DOWSING DEVICE TO DETERMINE THE TIME OF YOUR MAXIMUM LUCK LEVELS

The following is an idea which arrived as feedback from one of my clients.

He made up the chart below and used a pendulum to ask at what time of the day his maximum luck was likely to be. I tried it myself then recommended it to my client list.

Apparently there was a lot of success with it.

Merely swing your pendulum up the chart while telling it to "***give me a yes at my maximum luck period***".

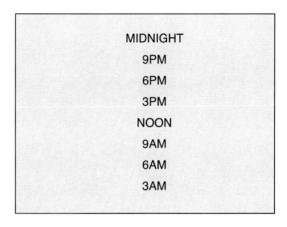

I also experimented with a similar chart to persuade the pendulum to tell me how lucky I would be during the high-luck period.

I categorized this from 0% to 100%

If the pendulum indicated I might only experience a 60% luck level for the day then I didn't bother to gamble. But once the pendulum indicated my luck level might exceed 80% then I usually had satisfactory results. Occasionally the predicted luck level was near 100% and on those days I normally did quite well at gambling.

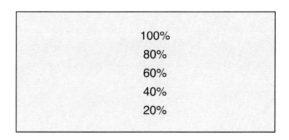

Ask your pendulum to *"give me a yes at my maximum percentage luck level for today"*

Copy both of the above charts on a sheet of A4 paper (or larger) so there is plenty of space between the lines. This will give the pendulum room to swing.

One interesting thing I have noticed over the years while playing slot machines is that just prior to a major luck run the machines "go dead". That is I cannot make any of the machines pay me. All of a sudden, usually within 10-15 minutes a large number of the machines give me good wins. This may tie in with the psychokinetic luck chart earlier in this book. You may like to experiment by watching what happens after you have a run of "bad luck".

WARNING
When experimenting with gambling methods do not spend more than you can afford to lose. Play carefully and sensibly. These mental methods may work brilliantly for you.....or....... they may not! I cannot be held responsible for any losses caused by wild overly enthusiastic play!!

12

THE CELESTIAL LUCK PROGRAM

AN ALTERNATIVE PROGRAMME FOR ATTRACTING LUCK

THE MOST POWERFUL MENTAL TOOL IN THE
UNIVERSE.....THE ABILITY TO KNOW WHEN
AND WHERE GOOD LUCK WILL STRIKE!!!

Learn how to program your mind
to attract LUCK...lots of it!!!!

There is nothing more satisfying than being in the right place at
the right time....to receive a totally unexpected windfall.

The program below will show you exactly how to achieve
this!!!

Firstly, before I share this new knowledge with you, let me recap on my original Fiscal PK Luck System, which I discovered in 1993.

After years of experimenting I concluded that luck is "an individuals personal psychokinetic resonance with their environment". As is well known, psychokinesis is the mind/machine interaction effect.

No other possible definition of luck can explain why some individuals are very lucky...while others are definitely not!

I found during experimentation that luck appears to run in cycles on a daily basis.

That is, it peaked at certain brief times during any 24 hour period. This peak may have lasted several hours....or only several minutes.

I also found that under certain circumstances the timing of this peak could be predicted a day or so in advance.

This was quite extraordinary new knowledge and I was able to use it to win a number of jackpots on the slot machines.

I developed this as a program and released it to a restricted number of gamblers worldwide.

The reported results were in some cases almost beyond belief.

It appears that most individuals experience this "high PK" (luck) window at least once a day. It also seems to wax and wane in strength over a larger cyclic period......... possibly 4-6 weeks, depending on the individual and there may even be a longer cycle.

I discovered that by supplying precise instructions to the subconscious mind (via a nightly cassette tape message) a person could raise their natural PK level to a point where they suddenly generated "bursts" of good luck.

I suggested that the easiest way for an individual to discover the timing of their daily luck periods was by randomly playing slot machines at various times during their waking hours. If they noticed a luck window peak, say, between 2pm and 3pm on a specific day, then it was likely that the same "PK window of opportunity" would appear 1-2 hours earlier the next day. That is, they could expect a similar run of high PK activity possibly starting from midday the next day.

Some of the original purchasers of the original *Fiscal PK Luck System* have confirmed that their luck window regresses in time each day. Others weren't able to confirm this.

I used poker (slot) machines initially as they contained the necessary electronic random-number generator software. This is somewhat equivalent to an electronic version of a heads/tails coin flipping device.

The PEAR Lab at Princeton University proved that a focused human mind can affect the otherwise random outcome of a random-number mechanism.

I took their findings and applied it to the gambling environment.

But....the original Fiscal PK method relied upon the user artificially generating sufficiently strong psychokinetic bursts to affect their own personal resonance with their environment...i.e....their luck.

The brand new method, which I'll explain shortly, enables your mind to *let you know* when you can gamble to win, without the necessity of applying excessive artificial PK influence.

BRAND NEW DISCOVERY

Since I developed the original system some years ago, I have made a number of quite startling discoveries.

One of the more interesting ones is that there definitely appears to be an overriding longer-term cycle, possibly in the 4-6 week range.

And this may well turn out to be a 5th biorhythm.

When this longer cycle is near its strongest point I notice that I start to win "clusters" of jackpots on the slot machines. It does not matter whether they are the electronic or mechanical types...both are absolutely controlled by a central computer chip.

As I write this I have recorded in my "jackpot logbook" that I have won 5 small jackpots in the last 4 days. Nothing big....most were round the $100 mark. But....very satisfying, because once again I was aware that this "higher PK luck surge" was due and was able to take advantage of it.

I also had the "urge" to buy a scratchit ticket this morning. Something told me to select a cheap $1 scratchit, instead of my usual $5 one. I scratched off a $50 prize! Nothing big....but once again...very satisfying.

THE HISTORY

Now what has happened over the past 4 years is this:

I had discovered the *Fiscal PK Luck method* and had fiddled with it for some time....making minor improvements and tabulating results with the help of customer feedback. It was the first of its kind in the world, so I had nothing to compare it with.

But I felt I had gone as far as I could go. It needed a new approach... one that didn't involve extended periods of slot machine playing to establish luck cycles.

I needed something simpler and easier to use. Some sort of "automatic alert" program in my mind that would direct me *exactly* when to take a punt....a subconscious instruction that would indicate exactly what I should do.

I knew this was possible, but I just couldn't figure exactly how it could be achieved.

I dwelt on this for months... and...very slowly.......a possible solution emerged. In fact the more I thought about it.....the more convinced I became that the answer lay in a staggering bit of information uncovered by the USA Military Remote Viewers.

In the short time I had been involved with the military Remote Viewing training program I had come to the realisation that the mind has access to all knowledge....past, present and future......and it is fully capable of tapping into the source of this "all-knowing".

This is the very basis of Remote Viewing. And it works beautifully.

The mind will tap into this knowledge *if you specifically instruct it to*, but unfortunately, the answers arrive in your subconscious mind...and are never permitted to seep through into the conscious mind. Occasionally of course, this does happen...and an individual has a vivid dream (or something similar) directing them to take a ticket in a specific lotto, or whatever. There are plenty of documented cases in Australia where this has happened.

I felt that the answer to this dilemma was to set up a mental training program to firstly instruct the mind to tap into future luck knowledge... and secondly....to transfer it to the conscious mind in a manner that was clear and precise.

I was also fully aware that the language of the subconscious is that of pictures and emotions....not of words and languages.

NEW DEVELOPMENT

With this in mind I set about developing a mind-training program that would tap into a persons future luck knowledge, then transfer it by strong impressions or emotions into the conscious mind.

I felt that if a punter could receive sudden strong impressions or emotions impelling him or her to take a certain course of action, then he or she would enjoy financial windfalls on a regular basis, without having to plot luck cycles.

It took me over 12 months of experimentation with different alpha/theta formats before I hit on the exact wording of the training instructions to my subconscious mind.

And did it finally work?

It was absolutely brilliant!!!

Earlier on it was producing only mediocre results until I developed this strong urge to change a few words in my experimental mind training cassette.

I changed them....and the immediate results were quite startling.

The improvement in my own "luck recognition" urges were "out of sight".

What I had done was to develop a simple cassette tape program which I turned on just as I was about to fall asleep at night. This played for around 30 minutes and the dynamic message impinged slowly on my subconscious mind...and gave it precise training instructions.

The upshot was that during my waking periods I would develop a sudden "urge" to buy a lotto ticket, play a specific slot machine, buy a certain scratchit, or back a certain racehorse...and to my stunned amazement......I almost always won!!

Due to the tape program, my subconscious had tapped into this "future knowledge" and successfully transferred it to my conscious mind...so that I was consciously aware of it.

That is...I had consciously become aware of imminent potential windfalls.

This, tied in with my existing knowledge of luck cycles, has turned out to be a very powerful tool.

So powerful in fact, that it is sometimes a bit scary.

After all, the average person is not always mentally prepared for a phenomenal run of luck.

In fact, when an ordinary individual has a superb run of luck...they automatically prepare themselves for "when it will stop running".

Correct?

But with this method that you're about to learn, the runs of luck just keep going...and going....and going.

And you automatically accept that this will keep happening!

USING THE PROGRAM

After using this nightly program for a couple of weeks you will find an automatic acceptance of your sudden change of fortune. You will start to "expect" lucky events...and they will continue to happen.

And there is so little effort required on your part to make all this happen. In fact there is no effort at all.....because you will be *sleeping* on it!

While you are sleeping your mind will be training to work for you...not against you, as it is currently doing.

WHAT TO DO

All you need to do is to play your cassette just before you go to sleep at night. The repetitive message on it will do all the work for you. (I'll tell you how to make this in a moment).

Your subconscious will hear the instructions crystal clearly...and fully understand them.

This will work while you are asleep...or in the very drowsy state just before sleep and just after waking. Basically the program will impinge on your subconscious only when your conscious critical mind is disabled.....as in sleep, alpha, theta, delta, or hypnosis.

You do not need to have your cassette volume turned up high. In fact it can be turned down so low that you can barely hear it. You can place your cassette player (or a set of headphones) under your pillow so that your partner is not disturbed. The message will be heard clearly through your pillow. The idea is to turn it down so that you cannot quite consciously hear the words being spoken........ but your subconscious will hear each word perfectly clearly.

I turn mine down so low that I am sometimes uncertain that it is switched on. It is a well documented fact that your subconscious mind can hear a low-level sound that is too soft for your conscious mind to hear. This is how subliminal tapes work. The actual message in that case is slightly below the level of the background music....but the subconscious mind of the listener still hears it.

This is similar to the situation where you enter a room of noisy people. All the conversations in the room create a simultaneous babble. But suddenly you hear your name mentioned across the room....and you focus intently on the sound source. In fact your focus is so concentrated that all other sounds fade out. Your subconscious mind is capable of locking in to a low level sound source in this manner.

THE CASSETTE TAPE

I have printed out below the exact words used in the tape message. This simple short message is repeated over and over.

All you need to do is to place a blank cassette tape in *any* recorder, even a dictaphone. Repeat the message below about 30 times, leaving a 20-30 second space between each message.

So you will end up with the same message repeated 20-30 times.

If you are able to record this on your computer via your sound card you will probably only need to record the message once....then let the "continual replay" function repeat the message over and over so that you can record it on to a cassette tape. If you do it this way add a small amount of reverberation/echo for reasons mentioned earlier in this book.

Some users will find that this program works almost immediately. Others may find that it takes several weeks to "sink in". It is just that each and every mind has its own bank of built-in programs already running.... and every one is different.

This new program will have to over-ride some of the existing belief systems.

I'd suggest you play this cassette every night for a week...then give it 2-3 days rest.

Then repeat the whole process for as long as it takes. You can do yourself no harm by becoming more attuned to your environment. And the health suggestions on the tape will be beneficial to everyone who uses it.

The 2-3 days rest break between your weekly playing sessions will give your subconscious time to assimilate and install the program.

However if you notice any unwanted side-effects then either stop using the programme or use it cautiously.

AWARENESS

The first thing you will probably notice is an improvement in health and well-being...and an ever increasing awareness of luck and synchronicity.

It may even appear for a while that nothing much is happening, but rest assured that your subconscious is taking it all in....and acting on it. It has to....it is receiving nightly programming. There is no way your subconscious can ignore it all!

I have spent well over a year developing this program....but I cannot install it in your mind as I could in a computer.

You have to do this.

It is now over to you.

Remember, the subconscious mind is like a computer hard-drive.... you can install virtually any compatible program on it, but until it is fully installed........it will not work.

Over the past 4 years I have proven conclusively that the human mind can....and does..... have a psychokinetic affect on the environment. And that was what my original fiscal PK method was all about.

Your mind affects your environment. Specifically it can affect your general luck environment.

This new program actually works the opposite way round. It tends to "extract" the windfall luck knowledge out of the mental environment .... and makes you consciously aware of your potential windfalls.

Once you have this knowledge, you can use it to your personal advantage.

The simple trick is to transfer this knowledge from your subconscious to your conscious mind....in a manner that you can recognise....and act upon.

And that is what this new method is designed to do.

Good luck...and remember......when you start collecting these substantial financial windfalls please share them with others who are less fortunate.

Your subconscious mind will react to this generosity and create even greater wins for you.

What goes round....come round!

MESSAGE ON THE CASSETTE TAPE

*"From this point on your subconscious mind will search for....
and alert you to....wonderful luck opportunities.*

*It will transfer this knowledge to your conscious mind in a
manner which you will easily understand.*

*You will act on these hunches as they are your instructions for
unlimited wealth creation.*

*You will become increasingly aware of potential luck opportu-
nities in your environment.*

*Each morning you will wake up feeling refreshed and
enthusiastic. Your health and well-being improves daily.*

*Every time you take a drink of liquid this program will reinforce
itself."*

13

EXPECTATION INTENT PSYCHOKINETICS AND MANIFESTATION

EXPECTATION AND INTENT.....
The force that drives the universe

Here is a scenario that explains the importance of consciousness coupled with intent and expectation. I'd suggest you find a quiet place to relax while you read it:

Imagine yourself walking into a pitch black aircraft hanger in the middle of the night. The hanger is huge and you know that it is absolutely empty. You walk for several minutes until you estimate you are in the centre of this vast space. Everything around you is absolutely black. You mentally compare this to the known universe made up of matter. Every single thing in the known universe consists of matter (which springs from "solidified" energy). You stand there for several minutes with this analogy running through your mind. Then.....you light a candle and hold it above your head. You realise that this candle flame represents *consciousness*, the only known condition apart from "matter" in the universe.

The candle flame is throwing a weak light in all directions....it has little impact upon the impenetrable darkness around you. Finally, you detach a high powered focused spotlight from your belt and turn it on. It cuts through the blackness and focuses on the rear wall of the hanger. You realise that this is the equivalent of **focused consciousness** in a mind boggling sea of matter. You swing the spotlight over this wall until it impinges on a doorway in the distance. You have become rather disorientated in this hanger and you are very happy to find this doorway. . It is your *intent* to exit via this door and you *expect* to be able to do so. Eventually due to the intent and expectation of your focused consciousness you find yourself outside the hanger looking at the stars. You realise then that the only thing more important than general consciousness is *focused consciousness coupled with **intent and expectation.*** You sit down on the grass and realise for the first time ever that consciousness is a vastly more significant event than mere matter.........and that focused consciousness in the form of **expectation and intent** is vastly more significant again.

From this simple exercise you have been forced to realise that expectation and intent are mankind's driving force in an otherwise sea of mundane matter.

Expectation and intent drive your natural psychokinetic abilities to create results.

It has been said that nothing can stop a determined human mind. When you look at what the word "determined" really means you realise that it embraces *focused intent* and *expectation*.

This is the reason that success in all its forms comes to people who utilise these great universal concepts in an intelligent and dedicated manner. And this does not require superior intelligence. Intelligence in an individual has nothing to do with him or her using focused intent and expectation to achieve an end result. In fact some of the most intelligent individuals on this planet are totally unsuccessful in life, due to their inability to understand and apply the above concept.

Intent and expectation can be used in a number of ways:

For example, your "intent" before you enter the alpha or theta states will largely determine the experience you have while in these states. That is, if you dwell intently on a specific subject as you enter these states, your subconscious mind will assume that you wish to explore that particular subject in depth and will automatically focus its attention in that specific area.

On the other hand you may have no specific subject to explore when you enter the alpha/theta state but you may elect to <u>instruct your subconscious to "dwell" on a subject</u> <u>that is of importance to you</u>....without initially knowing what it is.

When you are actually in your meditative state you may find yourself thinking automatically about a specific subject and you can assume that your subconscious considers this important....<u>even though consciously you may not previously have attached much significance to it.</u>

Often when you have a serious problem to solve you go to sleep thinking about it....it is playing on your mind. And you are sometimes amazed to find that when you wake up in the morning the correct solution just pops into your head. The reason for this is that you expect to solve this particular problem and because you keep dwelling on it your mind assumes that you *intend* to solve it....so it obliges.

This is rather similar to the situation where a certain musical "tune" keeps running through your head. This is quite often your subconscious giving you a message that you should "pay attention". Perhaps the words of the tune or the message in it are significant to you at this particular point in time. Or perhaps you first heard this tune under rather dramatic or unusual circumstances and your subconscious is suggesting you recall those circumstances and dwell on them. Whatever the reason, there is usually a message for you to decode.

You can also use a dream to materialise your intent and expectation. At one point I was running a simple program to improve my financial position. Just before I went to sleep at night I would repeat to myself (20 times or more) ... *"I will have a dream that solves my current financial woes"*. I ran this program on and off for about 10 days....at the end of which I had a sudden unexpected financial windfall. It was only a few thousand dollars but in those days this meant a lot to me. I have no idea what the dreams were about, but whatever they were....they worked!

PERSONAL THOUGHTS AND INTENT

Individual thoughts do not remain within the boundaries of the individual, a fact which has been proven over and over by the communication mode of telepathy, which most individuals have experienced at least once in their lives. A thought is usually regarded as a personal intimate possession belonging to the individual who created it. Because of the constant subconscious communication going on between all individuals at any given time.....this thought cannot remain private. And if you should be standing in front of another individual, whereby your concentration is focused on them, then your "personal" thought has a far greater chance of impinging on their subconscious. This may cause confusion in their minds as you are verbally saying one thing, your body language is saying another and your subconscious message is conveying something totally different yet again.

This can be proven conclusively by using a mental projection technique that the more advanced mind-power individuals know about.

Next time you are talking to someone you don't particularly care for and who is annoying you, project mentally at them "<u>Danger, Danger, Danger....Look out, Look out, Look out....Run, Run, Run</u>". You have to mentally 'scream" at them as if you were a castaway on a deserted Island and you were trying to attract the attention of a nearby passing ship. You might be quite amazed as the other individual suddenly looks alarmed and you will usually see their eyes quickly search your body for weapons. It will usually stop their conversation in its tracks. You can add to this by mentally screaming "Freeze, Freeze, Freeze". The two concepts together can mentally overload the individuals mind temporarily. I sometimes add "<u>Confusion, Confusion, Confusion</u>".

At this point the other persons' eyes usually develop a dazed look while their brain attempts to make sense of the incoming conflicting information. This is the principal behind "instant" hypnosis.

If at this point you walk 10-15 feet away from the person then when they become "undazed" they will perceive you as suddenly having "jumped" some distance away. Their brain has even more trouble with this and don't be surprised if they suddenly run from the room in panic.

Women can use this principal for self protection, particularly if being accosted on the street.

What this exercise proves is that you are in constant communication with other people on a deep down level and you can accentuate this by evoking a fight or flight response to a perceived danger.

Following from this it is obvious that it is difficult to hide from another person your true intent. Other people will sense your intent to a greater or lesser degree. The point here is that it is really very difficult to retain a "mental secret". Your thoughts do not circularise only within your physical body and stop at your skin.....they emanate outwards.

When you speak verbally your personal thoughts are projected outward to anyone within earshot......the same applies to your unspoken thoughts. So if you are talking to someone who does not particularly impress you it is important to think rather generous thoughts about them, otherwise they are likely to pick up on your true feelings.

You will have had several experiences with this subconscious communication when you are desperately searching for a car park on a busy street. Suddenly, for no reason, a car pulls out just in front of you and you grab that car space. In fact you can pre-program for this by focussing on a car park as you drive into town. I do this constantly.

What happens is this: Out of all the dozens of drivers who own cars parked in the area you wish to park in, one will receive your "mental desire" for a park and will decide on the spur of the moment that they have had enough of shopping. Their subconscious mind can judge exactly when you will arrive and they subconsciously time their actions so that their car pulls out of the parking space *just as you drive up.* In fact there may be several motorists ahead of you who could leap into this space but they don't! This whole process happens because of your dedicated intent and expectation.

The core of individuality is the individual's expectations and if a person wants to change their fate mere desire is not enough....it must be coupled with the absolute belief that the desired event will happen. This is why programming for your desires in the alpha/theta state is so important. The mental "picturing" of the required outcome in these deep meditative states will provide the subconscious belief system necessary and trigger the universal mechanisms required for the event to materialise.

An expectation of danger will create danger while an expectation of success will create success.

<u>Expectation is the force that triggers psychic realities into physical construction.</u>

Expectations are formed by the emotions so you must manipulate your basic emotions to set up a "success" mindstate. This is easiest done in the meditative states.

The subconscious represents a tremendous raw power that triggers forth constructions in accordance with the expectations that you have formed. Many of your expectations are formed in childhood from parent and peer pressure and they might be quite restrictive ones. All you have to do to overcome this is to look at successful people that you know and consider what *their* expectations are. How are they different from yours? Have they got superior intelligence to you? If you do deep analysis you will probably find that they are no different from you, but through life have developed higher expectations than you have currently got. They build on their small success (of which you will have had plenty also) and gone on from there.

It would be a great personal exercise if you sat down in some quiet place and wrote down exactly what your current expectations are....in the field of business, personal and emotional. When you have completed this list look hard at it......*are your expectations high enough*? Or are you aiming too low.

Probably the most important thing to you is your personal life.....you personal success and happiness. Ask yourself.... *"What do I really expect from life? What are my real aims and desires? Have I achieved the aims and desires I planned 5 years ago? If so, am I just cruising with no replacement aims planned?"*

Once you have identified where you're at you might like to consider "raising your game" a little, by setting aims and desires that are currently slightly out of your reach. If you write down clearly what you want then work on your mind to produce the necessary *expectation* level, you will find that these objectives will materialise in due course, in the same manner that your previous batch of objectives materialised. The point here is that if you don't keep stressing your comfort level slightly, you will be unlikely to make further progress.

Once you set your new objectives you will have to fully *intend* to pursue them.....and you will have to modify your mind-state to *expect* them.

There is a vast difference in "wishing" for something.........and planning for it via intent and expectation.

<u>Your subconscious psychic powers will only materialise constructions that you believe you are currently capable of.</u>

If you limit your expectations you limit your results and no amount of mere "desire" will overcome this basic belief limitation.

It has been said that sometimes an individuals' expectations are too high for their abilities but it is an observable fact that *expectations form abilities.* If your expectations are higher then your abilities will flourish.

TECHNIQUE FOR RAISING EXPECTATIONS

Lie back and relax. Close your eyes. Go into alpha or theta if you can. Now imagine yourself as a portion of the total universe. Imagine this universe to be alive with throbbing, pulsing energy. You can think of this universe as having the form of a body. See the suns and planets as your cells...realise that they are part of you...and you, them. See incredible energy everywhere, just waiting for you to unleash it. Now see this energy exploding into your consciousness. It is incredibly bright. Feel the throbbing of this energy as it enters your consciousness and body. Direct this energy to any point in your body that needs it. If instead there is an event that you wish to materialise then use that burst of energy to imagine its occurrence as clearly as you can. See the event taking place....filled with this magic energy. Maintain this image for as long as you can without strain....then let go and relax. Know for certain that this energy filled event will take place.

PSYCHIC RECHARGE

At dawn or dusk go for a walk among some trees. Stop and sense the colours and smells. Close your eyes and repeat this exercise. Breathe in the vitality and fragrance of the surroundings. Take deep breaths and imagine yourself breathing in goodness and vitality. Touch some of the leaves with eyes open then closed. Immerse yourself in the environment. Amble along and repeat the above exercises a few times. Forget all personal, emotion or business considerations....simply be at one with your environment. Feel the psychic relaxation sweep over you. When you have had enough, go home.

You might be amazed at the effect this simple exercise has on you for the rest of the day.

Prior to doing the above you can also mention your current desires and expectations to your subconscious.....then the act of immersing yourself in the environment will cause your inherent psychic abilities to flourish, with sometimes quite stunning outcomes. Do not dwell on these expectations while you are actually involved in the exercise.....program them in before the exercise.

Another simpler exercise is to merely lie on a grassy patch among bushes, maybe in your garden. In this case close your eyes and "sense" you environment. Become aware of smells and sounds.

This is the type of activity that free-form remote viewing trainees undergo.

Most importantly, if you are looking for inspiration takes frequent breaks away from your everyday environment. Visit some place that is the opposite of your normal situation.

Expect to be psychically recharged....and you will be!!

THE IMAGINATION, BACKED BY INTENT AND GREAT EXPECTATIONS, CAN MATERIALISE ALMOST ANY REALITY WITHIN THE RANGE OF POSSIBILITIES.

EXPECTATION, PSYCHOKINETICS AND MANIFESTATION

EXPECTATION AND MANIFESTATION

Expectation (particularly the subconscious type) is absolutely vital for the construction of physical objects and events from subconscious inner data flows. All visible objects are constructed of atoms which are a conglomeration of sub-atomic particles which in turn are basically solidified energy. According to Einstein matter and energy are interchangeable based on his formula $E=MC$ squared.

It is also vital when this internal data is sifted and categorized, within the framework of the individual's personal belief system. This individual belief system has developed and polarized over the years based upon the successes the individual has experienced in his or her life. It is the expectation, based on this belief system, that enables the individual to manifest situations, events and material objects.

For example, if a person *absolutely knows* that they are naturally unlucky then they will never be able to successfully manifest "luck" events without a serious change of mental programming.

Expectation characterises the belief system of the individual and portrays the innermost aspects of his or her personality. It represents the psychic building blocks from which the physical constructions will be successfully constructed.

Expectations are basically formed from your emotions. If you can develop "emotional excitement" about potential physical constructions (such as events) then you will find it much easier to manifest that which you desire.

Individuals who are temporarily "emotionally burnt out" will simply not be able to manifest in a satisfactory manner. In fact the reverse might happen. That is, events that you *don't want* may materialize.

It is therefore vital that you keep in touch with your emotions and if you should feel yourself becoming emotionally "bogged down" then it is time to take a break from your everyday activities and give yourself time to recover. It appears that a person's expectations are the result of their emotional heritage….and their own ability to understand and manipulate that heritage.

If you have trouble getting in touch with your emotions then think back to events that really profoundly affected you. Think of happy events from your childhood. Dwell on them and try and recapture the emotion at that time.

I find that listening to certain kinds of music gets me slightly emotional.

Each and every individual is constantly receiving a stream of inner data and the individual will accept data only that is in line with their personal expectations.

If a person wants to change their fate then mere desire is not enough… it is expectation that will cause the manifestation of desires into reality. It is actually expectation that triggers inner data into physical construction.

An expectation of success will encourage success, whereas an expectation of danger will attract dangerous circumstances to the individual.

Expectation coupled with deep emotion is the force that triggers psychic realities into physical realities.

Your expectations have a dramatic effect on your life. If, for example you believe that wealthy people are inherently "bad" and have obtained their wealth by fraudulent means, then in the event that you should suddenly acquire a large windfall (maybe from a lotto win) you will probably find that you lose most of it fairly rapidly, due to your expectation and belief system. This has happened many times in Australia to people who have suddenly won, then flitted away several million dollars......and in a short period of time gone broke.

MATTER AND ANTIMATTER

All the physical objects that you see around you are constructed of energy. The atoms and subatomic particles that are part of the furniture that you have in your lounge are originally formed from energy quantums. The fact that your furniture appears to be "solid" is an illusion created by your outer senses. The matter constructing your furniture is actually switching on and off at too fast a rate for your senses to perceive. And as you know the space between the individual atoms of your furniture is vast.... comparable with the spaces between the planets in our solar system. In actual fact there is almost no solidity in your furniture.....the construction is mainly empty space....with the illusion of solidity.

Material in our field is composed of constant energy pulsations...half the time it is switched "on".....and half the time switched "off". Each new pulsation is an energy burst which manifests itself as matter. The basic underlying energy is always present but switches itself from "negative" to "positive" in the same manner that alternating current switches from negative to positive.

The is considerable proof these days that all material is energy which manifests in our physical world into patterns which have been prepared for it either by individual consciousness or by mass universal consciousness.

Our own outer senses react too slowly to perceive the on/off energy pulsations as the quantums of energy that create material rhythmically disappear completely and are replaced by new quantum particles.

Basically matter is created and manipulated by psychic means, something that our scientists are now starting to suspect. This process operates in the subconscious realm at a level that we are not consciously aware of. The conscious mind usually has no knowledge of this process and it is almost impossible for the conscious mind to interfere with it.

It is considered that conscious awareness of subconscious manipulation of matter may arise in a manner that causes the subconscious to follow the desires of the conscious mind if emotional expectation and desire are present. In this scenario the conscious desires must be parallel and resonant with subconscious expectations, along with sufficient emotional yearning. For the above to happen then the communication between the conscious and subconscious must be of a high order. This can obviously happen during deep alpha/theta meditation states.

By itself a conscious desire to achieve a specific goal may conflict with the desires and expectations of the subconscious, in which case it is unlikely that the goal will be achieved. Where the emotional need is strong and there is no conflict then the materialization of the desire is more likely, over a period of time.

The combination of thought, expectation, emotion and desire creates form which is created by subconscious manipulation of the basic energy units of the universe.

It is for this reason that if you focus strongly on some desired event in your future it is likely to happen, given that you add the necessary emotional yearning and expectation.

Matter as we know it is merely energy units converted into solid perceptible items that we can either perceive via our physical senses or measure on scientific instruments.

Once again this matter is not permanent as we understand the meaning of "permanent", but switches itself on and off at a vibrational rate so rapid that we cannot perceive the "off" states. If you look around you every single item that you see is switching itself on and off. It spends as much time in the anti-matter state as it does in the positive matter state that you perceive. Matter is not permanent.....it only appears to be so.

If you are able to enter an out-of-body state you will notice that everything you see in this state appears to have a glowing vibrational quality. That is, you are aware of the molecular vibrational qualities of the object matter you are observing. It is almost as if you are aware of the individual atoms from which the object is constructed. It is a very strange eerie feeling and can leave quite an awesome impression.

As matter is constantly being created then what we perceive as physical growth of a living structure is not growth at all, but a constantly updating reconstruction of the structure to a newer slightly updated pattern or form. Your entire human body is constantly being updated within your body's template which as time goes by tends to disintegrate so that you appear to age.

My understanding of the Seth material (The SETH books explain a lot of these mind techniques) is that as this template loses its initial psychic impetus then the template loses its "initial sharp focus" and starts to "fray around the edges". The body then deteriorates and loses its initial sharply defined form. As death nears in old age the template disintegrates significantly and noticeably.

The initial psychic energy behind the original pattern weakens which causes the physical pattern to blur. Each recreation of the pattern becomes less perfect until the sharpness of the original pattern is completely lost. It can be compared to placing a good quality photo on a photocopier and making a sharp copy. This copy is then placed on the photocopier and a copy made "of the copy". If you do this 20-30 times all definition is lost and the picture in the end might only just be recognizable.

To sum up, matter is the result of molecular composition…..the molecules being converted from pure energy by psychic pressure. This is triggered at a subconscious level by expectation, emotion and desire.

The creation and manipulation of matter might be considered as a <u>psychokinetic event</u>.

If you look around your lounge room and view the separate items of furniture, you will observe that the space between the items appears to be empty air. In fact the empty spaces are full of the same molecules as those constructing the furniture. It is simply that you have not subconsciously created a construction in this empty space.

There are many cases whereby you create or dissolve a construction without conscious knowledge. Occasionally you become aware of this psychokinetic feeling and it can be emotionally uncomfortable. These PK events are happening to you constantly but unless you pay specific attention to them then they will not impinge upon your consciousness.

Lately I have become increasingly aware of these sometimes quite startling events.

Recently I tried to locate a portable compass which I knew for certain was in an airline carry-bag which I had beside my bed. I tipped the contents of this bag out on the bed and was highly puzzled that the compass was not there. I had placed it in the bag the night before. In the finish I gave up looking. The next morning when I woke up I remembered my search for the compass so I got out of bed and tipped the contents of the bag out again. Sure enough….the compass was there, exactly where it should have been. There were very few items in the bag and the compass was a fairly large shiny metal encased object so there was no way I could have missed it.

This incident was particularly startling as I had only that day read a chapter in a book explaining how this happened. I can only assume that my subconscious wanted to reinforce this vital piece of knowledge and was "kind" enough to supply a real-life example!

I found all this extremely puzzling especially when I thought back to when I was a child and I was always finding money (in the form of coins) on the footpath. Dozens of people had walked by but I was apparently the only one who found coins. My parents and Aunties thought this very strange and so did I.

It wasn't until I became absorbed in mind-power research in later life that I realized these events always occurred when I had a deep emotional necessity and burning desire.

I have slowly come to understand that our belief system causes us psychic imprisonment.

An absolute blind faith in the reality we perceive around us can cause this.

In fact our individual belief systems came originally from our parents and peer groups…..who got their belief system from their parents and peer groups…and so on.

What is very obvious to me is that in some cases an individual's belief system can be

traced back 4-5 generations. That is…..80-100 years!! The family chain has never opened its collective mind to new knowledge. You can see plenty of examples of this around you. Makes you stop and think, doesn't it?

From all of the above you can get an idea of how psychokinetic manipulation can rearrange events in your life to your financial and emotional advantage. You can now also understand why individuals with a burning dedicated obsession sometimes achieve miraculous results….. sometimes even way above their own expectations.

At some point in their lives every individual has visited a locality and noticed a feeling of comfort, familiarity or sudden peacefulness. Or maybe while driving through an area in a car a particular spot seems to stand out….for no obvious reason.

Your own emotional intensities will trigger one of these points into magnifying your thoughts….whether good or bad. Your emotional desire will suddenly resonate in the same manner a bell rings and resonates when struck.

These coordination points cause mental resonance which enables manifestation to occur.

Greater energy will therefore be added to the original thought or emotion, thereby facilitating its projection into physical reality.

……… *"Mental images, accompanied by strong emotion are the blueprint for the manifestation of a physical object, condition or event."*……….

The intensity (or emotional yearning) determines how effectively and quickly the desired event will materialise. A person who is in a critical situation and has developed an urgent burning emotional necessity to relieve themselves of that situation, will often find that something happens quickly and "unexpectedly" that soles the problem.

The two factors that trigger this are the mental picture in their imagination of what they want the result to be and the actual emotional component fed into the desire.

The human race is capable of mentally picturing and of deep emotion….something the animal kingdom is not usually capable of.

It seems to me that the emotional component of a human mind is the most profound facility that any living creature can possess.

The other vitally important facility is "intent". The Unites States Military remote viewers discovered that *Intent* was vastly more profound than they ever realized. They eventually discovered that by using Intent they could access the matrix of timeless universal knowledge and retrieve information from the past, present or future with relative ease.

However the secret to achieving this was the very definite and precise use of *Intent*.

The process simply would not work without intent.

Their discovery of just how important Intent was happened quite accidentally.

They had been experimenting with remote viewing at the Stanford

Research Institute for some years and had evolved into giving the remote viewer (Ingo Swann) latitude and longitude coordinates of a geographical location to see if he could correctly identify what was at that point. One day, quite by mistake, the "tasker" jumbled the coordinates as he wrote them down so Swann was presented with reference coordinates that were basically nonsense. To everyone's stunned amazement Ingo "captured" the correct target. This experiment was repeated several times with the tasker allotting a random set of 6 numbers for each target, but *clearly fixing in his mind that the number set belonged to a specific target.* After some further months of experimentation it became clear that the only thing that mattered was the INTENT of the tasker when he prepared the targets.

Ingo was able to latch on to the intent of the tasker and access the correct coordinate position in the universal matrix to retrieve information about the specific target. This turned the whole remote viewing research program on its ear....no longer did they need outbounder target viewers...all they needed to do was allot a set of random numbers to a target and it could be accessed reliably. Most of the internet sites that contain remote viewing practice targets contain a set of numbers only. Sometimes you can click on an addition page to get a clue, but after you reach a certain level in remote viewing you don't need to do this.

When somebody rings me and asks if I will do a remote view I stop their conversation immediately and ask them to write down on a piece of paper an exact description of the target....then allot a group of 6 numbers to it. I then ask them to read out the numbers to me. I had an occasion a while back where a client did this and I got an immediate impression of a gold ring. I rang this client and asked if this target was in fact a gold ring. The client said that it was. When I did the remote view I gained the impression that the ring was located behind the leg of what looked like a bedroom table. I phoned this info to the client and within 60 seconds he had located the ring....it had fallen off the bedside table during the night and jammed itself behind one of the legs. He was of course totally delighted.

I was able to do this remote view only because of the mind-state of Intent.

Our existence within this particular physical universe involves immersing ourselves within the most intense self-hypnotic trance state (both individually and collectively) whereby our conscious awareness is totally and utterly focused in a specific direction which effectively negates any possible awareness of other realities.

It becomes obvious from all of the above that such apparent aberrations as psychokinetic effects actually have a place in the overall scheme of things, even though our current physical laws do not appear to allow for them. Based on the above there appears to be no reason why a physical object could not suddenly be materialized in the space between armchairs in your lounge room. All the basic components for this already exist in that current blank space. The atoms and molecules are already in place. The universal energy is already flowing through it. All that is then required is the focused pressure effect of consciousness to enable the basic energy units to manifest themselves as the desired object.

We have seen macro PK effects produced that absolutely prove the existence of consciousness influence over matter......in the form of the PK spoon bending parties initiated by engineer Jack Houck in the U.S.A. The "parties" have spread throughout the world and require the presence of a group of people who through emotional manipulation develop a "mind-lock" whereby their minds tend to lock together to enable the necessary group consciousness state which will effect the molecular structure of metal in such a manner that it appears to soften. At this point the metal can be bent easily and sometimes even bends by itself.

This group consciousness effect is also evoked for fire-walking sessions whereby participants can walk over burning coals without burning their feet.

The above two PK examples prove conclusively that the effects of consciousness can override some laws of physics, which we have always assumed to be absolute.

With the advent of quantum physics and the Superstring theory scientist now realize that all is not what it seems. Indeed, some of the scientific community have realized that there are so many flaws in our scientific assumptions that we might have to go back to ground-zero and start from the beginning again.

14

HOW TO BE
A WINNER
IN LIFE

What does it take to be a winner?
Most successful people do not know how they achieved their success.

Success for them just arrived and was a very pleasant and satisfying experience.

If you stand and talk to a successful person for any length of time you will notice that their attitude and belief system is somewhat different to that which you are used to.

They seem to have a different angle or slant on things which you usually find quite refreshing.

If you could get close enough to these successful people to analyse their belief system you will find that they do none of the following..........

THE 10 SECRETS OF FAILURE -

1   Remain positive all day long ....for no reason. This is emotionally unnatural!

2   Discuss your life's objectives with negative family and friends.

3   Accept gratuitous advice from unsuccessful people.

4   Follow-the-herd....because that is what everyone else is doing.

5   Watch TV "soap" regularly...this is guaranteed to destroy all creativity.

6   Heavily mortgage into debt and absolutely guarantee high stress for years to come.

7   Remain in a business/personal situation where you are perpetually unhappy and stressed.

8   Tell yourself continually that you are naturally unlucky.

9   Become petty-minded and envious when someone you know has a major windfall.

10 Make lifestyle decisions based on spur-of-the-moment emotional feelings.

It is not what winners do that makes them so successful, it is what they don't do!

They totally avoid the above 10 secrets of failure, either consciously or subconsciously.

Now let's analyse each of the above 10 items and see how winners and non-winners handle each of these situations.

ITEM -1   REMAIN POSITIVE ALL DAY LONG.

Over the years you have been encouraged to think positively..... that is to remain positive all day long...no matter what. This is unnatural because your emotions go through cycles. Sometimes you feel cheerful and happy while at other times you feel slightly depressed. This is the way your emotional system is supposed to work. When you try to alter it by consciously remaining positive you mess up your natural emotional rhythms. This can have serious backlash effects. The correct way to handle this is to make lifestyle and business decisions while you are feeling positive and cheerful and avoid making these decisions during your negative emotional periods. Accept the fact that you will go through negative periods and mentally allow for them. If you try to act positively when you are feeling "down" you will feel unnatural because you are not in harmony with the universe.

ITEM - 2 DISCUSS YOUR PLANS WITH NEGATIVE FAMILY OR FRIENDS.

It is a sad fact that many of those people close to you will be living very mediocre lives and it will get "right up their nostrils" if you suddenly become an achiever. In Australia it is called the "Tall Poppy" syndrome. Small minded individuals simply cannot stand the thought of someone they know achieving success....because it will tend to show them up for what they are....non-winners.

It is vitally important that you keep your plans to yourself otherwise these small minded envious individuals will try to place every obstacle possible in your path. They do this because they haven't got the mental drive and dedication to aim for the goals that you are aiming at. After you've succeeded visit them in your new Mercedes....that will really give them something to think about!

ITEM - 3 GRATUITOUS ADVICE FROM NON-WINNERS.

If you tell others what your dreams are, you will be inundated with advice...usually negative. It is a different story if you ask a specific person for specific advice. But when all the losers around you offer advice.... whether you want it or not.....then you can safely ignore it. Just say to them...."What qualifies you to give advice? Are you an expert in this field?"......If they persist just laugh at them and walk away. You will eventually cut these people out of your life....so don't worry if you offend them right up front!

ITEM - 4 FOLLOW THE HERD.....

...after all...the lead animal knows where it's going, doesn't it?

It is a sad fact that people like to be led!

That is why they go to church...they want leadership.

And people who join cults have totally given up on any original thought and responsibility....they want to go through the rest of their life in a hypnotic daze.

Since your early days at school you were in a position where you were "led". At school you had your teachers....out of school you had your parents.

Then when you got your first job your boss took over the leadership.

Think about it....you have always been led! But....once you decide on an original and provocative course of action....you are on your own. You have cut all leadership from your life. You are standing alone with your own dream. You have left the herd. A lot of people find this uncomfortable and seek to rejoin the herd. But after a while you become used to the strangeness of total self-responsibility and you revel in the feeling and success.

ITEM - 5 IMMERSE YOURSELF IN NON-REAL MEDIA SOAP PROGRAMS.

If you are one of those people who feel compelled to sit down in the middle of the day and watch mind-numbing soap programs...then you are a lost soul. Success is not for you. Non-winners give their minds over to this type of garbage input....winners will have nothing to do with it because it is non-creative and intelligence insulting. If you are going to become a winner you must select mental input that is creative and inspirational. You must seek out new knowledge that embraces your dreams. If you have a goal you are working toward seek out mental input that embraces this goal. Do not let yourself become distracted by the mind-numbing garbage that accounts for 90% of free-to-air TV. After all.....this is your life. It is with you now....it is not a practice run. You either live it by shooting for the stars...or you give it all away and go to your deathbed regretting all the lost opportunities.

ITEM - 6 OVER-MORTGAGE YOURSELF FOR GUARANTEED STRESS.

The one thing that totally destroys creative thinking and shooting-for-the-stars dreams...is stress. And the majority of stress in a younger adult is money related. That is....they are encouraged by society to keep up with the Joneses. So they go heavily into debt for a house and a car...then spend the next 5-10 years stressed out trying to keep up with the payments. A winner does not get into this over-mortgage trap. The winner would initially purchase a cheaper home or a house with a granny flat (which would be rented to partially offset the mortgage). The winner would save and pay cash for a quality second-hand car.....and pay no attention to what his/her friends and associates are driving! The winner would work his/her finances out logically so they could achieve a roof over their heads and comfortable transport without stress.

Because......when you are stressed about money you cannot think clearly....it eats away at you. It is a tragic fact that in Australia today 95% of the population are non-winners. They simply follow the herd.

ITEM - 7 UNHAPPY BUSINESS/PERSONAL SITUATION.

Every free sane individual, at any point in time, is either doing that which makes them happy...<u>or the least unhappy</u>.

And the majority of individuals spend a lot of their time unhappy. This can be caused by financial stress or worse still...emotional stress. If they are in a long term relationship that has fizzled they are "living a lie". It may be that they are stuck until the kids grow up but the fact is...they are unhappy.

If you are prepared to tolerate this state then it is going to be far more difficult to become a winner. You have extra hurdles to overcome before you can succeed. Or to put it another way you are "behind the eight-ball". If you take a long hard look at what is making you unhappy then you will probably be able to work out ways to remove at least some of the unhappiness. But as 95% of the population suffer from "emotional inertia" then you might be accused of "rocking the boat" if you attempt to better your lot in life. You might have to make some hard decisions if you are in this situation.

ITEM - 8 CONSIDERING YOURSELF NATURALLY UNLUCKY.

Unlucky people are exactly that....unlucky! They "know" they're un-lucky....so they are.

It's as simple as that. Luck is your personal psychokinetic resonance with your environment. It is controlled entirely by your subconscious belief system. If you deep-down believe you are unlucky then you will be. Actually this is one of the hardest belief systems to break. The easiest way is to write down on paper all the successes you have had in life....and keep referring back to them so that your subconscious accepts that you want to change your belief system. Tell yourself that you have had these particular successes in life and you want more. Then focus on the good things that happen to you each day.....instead of the bad things which are usually easier to focus on. After a while this will become a habit and you will develop a deep-down feeling that you are becoming a winner.

ITEM - 9 ENVY AND PETTY-MINDEDNESS.

I always have a laugh when someone who has never had any money before appears on TV as the latest lotto winner and states that "this will not change my life...I am going to keep working at my job". What happens is this: The lotto winner gets into work the next day and all his/her workmates offer congratulatory remarks. But within a day or so the snide remarks start....such as..."here comes moneybags". Do you get the picture? The envy and jealousy from the small-minds starts to surface. Guess what? Within a week the winner usually gives up the job in disgust.

I had this happen to me when I won the major slots jackpot at Jupiters Casino in Australia. Each time I went back to the casino one of the regular woman players (I think she lived there) would make some snide comment such as..."well, you don't have to worry about running out of money do you?".....or....."here's moneybags again".

I ignored her for a while but after one particularly nasty comment I turned to her and said...."Do you realise that people here in the casino refer to you as the GCSW?"

She said..."What's a GCSW?" I calmly replied.....Gold Coast Silly Woman!!

She has never spoken to me since. Funny that? I wonder if I offended her?

You are surrounded by petty small minded people who would take great delight in seeing you fall on your face. Don't give them the opportunity.

ITEM - 10 MAKE EMOTIONAL NON-LOGICAL LIFESTYLE DECISIONS.

It never ceases to amaze me how otherwise intelligent articulate individuals will make a major lifestyle decision on the spur of the moment.... based on an altered emotional state. They may have been pondering this problem for months but instead of sitting down and calmly analysing it out....suddenly leap off their chair after a few beers (or whatever) and announce to all and sundry that they are going to leave the wife and kids and shoot off to Antarctica to count polar bears. Or something equally brainless.

I remember years ago meeting a character in a mobile home park who had sent his wife back to NZ while he spent 3 months in Australia making a "lifetime fortune" out of this fabulous idea he had been introduced to. He told me that within 3 months he would have earned enough money to set him and his wife up for life. And the brilliant beyond-belief idea....AMWAY! He had signed up to become an AMWAY distributor. He had made this brilliant decision after consuming what I took to be a 44 gallon drum of cheap wine one Saturday night. After the 3 months was up he had made virtually nothing and could not afford the airfare back to NZ. Then his wife rang from Christchurch to say that she was "shooting through" with a guy she had met at a party. Maybe they deserved each other.

Do not make any major decision unless you are extremely clear-headed. Bear in mind that this single decision could affect you for the rest of your life.

The big trick is to make sure your belief system is based on reality... then you can generate your dreams from there. But if you are already in dreamland then anything else will be non-achievable fantasy.

CREATING AND MANIPULATING YOUR OWN REALITY.

You must learn to listen to the voice of the inner self and work with it.

You may also simply ask the inner self to make the answers to problems available on a conscious basis.

You create your reality according to your beliefs and expectations, therefore you should examine these carefully. If you do not like some aspect of your world, then examine your own expectations. Your world is formed in faithful replica of your own thoughts... If you think positive suggestions to yourself about a situation you send telepathic ammunition for positive use. You must learn to erase a negative thought or picture by replacing it with its opposite. But do not attempt to think positive thoughts all day long. Let your emotional swings work in the normal manner.

You should tell yourself frequently "I will only react to constructive suggestions." This gives you positive ammunition against your own negative thoughts and those of others.

A negative thought, if not erased, will almost certainly result in a negative condition.

Say to yourself ...... "That is in the past. Now in this new moment, this new present, I am already beginning to change for the better." It does not do to repress negative thoughts, such as fears, angers, or resentment. They should be recognized, faced and replaced. Recognize resentment when it is felt, and then realize that resentment can be dismissed. Initial recognition must be made. Then you must imagine removing the resentment "by its roots" and replacing it with a positive feeling.

You must watch the pictures that you paint with your imagination. Your environment and the conditions of your life at any given time are the direct result of your own inner expectations. If you imagine dire circumstances, ill health or desperate loneliness, these will be "automatically" materialized, for these thoughts themselves bring about the conditions that will give them a reality in physical terms. If you would have good health then you must imagine this as vividly as you fearfully imagine ill health.

You create your own difficulties. This is true for each individual. The inner psychological state is projected outward, gaining physical reality - whatever the psychological state may be - the rules apply to everyone. Knowing this, you should try to realize what your psychological state is and change your conditions for your own benefit. You cannot escape your own attitudes, for they will form the nature of what you see. If changes are to occur, they must be mental and psychic changes. These will be reflected in your environment.

Negative, distrustful, fearful, or degrading attitudes toward anyone work against the self. If an individual sees only evil and desolation in the physical world it is because he is obsessed with evil and desolation and projects them outward, closing his eyes to other aspects of reality.

If you want to know what you think of yourself, then ask yourself what you think of others and you will find the answer.

MENTAL PREPARATION

Before you can even think about joining the winners in life you must ground yourself in absolute reality by removing all non-reality based beliefs which would otherwise cause confusion and chaos as you try to live your dreams.

The material you have read so far is designed to help in this and the next couple of pages carry this a stage further. After you have read and assimilated these reality concepts you will be ready for the final process of preparing to become a winner. But you will have no success at all unless you clearly understand and accept the preparational material that has been presented so far.

If you are in a position where you feel compelled to comply with the wishes of a peer group then you are not mentally free enough to become a winner.

I experienced an example of this in Las Vegas several years ago while I was on a remote viewing course. I had become quite friendly with one of the other advanced students and he had expressed an interest in trying his remote viewing skills on the Roulette tables at one of the local casinos. I suggested that he come back to the place I was staying at (which was the MGM Grand) and try the RV process on a roulette table there. He was deeply interested in doing this but told me that his religion did not permit its members to enter a gambling environment. I looked at him and said...."You're bloody joking!" (Actually I put it a little more expressively than this). Here was an otherwise intelligent individual allowing his life to be run by a group of people who wouldn't know reality if it leapt out of the bushes and bit them on their collective backsides. I really got stuck into this guy and finally asked if he was a man or a mouse. He finally agreed that it was worth the experiment and came into the casino. He not only won a ton of money but he thoroughly enjoyed himself.

A couple of weeks after this he emailed me and said that he had given half of his winnings to his church elders and they hadn't seemed to object at all!

The point is he had stepped out of his personal comfort zone and tried something different....and it was successful and memorable as far as he was concerned.

Here was a really nice guy who had spent half his life being messed up by someone else's dogma finally breaking out and doing his own thing.

For a brief period of time he dumped the manipulation in his life.

When you think about it we are manipulated from the day we started school. We were told what to do and how to do it. We were rewarded for doing things correctly and sometimes punished for getting things wrong. And worse still we were manipulated by anyone older than us...like the school bully.

When we started our first job we were manipulated by the boss. We had to "toe the line"....or else. We felt obliged to seek approval from others but by doing this we allow our emotions, thoughts and feelings to be subtly manipulated.

It is a sad fact that 95% of people take the line of least resistance.... and go with the flow.

Winners do NOT do this.

Winners let others know quite clearly that they will not be manipulated and when others realise this, they tend to give up trying to control you. They place you in the "too hard" basket and focus on the wimps and non-winners around them.

WHAT IS YOUR CURRENT SITUATION IN LIFE?

Have things gone well....or do you feel "stuck"?

Maybe your emotions have been burnt somewhat during the passage of life. And you feel desensitized.

Perhaps things have recently come unstuck for you......and you are back near square one. Maybe some of your previous lifestyle decisions were wrong and you're now paying the price for this faulty decision making.

If this is the case then there is one vitally important thing to realise.

When you were born you did not come with an instruction manual!

And as such the only way you can learn and develop your own belief system is through observation, trial and error. Mainly error!!!!

So if you have made some previously bad lifestyle decisions do not feel too bad about it because everyone else around you has also made faulty decisions in the past.

It is part of the learning process.

Everything that has happened to you up to now has been part of your learning curve.

If you take a piece of A4 paper and draw a straight line across the centre of the paper from left to right then all your "past" is represented by the area below the line. Your future is above the line. The line itself represents the here-and-now...that is....today.

Sit down in some quiet place and think deeply about this.

The decisions you make today will affect the space above the line.... your future.

You might like to make a momentous decision and say to yourself......"*today I have finished school and learned life's lessons. From here on I use these lessons to become a winner in life*"......

You can now prepare yourself for your future winners life by taking another piece of paper and writing down all those things you do that make up your existing lifestyle. This may take several pages of paper.

Then divide this list of items into 2 separate lists.

The first list will contain all the items that are necessary only for your personal happiness and wellbeing.

Be totally ruthless about this.

The second list will contain all the remaining items. Go through these items one at a time and ask yourself...."Does this particular item have any real value for me? Will it help me become a winner?"

If the answer is NO then cut the item right off your list.

If you have trouble sorting these things out then there is a very simple way to do this.

Imagine what would happen if your doctor told you that you had an incurable disease and had only 4 weeks to live. And after getting a second medical opinion you found this horrifying diagnosis to be absolutely correct.

What items on these lists would be important to you in these final 4 weeks on earth?

I'll bet that you would find 75% of them totally superfluous.

Your final short-list would be the things that are vital to you in the final 4 weeks.

Now imagine that you go back to your specialist and he tells you that due to a recent medical breakthrough he can give you some tablets that will extend your life for a maximum of 12 months. Upon hearing this

"

good news you add a couple of items back onto your shortlist and determine to get on with life while you have it.

The reality of the situation has forced you to review your remaining life and ruthlessly cut the garbage out.

And it is a sad fact that you do not know when you are going to exit this life. So why not live life as though you had little time.

Cut the garbage and insignificant things out of your life. If dear old Aunt Matilda expects you to come for tea every Saturday (mainly because you've been doing this for years) then tell her you can't any more because you've taken up skydiving and want to spend time on your new jetski.

Sure....this might upset Aunt Matilda but she'll get over it as soon as she finds someone else to manipulate.

Do you get the picture? Dump all manipulative situations for a start. If you found you had only 4 weeks to live you would certainly be doing this and getting on with what was important to you.

The rest of your life is above that line on the paper. What is below that line is closed off and finalised as from NOW.

Some of the things that you will be doing from now on might take you out of your personal comfort zone but this is a small price to pay for becoming a winner.

Winners are used to stretching their comfort zones.....this is how they find where their limitations are.

A lot of the items below your line on the paper (your life up until now) are the result of your belief system. That is....the accumulation of all the things you have ever believed in. If you sit down and analyse your major beliefs...in the light of reality.....you might be somewhat dumfounded to find that a number of them are totally without a reality foundation. They might have been legitimate beliefs 5-10 years ago but now they are obsolete.

You must ruthlessly replace these with new beliefs based on current actual reality.

It is a sad fact that a great number of people produce "wish lists" of nice things that they would like to happen. These lists do not come from a reality base......they usually come from an airy-fairy belief system and as such have little chance of success. They are not converted into dedicated desires and backed with planned, active visualisation.

If you want to create a fantastic stress-free lifestyle for yourself you have to prepare your mind by laying the belief groundwork (which is what we've been doing so far) then lay out a visualisation and action plan. On this basis it is highly likely that what you seriously and emotionally want to achieve will happen. Maybe not in the time-frame you want but it usually happens eventually.

Another factor that holds people back is the subconscious fear of success. These people have been taught from birth that struggle is noble. It is NOT! So when they start to sense success just around the corner they carry out some action which will absolutely guarantee their failure.

I have seen this literally dozens of times in my life while watching others self-destruct. Some of these self-destruction sequences have left me literally with my mouth open.

As an example I'll tell you about a character I met on a boating trip in NZ many years ago.

(This item has appeared earlier but I'll repeat it as it is important.)

He had been declared bankrupt (for the third time) and was working his way through this situation. He was an extremely clever individual and was into inventing things. He had come up with this beyond-belief brilliant idea of a new way to construct a cheap family home. He had built one of these in a friends' large backyard and it was ingenious. It could be completely assembled in 3 days, was totally insulated against the weather....and cost 25% less than a conventional home.

He had negotiated with some investors and a construction firm and had applied for a patent on the concept. A new company was set up in which he had a major shareholding and a marketing plan had been devised which would bring this man in at least $1m in royalties and fees over the next 5 years. It looked like he was set for life.

Then.....his fear-of-success started to kick in and he began to cause problems by accusing the other shareholders of dishonesty, etc.

He became quite obnoxious and refused to turn up to meetings. His wife had seen all this before and simply threw up her hands in despair. As far as he was concerned he was convinced "everyone" was out to get him.

Well, within 2 months the whole thing had collapsed and he was without backers. I asked him why he didn't sell the others the patent rights.... that would have bought him in at least $200,000.

And do you know what he said? He told me.....*"I wouldn't give them the satisfaction. I'd rather go bankrupt again than see those bastards make money from my ideas"*......

I cut off my friendship with this character fairly quickly after that.... who needs professional losers in one's life?

Tied in with the fear-of-success is the belief that money is evil.

This belief is absolute garbage.

I was told this consistently as a child in Catholic School. It wasn't until I grew up and found out that the Catholic Church is the world's wealthiest institution that I realised that I had been "had".

Let me explain where money originated from.

Originally way back in time debts were settled between merchants by transferring gold bars, which were stored in a "bank". As time went buy ownership certificates were transferred instead of the actual gold. These ownership certificates were used as a storage mechanism. This made the settlement of debts easier and safer.

Eventually these "gold receipts" evolved into money as we know it today.

Prior to this goods and services were traded (exchanged). If a farmer grew a crop of potatoes he would trade them for tomatoes, flour, oil, etc. from the local market.

Goods were traded directly without the need for money as we know it.

Now if our above mentioned farmer had a bumper crop of potatoes one season and produced 3 times as many spuds as he normally would.... then he could trade for 3 times as many of life's necessities than he obtained the season before. That is as far as he was concerned he had acquired unexpected wealth.

And did he feel he deserved this?

Of course he did!

He had plotted and planned and worked his field and he thoroughly deserved his success. He didn't get all emotionally hung up over the extra necessities he had suddenly obtained and he certainly didn't feel any guilt about it.

So when you think about it, since money is merely the "storage mechanism" for commerce and business.....then why should you suddenly feel guilty about having a cash windfall?

I'll tell you why. It is because the non-winners in society come out with statements like...."Money is the root of all evil!" Now think about this carefully and you'll see how blatantly ridiculous it is.

Money is merely a value storage mechanism which evolved to simplify commerce. In itself it is inert.

However if it was said that an obsession with excess money can be the root of some evil....then that would be reasonably accurate.

Likewise an obsession with excess alcohol and excess road speed is also evil....and sometimes kills people.

I have never heard of a $10 note committing murder!

However we have all been aware of this detrimental belief system about money since our childhood.

And if you think back very carefully to the sort of people who kept telling you this you will come to one unalterable conclusion....they were either non-winners or born losers.

So it is vital you recognise exactly what money is. If you have gone through life so far with little money yet you have worked and studied hard then don't you think it only fair that the universe dump a reasonable cash windfall on you?

There is a saying in country music.... *"the old boy's paid his dues"*....which means that the struggling artist, after years of penny-pinching and serious endeavor, has suddenly become a recording hit. Everyone is happy for him....because he has paid his dues. It is generally recognised that he got nothing for free and paid the price in full.

Now wouldn't YOU consider that you have paid your dues in life?

Isn't it time that the equivalent of the recording contract landed in your lap.

But....the losers in life around you will try to convince you that you will never pay your dues and that your soul will be dammed forever if you try to better yourself.

The bottom line is that you have already paid the price. You were issued without an instruction manual and you have had to figure things out for yourself. It has cost you blood, sweat and tears. And you want to be paid for this!

In fact you insist on it.

Or else!

Hold your hand out to the universe and get what you deserve. It is your natural entitlement and heritage.

You may not want value storage (cash) but you may want happiness and serenity.

Demand it.

But the choice is yours. If you want that windfall that the universe is prepared to hand you then you must "set up" your belief system to accept it.

This is why I have used up a dozen or so pages so far in this book to make sure you are fully grounded in reality. You are surrounded by dreamy "space-cadets" and the only thing these types will ever attract are other space cadets. Perhaps this is where UFO's come from!! Avoid them like the plague.

Now let's get on to the formula that you use to persuade the universe to give you what is rightfully yours. This is the formula and belief system that I have used for the past 15 years. In that time I have evolved it to the point where others are using it successfully after following my instructions.

It is the basis of wealth and happiness and emotional freedom.

THE WINNERS FORMULA

   1 **Accept reality as it really is....not as you would like it to be**
   2 **Focus intently on what it is you desire**
   3 **Use active visualisation techniques to trigger the results you want**
   4 **Mix only with other winners**

Now we'll look at each of the 4 items listed above and expand on each one in detail.

At the end I'll summarise the process so that you can easily understand what is required....and start on the WINNERS process immediately.

1 - Accepting reality as it really is.

You now know exactly and precisely how to determine your absolute reality. I've covered this process in the major part of this report. Many individuals go into visualisation techniques expecting wonders....and become frustrated when nothing happens. This is solely and simply because they have not grounded themselves in reality first. For example, if you were a runner and you were about to start a 100 meter race, you would make sure you were correctly set up with both feet on the ground and in a semi-crouching position. You would not start the race in a standing position with one foot off the ground and your arms wind milling around.

Yet almost all visualisation methods totally ignore this initial grounding preparation.

The trick here is to read through this report once every day for a week, just before you do your 5 minute visualisation exercise (explained shortly).

After you have read it a total of at least 7 times the grounding/reality message will have sunk in. This is why I have gone to so much trouble to explain it all.

2 - Focus intently on what it is you desire.

During this WINNERS process you will be asked to mentally picture what it is you want. Some people will be able to visualise this clearly while others will only be able to imagine it. But the final result will be the same.....because this process is causing you to intently focus...and that is all that matters.

3 - Use active visualisation techniques.

This is something you might have to work on for a few days before you are happy with it. It is a simple 2-stage "mental picturing" process.

Here is what you do:

Mentally picture, imagine, or visualise the result you seriously desire. Let us say it is a large bank balance. You generate a picture in you mind of a bank statement with your name on it, and a large amount of money in the credit column. Now picture this as clearly as you can for about a minute....then place this mental picture to one side. You now generate a second picture. This one is relatively easy. During all this you are relaxed with your eyes closed. Picture yourself flying off into the depth of the universe and landing in the centre of the Milky Way. There are billions of bright points of light all around you. Feel the vast energy present. Feel the "hum" of the universe. Now place your mental picture of your bank statement right in the centre of all this energy filled brightness and "see" all this energy flowing through your bank statement. See your statement "shimmering" with energy.

If it is an object you desire such as a new car then use a mental picture of the car instead of the bank statement. If it is happiness and serenity that you desire then generate a mental picture of yourself as if this fabulous result had already happened.

Whatever you elect to picture imagine it as if it had already occurred. That is, you feed into the universe a picture of the end result as you want to happen.

This is vital!

You must present the end result. Do not even try to imagine how this will occur.

You are imparting universal energy into a picture of your end result. Let the universe figure out how it will all come about.

Now you do this picturing process for a maximum of 5-10 minutes per day only.

Put all your mental energy into it. You might feel slightly drained at the end of each session but that only means that you are getting the process right by expending a large amount of psychic energy.

When this happens you know that you are succeeding with your active visualisation. Ordinary passive visualisation draws no psychic energy at all and does not tire you.

4 - Mix only with other winners.

This is self explanatory. After a little while you will start to detect the shallowness of many individuals close to you. Start the process of gently easing them out of your life. Do not tell them what you are doing...they will sense the change in you and start to perceive you as a different person. As such they will probably not miss your company after a while. Search out the company of others who you perceive to be winners. These people will eventually sense that you are "their kind of person" and welcome you into their circle. But this will not happen until you are fully grounded and well down the line with your active visualisation.

When you first start associating with winners it is vital that you keep all your comments positive. Winners do no like to listen to negative talk.

Explain that you have just started a major self-help program and expect it to run for a year or so. Winners like to hear this sort of thing. For the first week read this WINNERS chapter from start to finish each day first....then do your universal picturing. This will probably take you 15-30 minutes a day for the first week, depending on your reading speed. After the first 7 days there is no longer any need to read the grounding material....your subconscious mind will have assimilated it.

Continue the visualisation process for approximately 3 weeks....preferably each and every day at the same time. Then give it all a break for a week. After this start again with the visualisation process only.

SUMMARY

Read this entire chapter once a day for 7 days....this will ground you in reality.

Use the visualisation/imagination technique to overlay your desire into the energy of the universe. Do this for no more than 10 minutes per day.

Mix only with other winners and act as though you have already achieved your desire.

15

MENTAL WIZARDRY PROGRAMMING UP GOAL & HEALTH INDUCING DREAMS

Cure the body and mind through innovative dream control

The secret of therapeutic and happiness dreams.

An eye-opening story from the writer of this report:

A strange thing happened just after I retired at the end of June.

I suddenly developed a minor problem with my left shoulder known as "Bursitus" or "lazy shoulder". I could not lift my arm without pain. Some days it was bearable but other days were a serious inconvenience, especially in bed at night. That was when I really noticed it.

I figured it was something to do with the sudden release of stress after 29 years in business. I went to my doctor who told me it would go away eventually. Great help!! Then I went to a chiropractor who made a series of adjustments which only partially helped.....temporarily.

I mentioned this to one of my clients who had telephoned for a general chat.

He told me that a friend of his had used dream control to remove an identical problem.

I went onto the internet and did a fair amount of research on this subject and finally figured how I might make it work.

After 6 weeks of putting up with this pain I tried the dream control technique on a Friday night. The next morning I woke up feeling "different". It took a couple of minutes to figure out what it was. You guessed it......the pain was not only totally gone but my arm had full and free movement.

I was slightly amazed to say the least.

Two nights later I tried another technique relating to dream control.

I should point out here that all this was quite a few years ago while I was still learning the potential of the mind.

I programmed up a dream which would cause me to feel happy and relaxed the next day.

And sure enough from the moment I opened my eyes the next morning I felt not only happy and contented....but at peace with the world.

At one point I was a tourist on a cruise ship exploring the Indonesian islands.

While chewing on some Indonesian food on the beach my teeth hit a nut or something similar in the cookie. This broke the top off one of my back teeth. This was hurting like hell so I gave up scuba diving for the day and headed back to the ship to see the doctor. He could not help me and there was no dentist available until we got back to Darwin six days later.

So...that night I programmed up a dream in an attempt to kill the pain and the next morning it was 90% free from the toothache.

To say that I was impressed would be a gross understatement!

I had been totally unaware that pre-programmed dreams could be used in this manner.

The bottom line is that the *Inner Self has the ability to cure the body and mind.*

I obviously started to develop a serious interest in this process and during the course of a phone conversation with one of my regular clients learned that she was feeling rather depressed and miserable. As an experiment I explained the basics of this dream method and suggested she try it. She wasn't all that enthusiastic but half-heartedly agreed to "give it a try". I asked her to let me know how it went.

Two days later I received a very excited phone call from this lady....she was feeling "fantastic". All her "blues" had vanished and she told me she was feeling the best she had felt in months.

About 2 weeks after this incident a business client rang me looking for advice on how to complete a tricky business transaction that clearly meant a lot to him.

He was actually after specific Subjective Communication techniques and after discussing this new dream method I suggested he give it a try. He sent me a fax a week later to tell me that the process had worked "beautifully" and that the deal he was working on had actually happened without hitches. Apparently he had been trying to put this together for 3 months and all of a sudden "everything happened", as he put it.

This gentleman was totally delighted as it saved him all the effort involved in setting up nightly Subjective Communication sessions.

Dreams can completely reverse moods of depression by simply pre-programming up the necessary dreams.

The technique is to give yourself suggestions as you go to sleep to have dreams that will bring about the desired results.

THE TECHNIQUE

After you go to bed at night and are fully relaxed prior to sleep say to yourself (over and over) .... *"I will have dreams tonight that will solve my problem of -------"*.........

Your problem might be one of an illness such as flu. In this case you would repeat over and over ...... *"I will have dreams tonight that will solve my flu problem and cure it"*.

If your problem is one of unhappiness and discontent you would repeat over and over .... *"I will have dreams tonight that cure my unhappiness and make me feel happy and contented"*.

If your problem is one of a general feeling of unwellness then you would repeat over and over .... *"I will have dreams tonight that make me feel fit, well and bursting with energy"*.

If your problem is one of negativity then you would repeat over and over .... *"I will have dreams tonight that make me feel positive and contented".*

If your problem is one of a feeling of failure then you would repeat over and over .... *"I will have dreams tonight that make me feel successful and fearless".*

If your problem is one of a lack of confidence then you would repeat over and over .... *"I will have dreams tonight that make me feel confident and dynamic".*

If your problem is one of aggressiveness and short temper then you would repeat over and over .... *"I will have dreams tonight that make me feel patient and tolerant of others".*

If your problem is one of a general lack of interest and listlessness then you would repeat over and over ....*"I will have dreams tonight that make me feel dynamic and interested in life".*

If your problem is one of financial stress then you would repeat over and over .... *"I will have dreams tonight that cause me to have financial abundance and freedom from stress".*

If your problem is one of loneliness then you would repeat over and over .... *"I will have dreams tonight that solve my loneliness problems and attract emotional happiness and fulfillment".*

If your problem is one of a feeling of general desperation then you would repeat over and over .... *"I will have dreams tonight that bring relief from my feelings of desperation".*

If your problem is one of a lack of suitable partner in life then you would repeat over and over .... *"I will have dreams tonight that attract the ideal partner into my life".*

If your problem is one whereby you have a close friend or family member who has a serious problem or illness then you would repeat over and over .... *"I will have dreams tonight that will help give (use their first name) relief from his/her current problem".*

If your problem is one of a general lack of *luck* then you would repeat over and over .... *"I will have dreams tonight that cause me to have immediate runs of luck"..*

If your problem is one whereby you need to achieve a specific goal fairly quickly then you would repeat over and over .... *"I will have dreams tonight that will cause my goal (name it) to materialise quickly".*

If your problem is one whereby you want to improve your conscious awareness then you would repeat over and over .... *"I will have dreams tonight that cause my conscious awareness and insight to improve dramatically"*.

If your problem is one whereby you want to improve your intuition and Remote Viewing abilities then you would repeat over and over.......... *"I will have dreams tonight that cause my intuition and Remote Viewing abilities to improve dramatically"*.

If your problem is one whereby you want to give up smoking then you would repeat over and over.......... *"I will have dreams tonight that cause me to increasingly lose interest in smoking until I give it up"*.

If your problem is one whereby you want to lose weight then you would repeat over and over.......... *"I will have dreams tonight that cause me to become aware of calorie intake and lose weight naturally"*.

If your problem is one whereby you want to feel less stressful during the day then you would repeat over and over.......... *"I will have dreams tonight that cause my stress level to reduce drastically so I feel calm and peaceful all day"*.

You may find that the desired result happens after the first night of trying.....or you may find that it takes several "bursts" to achieve that which you want.

Luck and goal-seeking aims tend to take longer.

The critical thing is to do your pre-programming thoroughly.

If you have trouble staying awake long enough to focus on this vital process then you might like to record a 10 minute message on a cassette tape and play it as you go to sleep. The tape will contain the desired program repeated over and over. Simply read your short message on to it.... leave a 5 second gap....then repeat the message. If you record the same message 20-30 times this should be sufficient.

It is a good idea to record 5 minutes silence at the start of the tape before your repeated message.

This means that as you start to feel tired you can switch on your tape then turn out the light and relax. The messages will start after 5 minutes or so and will catch you as you drift off to sleep.

It appears that this dream control technique could be used to replace the process of Subjective Communication in many cases.

Don't forget to leave a 5 minute "silent" gap at the start of the tape. This will give you time to scratch your nose, get comfortable, etc., and settle down ready for sleep.

It doesn't matter if you drop off to sleep while the tape is running..... your subconscious will still hear and react to it.

If there is something you particularly want to achieve that is not listed here then you should be able to easily assemble the desired message from the examples given above. The beauty about this particular program is that nothing is critical. You know what it is you want to achieve and providing you convert this to an approximate message your mind will understand exactly what it is you require. Then it will arrange a dream to suit your requirements.

You will probably not remember this dream (or dreams) but you could safely assume they have occurred. Particularly if you have run the identical program several nights in a row.

I have a feeling that it is important you only run one program at a time.....don't try to double up to produce multiple results otherwise there may be confusion.

Up until recently there has not been a great amount known about dreams. There are a number of books on the market which claim to be able to "decode" your dreams but these are usually highly inaccurate. The only thing that has been widely known and accepted is that if a person is deprived of their normal dreaming cycle then they often suffer emotional problems.

It seems logical then that we should be able to program up specific dreams to solve problems in our physical reality.

I have a feeling that there will be some interesting breakthroughs in this dream research but in the meantime you have been given an innovative new concept that you will be able to experiment with to discover the parameters.

My thinking is this: If you can call up a dream to make you feel blissfully happy the next day or to solve an illness problem......then you should be able to program up dreams to accomplish any thing you seriously need in your life.

Exactly the same results can be achieved of course by hypnosis but what you are doing with dream control is a form of automatic self hypnosis.

It seems to me that we have a brand new *tool* at our fingertips and all we have to do is experiment until we figure how to use it to maximum advantage.

And the real beauty is that it is the *simplest* tool I have come across yet!!!

Happy dreams!!!!!

16

THE *NEW*
MENTAL PENDULUM
TRAINING TECHNIQUE

Earlier in this book several methods were described to help you trigger off the autonomous thumb twitch effect which I have called the mental Pendulum.

After receiving a lot of feedback from individual clients over the years it has become obvious that the best overall method is to train the thumb muscles by example. That is, you intentionally twitch your thumb muscles while telling your subconscious that this is what you want to happen.

The method that has slowly evolved over the past couple of years is as follows:

Place both your hands flat on a table at which you are sitting. Close your eyes and relax....drop down to the alpha state if you can.

Say the following out loud:

"Subconscious, I want you to give me a yes and a no twitch in my thumb muscles when I ask a question that can be answered with a yes/no answer".

Repeat this a dozen times or more so the subconscious clearly knows what it is that you require.

Remember, when dealing with the subconscious, treat it as a 10 year old child.

Then say out loud the following:

"Subconscious, I am now going to twitch the thumb muscles in each hand so that you can see what I want".

At this point intentionally twitch the thumb muscle in your left hand several times....then do the same with the right hand. Don't rush it...... take your time.

As you trigger each "twitch" say to your subconscious.... *"this is what I require you to do automatically when I ask yes/no questions".*

You will note that we are talking in very basic language to the subconscious....almost in a childish manner.

The next step is to do the same exercise again....but in an imaginary manner.

That is you **visualise** your thumb muscles twitching in your mind's eye. Do not actually twitch them yourself.....simply close your eyes and mentally see them twitching.

You may find to your surprise that one of them actually does twitch as you do this mental exercise.

You then go on to the next step.

Pick a simple question to which you can easily obtain a yes/no answer.

The easiest question of the lot concerns your own name.

In my case I use my own name....James.

I say to my subconscious.....*"Give me a YES twitch in my left thumb muscle when I ask if my name is James".*

Repeat this 6-8 times out loud so that your subconscious clearly understands.

It may be that you have already had an autonomous twitch in one of your muscles, so you would then ask your subconscious to give you a YES twitch in one of your hands when you ask if your name is (whatever your name is).

The reason for doing this is that your subconscious may prefer to use your right hand muscle for a YES twitch....rather than the left hand one.

But if it has given you no indication at all so far then you may want to select, say, the left hand muscle as a YES.

This is how it works for me.....my subconscious selected my left hand muscle as a YES.

Other people get a YES in their right hand.

At this point you tell your subconscious (several times out loud) that you want your YES twitch to appear in your left hand. (Or your right hand if you prefer).

Then, with your hands still laid out flat on the table in front of you.... you say....."*Is my name James (or whatever)?*"

You then intentionally twitch your left hand muscle (if you have elected to use your left hand for a YES).

This means that you are now starting to train your subconscious to give you a twitch in the muscle of your choice.

You repeat this exercise until your muscle grows tired.

Then for a change you can repeat this whole exercise by asking for a NO answer in your other hand muscle.

In my case I would ask......*Is my name Fred?*"

As my name is obviously not Fred then I would intentionally twitch my NO hand....in my case...my right hand thumb muscle.

Carry on with this until this hand is also tired.

You may have to repeat all this for several days....maybe even a week or more....until your subconscious suddenly "clicks" as to what is expected of it.

The first twitch you get may be only just perceptible...that is....unless you are really observant you may miss it.

The first twitch I got was only just noticeable.

You may also notice a slight "muscle surge"....as if the muscle is trying to twitch.

This might appear as a tingle or some other subtle feeling. Watch carefully for this as this type of effect will indicate that your subconscious is trying to comply with your requirements.

If nothing happens in the first few days....and your muscles are feeling sore.... give it a rest for a couple of days then start the whole thing over again.

Slowly your subconscious will get the message but there is no reason why you cannot get this process up and running effectively as your subconscious has direct autonomous control over all your body muscles.

When you get a fright your subconscious causes your body muscles to jolt. In this case we are asking for a minor jolt reaction upon demand.

The main thing here is to keep asking the question (as detailed above) that requires a YES reaction......and demonstrating what you want by intentionally twitching the muscle you have chosen to represent a YES.

At some point a YES twitch may appear just before you intentionally twitch this muscle.

In fact, when I first stated doing this my muscles would respond 1-2 seconds after I asked the question. That is.....there was a delay in the response.

So when you are training the muscle....ask your question...then wait 2 seconds or so before you intentionally twitch the muscle. If your subconscious reaction is going to flick in and give you an autonomous response... then it has 2 seconds or so to do so. And to your surprise, you may find a weak reaction suddenly appear within this 2 second pause.

When it does happen...don't push it too hard. It may take some time for the effect to happen again. Be patient because you do not want to give your subconscious negative messages by wondering if the first twitch was a fluke...and maybe it wasn't real, etc.

The point is, once you have this up and running reliably you have it for life. And it will help you in ways that you can only now dream about.

There are a vast number of ways in which you can use this Mental Pendulum.

The main application is to identify problems, then use something like reverse Subjective Communication to solve them.

REVERSE SUBJECTIVE COMMUNICATION

You will already be familiar with the principles of standard Subjective Communication, whereby you program yourself to wake up in the middle of the night when you are mentally in touch with a person you want to influence. You then transmit a message to them that moves a situation in your favour.

However, if you program yourself to wake up when you are in mental contact with a large group of people who have expertise in the subject you are interested in, then you fire the problem at this imaginary group.... and **listen for answers!**

That is, instead of transmitting....you are receiving.

This is reverse Subjective Communication.

You can even go a stage further and set up communication with a group of people from some time in the future. You explain your problem....and wait for "voices" or impressions from the audience.

I have started to use this method quite a lot lately....and the more I use it....the more effective it becomes.

But initially, you have to know what the precise problem is. This is where the Mental Pendulum comes in. Sometimes the problem is either not obvious....or it turns out to be something different from what you expected.

I have found that the Mental Pendulum sometimes gives me the most unexpected answers and has me searching in an entirely different direction.

That is....it makes you think things out from different angles.

I have usually found that when using the Mental Pendulum on personal matters....it is highly accurate.

Let us now look at various scenarios where the Mental Pendulum can be of help.

I have broken these down into "example" categories....and gone through the whole process so you can follow my method.

DREAM ANALYSIS

Let us suppose you have a problem that is really bugging you. You know approximately what the problem is, but you can't seem to find an answer.

The idea here is to program up a dream and specify that you want to solve this problem.

(Alternatively you may not be able to identify the problem.....but you know one exists....so you program the dream to identify the problem)

When you wake up some time during the night (or morning) with a dream clear in your mind...the first thing to do is to make brief notes of the dream. Jot down all the points that seem to matter.

Then you start to ask your Mental Pendulum what it is all about.

You can also use an ordinary pendulum but this means you usually have to get up out of bed.

With the Mental Pendulum you can query the dream scenario there and then....while you are still lying in bed with your eyes closed.

Assuming you have your notes on the dream...or maybe you have just woken up from the dream and it is still clear in your mind......you can start to ask questions.

For a start I always ask if this is connected with either my business or personal life. If the pendulum says yes I then ask if it is my business life. If the answer is no I then ask if it refers to my personal life. Assuming the answer here is yes then I start to query what aspect of my personal life. I normally ask a series of questions such as:

Is this connected with my financial position?

Is this connected with my lifestyle?

Is this connected with my health?

Is this connected with my social activity?

And so on until I get a positive yes.

I then break this down with more questions until I precisely identify what is required.

Occasionally the pendulum tells me that the dream is not connected with either my business or personal life. In that case I ask if it is connected with my meditation life. If the answer is no then I have to really scratch my head.

But initially if you preface all your questions by asking if the problem is connected with your business, personal or social life then it will normally give you an answer to one of these....and you have narrowed down your search somewhat.

But before you do anything at all with the Mental Pendulum you have to give it a "pre-flight" check to make sure it is working properly.

You do this each time you use it to ask about a new subject.

A lot of people pick up an ordinary mechanical pendulum and attempt to use it without going through this checking procedure. And they wonder why they get false results. Sometimes the pendulum action reverses itself and gives a yes instead of a no. At other times it simply doesn't want to answer the question....and at certain times you may be too tired or stressed to use the pendulum. So the idea is to run through a checking procedure right at the start.

Here are the questions I ask the pendulum (or Mental Pendulum) prior to every session:

Is my name James? (This tests its polarity)

Can I ask question about this subject? (Specify the subject in your own mind)

May I ask questions about this subject?

Am I ready to ask questions about this subject? (Sometimes it may tell you No)

Am I too tired or stressed to ask questions now?

Am I receptive enough to ask these questions?

Will you give me answers better than 90% accuracy?

If the pendulum gives a No to any of the above then it may pay to wait for a while....then do the checking procedure again.

But normally it will give you a Yes to all the above check questions.

At this point in time you are free to proceed with queries on the subject matter.

FINANCIAL PROBLEMS

Let us suppose you have some specific financial problem. You know precisely what it is and you need to know how to solve it.

The first thing you ask....."Is there an easy solution to this problem... Yes or No."

If the answer is Yes then you start asking a series of questions designed to elicit the answer. If you have trouble achieving this then you might program up a dream solution and use the pendulum to decode the dream.

If the answer to the first question is No then you need to ask why the solution would be hard, rather than easy. Ask a series of questions designed to find out why the solution is hard. This may give you a lead on the correct line of questioning.

Obviously as I do not know which particular question you may need the answer to I cannot be more specific here.

The procedure is to slowly develop a line of questioning that gives you general answers to start with....then narrow the field down so you are asking more specific questions.

Start with general questions so you can sense the direction the pendulum is taking you...then get more specific.

You will often be totally amazed at where you end up. Sometimes the answer is not at all what you would have normally thought of.

The Mental Pendulum will sometimes amaze you. It is drawing answers from your deep subconscious and will usually steer you in the right direction. The fact that you might tackle the same pendulum problem day after day convinces your subconscious that you are serious about finding an answer.

HAPPINESS PROBLEMS

It may be that deep down you feel a sense of unease, disquiet, dissatisfaction or general unhappiness.

The first thing you would ask the pendulum (after your initial pre-use checks) is this...."Is there a genuine problem?"

If the answer is Yes then you would ask...."Is there something specific that is disturbing me or making me unhappy or apprehensive?"

If the answer here is Yes then you would ask...."Does this relate to my personal, social or business life?" If the answer is again Yes then find out which one of these three it particularly refers to by asking for as response for each of the three.

Once you have narrowed it down to, say, your personal life, then you ask a series of questions attempting to find exactly what it is in your personal life that is causing the problem. You might write down all the things you think could be wrong then go through each one with the pendulum until you find which item it is.

If you have trouble identifying the problem you might generalise the search again by asking if it applies to you at work...at home.......in a social scene, etc.

You simply keep at the questioning until it defines exactly what causes the problem. It might be something that you have attached no importance to....and surprise you somewhat. However, upon deep reflection you may realise that the pendulum has hit the nail right on the head, so to speak.

It gives you an extraordinary feeling of self satisfaction when you solve a problem this way for the first time. You suddenly realise the implications of what has happened....and what this ability will mean to you in the future.

SIBLING PROBLEMS

You may have trouble with one of your kids (who doesn't?) and want to know exactly what their problem is...and the solution.

You would first ask......"Does little Johnny have a problem at all"? (You ask this because there simply may be no problem at all and you have mis-read the situation).

If the answer is Yes then you ask general questions such as...."Can Johnny solve this problem by himself?" Then maybe...."Am I able to help him solve this problem?"

Then you can get into specifics and determine what the problem is.

The next step is to ask the pendulum a series of question designed to elicit a solution. In the end you simply ask the pendulum....."Is this solution likely to work?"

You could also add to this by using Subjective Communication to assist in solving the problem. But the Mental Pendulum identifies the real problem...something you might never have known unless you'd used it.

WORKPLACE PROBLEMS

It might be that you sense a problem in your place of work....or suspect that there is something going on that is causing you concern.

Firstly you would specify (either in writing or verbally) that you suspect there may be a problem. Then you would ask the pendulum to confirm this. If it says Yes then you start to ask questions attempting to determine the nature of the problem....in general terms. After you have narrowed things down you start to ask specific questions. Finally, if you determine there is a real problem (as opposed to imaginary) and it concerns other people in your workplace....then you can use Subjective Communication to modify the attitude of the other people concerned.

As always, do NOT tell others what you are doing....keep all this knowledge to yourself. It is an extra "weapon" that you can use to your advantage in life.

MARRIAGE PROBLEMS

If you suspect your marriage might have a problem you can use the pendulum as above to identify the problem. There are so many possible marriage problems (I speak from vast experience) that I can not even begin to present examples.

But you have to be very careful here. You might suspect for example, that your partner is playing around. If the pendulum confirms this then due to the possible emotion involved.....you may precipitate an emotionally based action....only to find that the pendulum mislead you to start with.

If you intend to ask your Mental Pendulum emotionally charged questions...then you may not get accurate answers.

But what it might do is to supply leads that you can follow. It may indicate for instance, that certain things are happening, or certain perceived scenarios are false. You can then use ordinary means to investigate these.

But if it leads you to various conclusions that you can verify by other means then you might even be able to use Subjective Communication to solve the problem.

Deep emotional problems can cause your intuitive pendulum to act abnormally.

In these circumstances, use it only a guide.

HEALTH PROBLEMS

This is a situation where the pendulum is normally fairly accurate.

I use it regularly so see if I am short of vitamins or minerals. I go through the pre-use check then tell myself that I am going to check for lack of any of the above. I then ask...."Am I short of vitamin A?".....("Am I short of vitamin B?"...etc.

Often it will give me a yes twitch......or a partial twitch.....which will indicate that there is a shortage of that particular chemical in my system.

You can ask about more serious problems, but remember that very serious problems may create emotional overtones which can cause the pendulum to malfunction.

In this case you can use the pendulum to get an indication as to where the problem might lie...then use standard medical procedures to confirm this.

You can also use the pendulum to determine the reason why you may be feeling depressed...or otherwise slightly low. You can also use it to ask for ideas to improve your state of mind....it may even tell you to go to the movies or something else very simple.

LUCK PROBLEMS

If you appear to be having a run of poor luck you can set up a series of questions to determine if there is any specific reason for this. For example you might ask if this is a cyclic thing. Or you might ask if there is something you can do to change your situation. If you can determine the reason for a low luck run then you might find that you can do something about it.

On the other hand the pendulum may inform you that there is nothing you can do in the meantime. In this case you would ask the pendulum how long before the situation corrected yourself.

You can ask it to count out the days (or weeks) by telling it forcefully to twitch your yes thumb once for each day. If it gives you 4 twitches then you can take this to mean 4 days.

SUMMARY

After you have this process up and running....and are confident with it... then you can start to transfer the twitch to other muscles....such as the eyelids.

Simply instruct your subconscious that you want the twitch to appear at your eyelid muscles. Train it if necessary to show it what you want....by intentionally twitching your eye muscles (if you can!)

After you have this working you might like to visualise a mental movie screen in your minds eye.......and see a yes answer as a flash of light on the left of the screen...while a no would be a flash of light on the right of the screen.

Or you may wish to reverse these two to suit yourself.

After you have used this process for a year or so you will find that the twitches appear almost the instant you ask the question...that is, there is no delay.

Also you may also notice that yes/no answers start appearing in your mind...as intuitive hunches.

This is the start of a full-on working intuition ability...where a specific question triggers an intuitive answer (or strong impression) in your mind.

You will then be in the position of having six senses working for you.... instead of merely five.

Makes life a whole new ballgame......doesn't it?

17

REMOTE
INFLUENCING

How often have you felt that someone was staring at you. You probably turned around and immediately caught the gaze of the "starer".

Or maybe you've unintentionally done this to someone else.

What has not been realised until quite recently is that when you focus on another person, either within eyesight or geographically distant, then that person subconsciously picks up on your attention. Further still, their physiology changes slightly. Their blood pressure increases for a start.... and there are other measurable changes.

Human minds appear to act like an international telephone exchange. When you focus on someone...you "connect" directly with them. There is no error....the connection is always made.

This fact was suspected for a long time, but until recently there had been no serious research on it.

Then along came the remote viewers. And what they discovered absolutely stunned the scientists who had an interest in this field.

The remote viewers found that not only could they "connect" with their target person in real time....but they could connect at specified times <u>in the past and in the future!</u>

That is...they would remote view (connect with) an individual....but before doing so would specify exactly the time and date that they wished to do so.

This is totally astounding knowledge.

In fact, all you have to do to remotely influence someone is to specify the exact individual...and also specify the time and date when you want contact established. You then focus intently on that person......and follow whatever procedure you have in mind. (More about that later).

The USA ex-military remote viewers are ALL familiar with remote influencing.....and most of them will deny that they have ever heard of it!

Let me now give you the background as to what has been discovered in the past...then I'll supply you with the latest up-to-date information.

You'll find in this report a number of different methods you can use to learn remote influencing. When you combine these methods together........ your life will totally change. Some of the methods will appeal to you.... and some probably won't. It is over to you to take the knowledge contained herein and apply it. As everybody has a different mindset then no one particular method can be recommended. Something that will work for another individual may not work for you.

The field is still in its infancy, so you will have to adapt the processes described to suit yourself.

But if you practice some of the methods described you will start to notice increasing success.

Please remember that each and every individual affects other people all the time.

If you drive your car down the road slowly and hold up traffic behind you...then you are affecting others.

The mere fact that you are reading this means that I have affected you. You could have been doing something else right at this instant.

All we are doing with remote influencing is affecting people in a slightly different way....remotely. It is merely an extension of your day to day interaction with others.

If you happen to be in a foul mood and enter a room full of people, then they subconsciously pick this up off you and avoid you. That is uncontrolled remote influencing. What you are learning here is controlled remote influencing. You can use it to your advantage...and to the advantage of the other person. If you use it to try and harm them....then you are likely to have the exercise bounce back on you some time in the future...with a considerable interest percentage added on!

Once you have mastered the process....you will simply find that things go your way. This is because you are <u>unconsciously</u> using subjective influence without even being aware of it. It becomes an automatic process.

When you focus on a project intently then your remote influencing abilities come into play and make it happen. It is really an automatic process and will appear to you as if you are suddenly having a run of good luck. Don't knock it...ride with it.

And don't be afraid of it because it is a natural talent that you were born with. For the first time in your life you will have it under control.

Some of the more advanced martial arts gurus have learnt how to affect a person at a distance by transferring emotion based on "moving-energy".

This process was tested out at the American Society for Psychical Research.

The process involved a visualisation as follows:

You visualise yourself as a hunting animal, such as a wolf. You are hunting someone or something that you dislike intensely. You "see" yourself stalking this target through the jungle or forest, thinking all the time how much you dislike the target. Then you visualize sneaking up on the target...leaping and striking. At the instant of the "strike" you throw the emotional energy of the attack at the person you want to remotely influence.

That is, your pent-up "killer emotions" are transferred to your subject.

The same method was used to break infra-red beams in a laboratory. Apparently quite a lot of energy is released this way.

You can also use a burst of frustration and throw this at you target. If you think of something that is totally frustrating you right at this moment... capture it in one "energy-ball......and project it at the person you want to influence...then you are likely to have success.

If you sit at one of those sidewalk cafe's watching people walk past, then you can practice throwing energy balls in the manner described above. By doing this you are also able to get instant reactions in people.... so you can judge how well you are doing.

A Czechoslovakian experimenter released details of Russian mind-projection experiments involving "negative-health" remote suggestion.

In these experiments the "sender" was asked to transmit bursts of emotion.

After the sender fixed the subject firmly in his/her mind's eye he or she concentrated on the anxiety of suffocation and conjured up racking attacks of asthma in the subject (victim?). In the experiments the subject several miles away had an intense choking fit. Their physiology had been changed by the intense focus on them.

When the sender concentrated on gloomy emotions the receiving subject showed the appropriate brain-wave responses on an EEG machine and began to experience strong head pains and a feeling of nausea that lasted for hours.

These are quite immoral procedures and you may want to avoid experimenting in this manner. The reason I have mentioned them is to show you what can be done with projected mind-power and to prepare you to repel such manipulation should another individual try this out on you. If you become aware or suspect that another is trying to mentally manipulate you then visualize a ball of high energy light around yourself deflecting incoming messages away. I have had several occasions in my life where I felt compelled to use this protection method. The point is there are always unscrupulous individuals who are prepared to misuse this process.

An individual who is totally psychotic and for no reason at all absolutely "hates" you can subconsciously project this negative material at you. And it can have quite a nasty effect on your mental health as they live and breathe malice towards you.

At one point I did some dream control programming and instructed my mind to wake me up if a batch of negative incoming messages started arriving. On at least 3 occasions that I can remember I woke up in the middle of the night and realized that I was being influenced.

Cleve Backster who made the extraordinary discovery that plant life reacted to human emotion went a step further. He scraped some cells off a subject's tongue and attached a pair of micro-fine electrodes to these cells. He found that the measuring equipment reacted when the subject induced a strong emotion. It was then further found that the cells did not need to belong to the "sender". They could belong to anyone.

Some of the scientific community have been looking hard at the effect Voodoo rituals have on an individual. There is now some indication that Voodoo, under certain circumstances, might actually work. Samples off the victims person...such as a hair....are used by the witchdoctor to caste a spell.

Cleve Backster's experiments indicate that there is some validity in this concept.

The Australian Aboriginals have a long history of successfully projecting psychokinetic effects at others.

RUSSIAN TELEPATHY EXPERIMENT

In an experiment with telepathy, the sender who was trying to transmit telepathically a message to a receiver some distance away found that when he or she transmitted a message, the receiver experienced a change in brainwaves, which they were unaware of. This was measured by EEG equipment monitoring the receiver's brainwaves. When the sender focused on the receiver and attempted to send a message, the brainwaves of the receiver responded. The way this was done was by giving the sender very small random electric shocks so he/she would get a slight electrical jolt. This shock in effect was transferred telepathically to the receiver. Then they went a stage further and instead of using EEG equipment to measure the receiver's brainwaves they put a little device on the receivers thumb which measured the blood pressure and the blood volume in the thumb.

They got the same result when the sender experienced his or her random electric shock...... the blood pressure in the receivers thumb changed. The conclusion here is that if the sender focuses intently on a distant human being he/she can modify their blood pressure.

One of the US Military Remote Viewers was deeply concerned about an "enemy" attempting to influence him at one point.

He said...."*I can feel them working away at me. You know how it is - you get that itchy jumpy feeling inside, as if someone's dragging their fingernails across your blackboard*"....

He explained that it was similar to the feeling you have when someone stands too close to you at a party - when some unthinking person is in your space.

He said that the only effective protection he knew was to create a mental energy ball and surround himself with it. You give it a reflective surface which deflects any incoming energy.

Recently I received a remote influence report from a physicist who was researching this field. I have "censored' it slightly to protect his identity. Here is what he has to say:

> "...Our thoughts are really a physical thing when we look at them from a quantum point of view, so it is quite logical that our thought forms also have a resonance with identical thought forms. I think this is the very basis of PSI phenomenon.
>
> I have for years been trying to find various ways to measure this resonance and ways to manipulate it. I have had some success, and so have a few other people.
>
> One of the studies that fired my imagination was the research by the Russian scientist Vasilev. He was one of the early researchers into the phenomenon of "Remote Viewing", which I am sure you are familiar with. He and his co-workers also did some experiments into what might be called remote hypnosis or manipulation. A group of them one night pooled their efforts and mentally summoned a co-worker from his sound sleep across the city to get out of his bed and come to the laboratory in the middle of the night. He shortly arrived, not being able to explain why he had come.
>
> My own thoughts were that even if we cannot explain the nature and forces of this phenomenon, there must be some formula by which we can enhance and improve upon it to make it more effective and reliable.

About 20 year ago I launched upon an experiment to do just that.

I was at the time living in Singapore, on the north side of the island. Every day I had to board a bus and travel a long and boring ride to the south side of the island. The bus passengers seemed to be ideal subjects to experiment on. So I started trying in various ways to mentally affect their behavior. I always sat near the rear of the bus, and I would pick some target near the front, of whom I had a clear view. I would visually concentrate on that person, watching their every move. If they moved their head, or an arm, I would visualize that I was moving that head or arm. After a short period of such concentration, I gradually built up a resonance with the mind of that person. Once rapport was established I would then imagine an outside event such as a fly had landed on the back of their neck.

The reaction was astounding. They would reach back to brush away the imaginary fly.

I also used Skinner's operant conditioning on myself to enhance my training. I had a great liking for cashew nuts, and I would carry a small bag in my shirt pocket. Each time I was successful in distantly influencing the other person's behavior, I would reward myself with one cashew nut. This may sound a little silly, but no matter whether we are intelligent humans of a laboratory mouse, operant conditioning works equally well.

I made great strides in refining my technique, and it certainly improved with practice also. For reasons that I have not yet been able to explain, I found it somewhat easier to manipulate women than men. Children were more difficult, although at times when rapport was well established with a child, they became almost like little robots.

I once influenced a women into getting off at the wrong bus stop. After we pulled away I could see her standing there scratching her head and no doubt wondering why she got off the bus.

Once you have developed the technique, it is quite natural in its use, very much like learning to swim, or ride a bicycle. I find I use in ordinary everyday life quite spontaneously.

I think almost anyone who is capable of a fairly focused concentration, can learn the technique quite easily.

The key is mental imagery. You must be able to visualize imagery well, and imagine feelings. The most difficult period is in the beginning. You must watch for every small indication that you are exerting some influence on the other person, and then build upon that. Like learning to ride a bicycle, it becomes easier as it progresses, and finally become almost like second nature. It is this very difficult initial step that keeps this phenomenon from being more widely used.

After you have become proficient, you will find that you do not need to see the person you are trying to influence, nor do you need to be in the proximity of that person. In fact distance seems to have no effect on the phenomenon, just as it has no effect on paired quantum particles..."

Remote projection, like remote viewing, requires a relaxed mind and body. This is where your alpha training comes in. With remote viewing you struggle to become aware of what is coming in from the matrix. With remote projection you are focusing what you are sending out. That is....you are projecting tightly controlled imagery. You clearly shape your thoughtform, fill it with the necessary energy...then release the thought to the target you have chosen.

You must be very clear in your mind exactly what it is you wish to project. Waffly half formed thoughts will go nowhere. That is the first step. The second step is in releasing the thought. You fire this compressed energy thought-ball at the target..... then promptly forget all about it. You DO NOT dwell on it.

This is the same process that is used for psychokinetic experiments. You fire the energy...then promptly think about something else. Most psychokinetic effects happen after you've stopped trying.

You really have to become aware that what you think and what you feel is changing the world outside yourself!!!

Your thoughts have energy....this has actually been measured. And when you <u>intently focus</u> these thoughts they develop a resonant energy. Then when you direct this resonance toward one particular person....with absolute single-minded intensity......that energy will impact on that target person <u>and affect them</u>.

Bear in mind that all day everyday each and every single individual is projecting his or her thoughts into the common consciousness. You are doing this remote influencing <u>whether you like it or not</u>!

So if you are one of those individuals who believe that what I have written so far is manipulative and dangerous (and possibly against your religious beliefs) then you might like to rethink your belief system, because you're involved in it anyway. You are part of the common consciousness process.

You can design your life circumstances by consciously designing and focusing the thought patterns and accompanying intensity.

In developing projective skills remember that whatever you project outward will be reflected in your environment so destructive projections will adversely affect your environment. There is an old saying...... *"what goes round comes round"* and this is particularly true of mind power. If you use mind techniques for the wrong purposes you might find that nasty things start to happen to you.

I've seen plenty of evidence of this in the past.

This is why people who dwell on things that they fear...and impart projective energy to these thoughts...usually self-destruct by creating their own personal disasters.

Once you learn these projective skills you <u>must never dwell on negative destructive activities</u>.

The purpose of developing this projective ability is to firstly improve your own life...then the life of those around you that you care for.

Here is another simple exercise for training yourself in projection:

Chose someone in a room of people as a subject. Obviously don't tell them. Produce a clear focused picture in your mind of that person scratching their neck. Now this is an autonomous response so they will not always be consciously aware that they are doing it. It is the same autonomous nervous system response that allows the Mental Pendulum to work. Focus intently...then let go. Try this on various people until you get a response. When you get your first response take a careful mental note of the exact thoughtform you projected...and use this method in the future.

This is a great exercise to do when you are sitting in a doctors waiting room....or an airport lounge.

Another simple exercise is to focus intently on a distant friend. Visualise them picking up the phone and ringing you. Keep practicing at this until you have some success. Even one successful attempt out of ten is great for starters. As you become more adept at it....your success percentage will creep upward.

Remember that this is a <u>new skill</u> that you are learning and as with all new skills....it takes time.

Do not become discouraged. You have been learning new skills since day one! It probably took you weeks to learn to walk when you were a baby....but you were absolutely determined. In fact you were probably so totally focused...that you made it happen! And this is what you have been doing throughout life.

You can also practice sending positive affirmations to loved ones who have troubles. You can "transmit" enthusiasm, encouragement, compassion, healing vibes, cheerfulness, optimism, love, and self esteem...to name just a few. You can watch their reaction to see if they received your message. You will probably find this works best when they are in a meditative or alpha state.

The professional Remote Viewers have an analogy for "influencing" -- as follows:

They "light up" the target...then fire!

In military terms this means that they "light-up" an enemy target with a laser lock-on...then fire the missile *down the laser beam.*

In projective influencing they "light-up" the target by remote viewing the person concerned...then fire projected thoughtforms back down the signal path....as described earlier on. It has been proven conclusively that when you remote view someone you lock on to their signal line. You also do this to a lesser extent by merely focusing intently on someone at a remote geographical distance. What you are doing then is to fire an intense thoughtform back down this signal line.

The most useful application of remote influencing is in the field of psychic healing. You can seriously affect another person's body cells at a distance. You simply visualise...with deep intensity....the cells in the body becoming well and normalised.

Obviously you'll be doing this type of projection to help others...I hope!!!

As you learn this new skill...treat it with the respect it deserves.

It is the single most potent mind-control ability you will ever learn. When used in conjunction with Remote Viewing and alpha/theta techniques....you are basically unbeatable!!!

CONCLUSION

After you have experimented with some of the exercises listed so far...... and have had at least a few success...then it is time to "tie" it all together and do some advanced experimentation.

Here is the process you will use:

(1) "Light-up" you target....by focusing intently on them
(2) Project your pent-up emotion at them (as in the example of the wolf attacking its victim
(3) At this instant of emotional release......instruct the target person what it is you want to convey to them, such as a healing process in their body.

In radio terminology.......you are *modulating* your energy burst with your instructional command. This is the secret behind remote influencing......the modulation of a focused mental energy beam!

From the above you can see that the process is one vital step beyond that of simple Subjective Communication. We include the projection of an intense energy force. You are basically "swamping" the target's mind with an instruction.......by overloading it with emotion.

You will need to quietly practice some of the earlier exercises in this report, to assure yourself that you are on the right track.

Do NOT attempt remote influencing until you have had at least partial success with one of the projective training exercises listed.

And finally....please remember...what goes round comes round!!

Use this extraordinary power to help yourself and others.

18

THE
MIND POWER
JACKPOT SYSTEM

This program is divided into 3 separate parts. You can do the first 2 parts in bed in the morning just after you wake up (or at any time during the day) with the third critical part being done in bed at night, before you go to sleep. If you follow this program faithfully there is no way in which it cannot change your circumstances for the better.

Firstly you must be prepared to accept mentally that your <u>subconscious mind</u> has absolute control over you psychokinetic resonance with your environment....that is....your *luck*.

After 7 years of research I have not only proven this conclusively but a number of my original **PK LUCK SYSTEM** clients have come to the same conclusion.

That is there are some dozens of people in Australia who have reported that this program has bought them significant benefits.

What this program does is change your belief system to accept financial windfalls as your right and heritage and as such triggers amazing bursts of what you commonly know as *luck*.

This program will also generate very pleasant side effects. You might slowly discover that life is becoming more interesting and that your health improves.

It is almost certain you will find that other people want to help you.... for no apparent reason.

This is because you are becoming fully resonant with the universe instead of being on the fringe of resonance.

One major result is that you develop a confidence in your future success that you have probably never had before.

This is simply because the program transfers your major past success and resultant mindset into your future.

There is no way this program can fail if you follow instructions precisely.

I suggest that in the first instance you read through the entire program so that you gain a picture of what it is all about.

Then you can start on part 1 immediately.

PART 1

The first thing I need you to do is to sit down in a quiet place, or maybe recline on a settee or bed. Focus on your breathing and relax until your muscles stop twitching and you feel calm. Now, read the following statement to yourself 8-10 times. There is no need to speak it out loud....you only need to mentally verbalise it.

MY POINT OF HIGHEST ENERGY

.......''My point of highest energy is right now. I cannot easily affect my past but I can and will affect my present and my future. My ability to affect my lifestyle and success is based on my actions and thoughts right here and now. I shall shortly dwell on a number of successes I have experienced in the past and I will project these into my future by accepting that they are repeatable.....no matter what my current circumstances. I fully acknowledge and accept that my current circumstances are the result of my own previous future projections weeks, months and years ago. I accept full responsibility for this. I also accept that my absolute peak point of resonant energy is right here and now. What I think and project now will become my future"......

It is important that you read the above a number of times..... preferably 8-10 times.......while you are relaxed and in a reflective state. After you start the program you will probably want to read the above just after you wake up in the morning, while you are relaxed.

The reason for reading it rather than listening to the message on a tape is that you are focusing more intently by reading the written word. That is a higher percentage of your attention span is focusing on the message.

SUCCESS HISTORY............

Now I want you to take a piece of paper and write down all the successes you can recall from your past. This might be when you first rode a bicycle without falling off....or when you passed a high school exam.

Or when you bought your first home. Write down as many as you can remember then think back over each event and try to recapture the emotion you felt at the time. Attach the emotion to the successful event.

Pick events that made you "glow" at the time.

Do not under any circumstances dwell on any failure.

Now the idea is to read through this list immediately after you have read the POINT OF HIGHEST ENERGY exercise above 8-10 times.

That is....you relax and read the POINT of POWER exercise multiple times.....then you read through your "success" list once while dwelling briefly on your past successes.

Do this for no more than 10 minutes.

If you find your focus wandering and you think of a negative occurrence then tell your mind.... "Cancel that thought"!

So that is Stage 1.

You read the Point of Highest Energy exercise and immediately follow it with your success remembrances.

Do both of these interconnected exercises together...do not separate them.

If you are not clear about the above then please read it all again, before you go on to the next stage, which is Part 2.

PART 2

This is where you do an active visualisation exercise once a day.

This can be done in bed at night (just before you do the stage 3 exercise) or at any other time during the day.

Almost all visualisation methods are passive. That is, they *request* help from the universal forces. This particular technique forces the universe to supply that which you require.

It produces vastly superior results. Here is the stage 2 visualisation exercise that you do once a day:

POWER VISUALISATION

........Place yourself in a comfortable situation where you will not be disturbed. Close your eyes and focus on your breathing while you feel the tensions wash away. Tell yourself that with each breath you take you will relax more and more. Now project you mind into the universe. You can do this by imagining yourself traveling at breathtaking speed away from planet earth and positioning yourself so that you can "picture" the universe. You can see the galaxies and star systems and one giant scintillating pool of energy. Then picture yourself wrapping your consciousness around this magnificent energy source and becoming part of

it. Feel it permeate your very being with its vibrancy. Feel it ex-
plode into your consciousness with its pure white brightness. Feel
it compressing in your mind so that the entire universe becomes
one ball of blue/white energy. Now picture the financial event you
require to happen and transfer the scintillating ball of pure energy
into that event. Picture the required windfall event actually hap-
pening while you are connected to this energy. Picture a jackpot
happening in front of you and feel the emotional excitement in-
volved.....

You may have difficulty with this visualisation to start with but if you keep at it you will find it becomes quite easy. (It took me 3 weeks to get this to work so I could feel the energy).

So far you have learnt the first 2 parts that prepare you for the final Stage 3 exercise that you do just before you go to sleep at night.

Incidentally, in case you are wondering, the above techniques are the most powerful visualisation methods known.

You are doing them at your absolute Point of Highest Energy.....your present.

They will not only affect your future but they will change your belief about your past. You are setting up a "successful" past for yourself by emotively recalling only your past successes and projecting them actively into the future.

By utilising these methods there is *no way your life cannot change for the better.*

If you follow the 3 stages in this program once a day...without fail..... you will find, as others have, that your world may change radically.

This may happen in the first week....or it may take several months.... but it *will* happen.

The results will depend on how much mental effort and sincerity you put into it.

If you take this program seriously it can not help but produce spectacular results.

PART 3

THE FINAL STAGE

This is the critical stage. The previous 2 stages create the correct mind-set for this final nightly procedure.

Important: Do not do this final procedure unless you have completed the other two earlier in the day.

All three procedures are required each day.

It is best to do stage one and two earlier in the day, perhaps when you first wake up.

But you can do the first two stages any time that is convenient.

The final stage must be done just before you go to sleep.

The idea here is that the first stages set up your mind for the most important Part 3 message.

<u>Here is the final Part 3 procedure:</u>
Do this sitting up in bed with the light on....so you don't drop off to sleep half way through. Here is what you dwell on prior to sleep:

MAKING IT HAPPEN!

Relax and focus on your breathing. Feel your tensions wash away.

Now start picturing yourself walking into your favourite club or casino.

See yourself walking toward your favourite bank of machines.

Mentally walk along the bank of machines and put coins into the ones that "feel right" in your imagination.

See yourself doing this until you find a machine that is "friendly".

Picture yourself putting more coins in this machine.

See it progressively paying out more and more.

See it suddenly pay a jackpot.

<u>Feel the emotion of the moment.</u>

See other players rush up and congratulate you.

Then see yourself walking out of the club with a satisfied smile on your face.

Picture yourself the next day using the jackpot money for goals that you have already predetermined. You might, for example, see yourself walking into a car dealer and paying cash for the vehicle you want. Or you might see yourself paying off all your debts with a smile and a tremendous sense of personal satisfaction.

FEEL the emotion of these events.

Attach emotion to the way you use these windfalls.

Picture yourself celebrating and people congratulating you.

Attach emotion, a sense of satisfaction and an "absolute knowing" that you can repeat these windfalls. The universal forces react strongly to emotion and without this emotional component things will not work properly.

After you have spent 5-10 minutes doing the above exercise turn out the lights and drop off to sleep. Do not think any further about your wins. Leave it alone.

Incidentally the procedure will work for almost any gambling situation. One of my clients use it (after only 3 days) to pick up a $7000 Keno jackpot at his local casino.

If you are involved in some form of gambling other than slot machines then change to wording of the above Stage 3 message to encompass your favourite gambling mechanism.

(You have now completed your exercises for the day)

SUMMARY

1   Sit in a quiet place where you will not be disturbed. Read your POINT OF HIGHEST ENERGY exercise 8-10 times. Follow this by dwelling on your past "Success List" for 5-10 minutes.

2   Do your POWER VISUALISATION exercise. This can be done immediately after the part 1 procedure above, or later in the day if more convenient.

3   Do your final part 3 MAKING IT HAPPEN procedure in bed at night. But make sure you are sitting up and not too comfortable and with the light on. This will prevent annoyance should you inadvertently drop off to sleep.

Do these complete procedures daily. Do them each _once only_ per day as instructed because your mind needs to recondition itself at its own speed.

If you do miss a day don't panic but it is best to keep going on a regular daily basis if possible.

It will not be long before you "feel" a difference within yourself. Other people may notice this and comment but <u>DO NOT tell them what you are doing</u>.

Keep at it and you will achieve personal miracles!

19

UNLIMITED
LUCK!!

A stunning new way to actually attract luck.
It's simple….easy…..and it works!!!!!

What do we know about the nebulous phenomena called luck? Well, we know naturally lucky people continually <u>expect to be lucky!</u> And they are!

We know that luck appears to run in cycles. A person can have a run of exceptionally good luck - then it fades away. Professional gamblers are well aware of this. We also now know that luck-runs can be artificially induced by running hypnotic mind programs - which appear to effect an individual's personal interaction with their environment.

In fact over the past ten years quite a lot of research has been done in this direction. Some participants in our early Fiscal PK Luck program have had extraordinary success with hypnotically enhanced luck programs.

For the first time ever the phenomenon of luck has been scrutinized and analysed. Some extraordinary discoveries have been made.

Until now, the term "Luck" conjured up thoughts of wealth, windfalls and happiness.

"It never evoked thoughts of the mechanism by which it worked."

UNTIL NOW!!

Since childhood we have been familiar with the term "Luck."

But nobody has ever explained what it is.

Scientifically put - luck is - "an individual's psychokinetic interaction with their environment." It is their inherent ability to manipulate (usually subconsciously) events within their environment to produce positive unexpected windfalls, which is very profound knowledge.

But most amazingly of all, there appears to have been no concentrated scientific investigation at all into this phenomena.

There has been vast well funded research into all sorts of quantum events, such as sub-atomic particles, cancer cures, atomic energy, space propulsion systems, digital information storage and transfer - but <u>no</u> known research whatsoever into the primordial paranormal events which impacts on 100% of the human race...... LUCK.

This is nothing short of an extraordinary omission.

Part of the problem is that scientific experiments in luck cannot be replicated in the laboratory. That is, no one has found a way to make "luck bursts" repeatable. In fact it is highly unlikely that any serious scientific research centre has ever considered investigating luck.

The reason is simple........funds would not be made available for such a nebulous concept.

Probably because no one before has ever considered luck to be a personal psychokinetic and sometimes synchronistic event.

SYNCHRONICITY

Synchronicity at this point can be defined as a series of seemingly unrelated events which are connected via a hidden agenda.

The recent publication of the SUPERSTRING theory indicates that there may well be ten dimensions in existence, not merely the four that ones senses are currently aware of. (Length, breadth, width, time)

There is now considerable mathematical proof to indicate that ten dimensions exist. And most quantum physicists have given serious consideration to this theory. It would appear that the "hidden agenda" of synchronistic events may be transparent and obvious in one or more of these ten dimensions, but become opaque and difficult to fathom when viewed in our current restricted four dimensions.

There is now at last a small amount of evidence to indicate that when an individuals subconscious mind-set is modified to encourage positive PK events (luck) then synchronistic elements may be set into play which materialistic as PK Luck events in our "real time" dimension.

What has been definitely proven however is that the mind-set of an individual influences their interaction with the environment, to an extent which can leave a person "stunned" at the positive results.

Until now, we have assumed that the only effective way to change our luck was to feed semi-hypnotic PK suggestions into the subconscious mind in an attempt to emulate the individuals who are "naturally lucky."

That is, the use of the tape program in our Fiscal PK Luck program tends to evoke positive PK events in some individuals. (It can also evoke negative PK events under certain mind-set conditions.)

But, we now find there is a better way of achieving this same result, which appears to be not only vastly more effective, but is much simpler and easier to use.

And it was discovered by accident.

Here is the history of how it evolved:

One of our lab researchers had gone to sleep at night after programming himself to wake up in the early hours of the morning for a subjective communication exercise. He awoke around 4am and effectively projected this subjective message to the person he was trying to influence. At the conclusion of this he suddenly and unexpectedly received a very clear and strong impression of "wiggly luck cycles" floating through this universe (or whatever.)

He was somewhat startled at the clarity of this mental impression and developed this strong urge to "call these cycles" down to himself. This he did. He clearly saw them looping down and passing through and around him.

Then he drifted off to sleep. The next day, he was totally stunned at some of the "lucky" events that occurred and this same thing happened the next day. On the third day, as he was about to drift off to sleep he had this sudden profound realization that these luck events were connected to him "calling down" the luck cycles.

As he put it "this was a stunning realisation." At that point he drifted off to sleep. The next day was back to normal …. no unusual luck events …. and he wondered if he couldn't program his mind to wake up at the right time of the night to "call down" another batch of cycles.

He did exactly that the next night.

And the next day …. A startling series of luck events happened all over again. He told me that he found this totally incredible.

Quite beyond belief.

Instead of playing his PK tape night after night - as he had been doing, he now found he could evoke a closer PK connection with his environment merely by programming his mind to wake him at the best possible time during the night and calling down luck cycles.

Over several weeks he experimented with different methods and finally settled on the following ….

> *As you go to sleep at night program your subconscious mind by repeating over and over "I will wake up at the best possible time to attract positive luck cycles and I will remember why I have woken up." This is to be repeated over and over as you go to sleep, as if you were going to do subjective communication. But - instead of using your mind as a <u>projective transmitter</u> you use it as a <u>passive receiver</u> to pull in any luck cycles floating around in the universe.*

This almost sounds too simplistic to be true …. But <u>it works!</u> I tried it with somewhat stunning results, so did a business associate who is familiar with subjective communication. He got the same positive results.

In fact right at the start this gentleman was a profound sceptic when it came to mind power techniques, but after reading and practicing Alpha - Theta techniques then evolving into subjective communication, he is now a firm believer. As he said "Life has changed dramatically for me since I started in this hocus-pocus." (He has a sense of humour too!)

He found that calling down luck cycles worked, and worked brilliantly.

When you think deeply about all this it makes sense, because people who "know" they are lucky invariable are.

<u>They are subconsciously calling down luck cycles because of their inherent belief system.</u>

It also has become obvious that luck runs in cycles - so it may work even better if you have PK cycles on an upturn.

It may even be possible that "calling down luck cycles" will work against you if done at a negative point on your natural luck cycle.

But the most important thing to remember is that you <u>do</u> have luck cycles - and that if your mind-set is negative during these peak periods you are more likely to scare away luck than attract it.

Put another way - if during this cyclic period when you are psychokinetically closer to your environment, you have a negative mind set regarding luck, then you are likely to attract bad luck - or "PK missing" effects.

This is where things work the reverse of what you really want.

Remember, you are researching a totally unknown field here.

Despite all the efforts science has made over the past 150 years to improve the quality of life. The most important human factor of all - LUCK - has never been seriously researched.

Yet - if the answer to this riddle could be successfully discovered, the whole human race could suddenly become more cheerful and optimistic.

Sort of makes you think - doesn't it?

As far as I know, we are the only group in the world researching that most important of human attributes - LUCK!

There is obviously still a lot we don't know about all this but our extended experiments have proven beyond doubt that the human mind affects environmental mechanisms in the vicinity.

And why shouldn't it?

Consciousness is a stand-alone event. Every single thing in the known universe is constructed from sub-atomic particles, which the unique event known as consciousness appears able to manipulate.

The implications for human endeavor and fulfillment are staggering!

Happy experimenting.

THE PROCEDURE AGAIN

1 **Program to wake up at the best time to attract luck cycles**

2 **Visualize these "cycles" floating around you then visualise them coming down around and through you**

3 **Go back to sleep <u>knowing</u> that your luck has been improved**

20

THE
ULTIMATE
VISUALISATION
EXERCISE

The following simple exercise is widely regarded as one of the most powerful visualization exercise ever discovered.

Relax with your eyes closed and focus on your breathing. Tell yourself that with each breath you take you are relaxing more and more. Now imagine yourself as part of the entire universe. The easiest way to do this is to project your mind at high speed out into space....see the planets then solar systems rushing by. See the universes rushing by until you have reached as far as you can go. When you look back you see all the matter of creation shimmering and pulsating in a large vibrant form before you. You can visualise this shape in human form if you wish (God?).

The suns and planets are your body cells, each filled with energy and power but awaiting your direction. You realise that you are part of the universe and the universe is part of you. Then see this image exploding into your own consciousness. It is unbelievable bright and full of love. Realise that this is only one portion of a far greater unseen multidimensional structure spread out over dimensions that are on the fringe of your conscious awareness. Feel the energy arriving from this entity then visualise this same energy passing into your mind and body. Let it fill your being then direct it physically to any place within your body that you chose. If you are looking for a financial or other physical event to occur in your life then picture that event as clearly as you can and transfer this massive vibrant burst of universal energy to that event. Visualise the required event actually happening while you are connected with the universe and full of this life-force energy.

21

CONTACT !!!

THE
EROTIC
INFLUENCING
REPORT

THE USE OF MIND-POWER TO ATTRACT OR RETAIN A SUITABLE ROMANTIC PARTNER!

* **Find a new romantic partner**
* **Revive a dying relationship**
* **Attract the things you really want in life**
* **Deter unwanted attentions and sexual harassment**

NOTE: This report was written for a profound reason. Every individual deserves the right to absolute happiness....and the greatest happiness comes from being in love.....that is.....having the right partner in your life. This report therefore covers the two aspects of erotic attraction:

Attracting the right sensual partner......and deterring unwanted sensual advances.

COMMUNICATION AND GOALS

It is now well-known that people communicate with each other on a subconscious level constantly.

Most of this communication occurs in the alpha or theta brainwave level .

We are constantly communicating with and affecting each other, whether we realise it or not.

Some individuals are naturally good at influencing other people and a handful of cult leaders and similar people specialise in controlling their victims by this mind control.

On top of this the human mind is goal-seeking and what the determined mind usually wants it gets.

Your goals and desires will manifest themselves by psychokinetic manipulation of the environment and by the direct mental influence over other people.

Influencing other people by direct mental thoughts is vastly easier than control over your environment by psychokinetic means. And it is a fact that most people want an emotional attachment to another special individual and this usually means that their mindset is already attuned to the possibility of mental influencing, because deep down this is what they want.

MANIFESTING CONCEPTS

Manifesting concepts and ideas can take quite a length of time but manifesting sensual attraction can be almost instantaneous because it involves deeply desired preconditioned emotions of potential love.

It is not necessary to visualise the person you want to influence in precise clear detail....... it is only necessary to be able to picture or imagine their overall gestalt. (A gestalt is a generalised overall picture).

In general most of your influencing will be done in the dreamy state of alpha but if you can manage to handle the process in theta you will generally find the results quicker and more profound.

DAY-DREAMING

Everyone is familiar with day dreaming and this is all you are required to do. The only difference is that you do a controlled daydream about a specific person with a specific result in mind. You will find this quite a pleasant, relaxed process.

You can do this influencing during the day or when you are in a naturally dreamy state just before sleep or while you are having a shower or bath. It is basically controlled and directed daydreaming. When you daydream about another person you are automatically influencing them anyway. This is the way human minds work. So if you feel that remote influencing is immoral or against your personal principles then the bad news is that you are guilty of it yourself! You cannot escape it.

When you are in this daydream state your mind is capable of becoming more focused because the usual wide-awake beta distractions are diminished.

The alpha range covers the 7-13 cycle per second brain frequencies while the theta range is from 3-7 cps.

The process you will be using involves "picturing" or "imagining".

These are simple forms of visualisation which is a process some people have trouble with. When you mentally imagine or visualise some event with reasonable clarity and considerable forceful emotion then after a period of time that event is very likely to happen. The whole secret of manifesting events is in the amount of emotion you can generate. Fortunately when it comes to love and sex it is quite easy to generate emotions....this is human nature and is the way it was intended to be.

ESTABLISHING A GESTALT TO MENTALLY INFLUENCE ANOTHER

Before you start mentally influencing another individual you need to get a reasonably clear picture of their overall "gestalt". (A gestalt as mentioned before is the overall mental picture of an object).

You do not need to be able to actually picture them clearly in your mind's eye but you need a couple of specific details so that your mind latches on to the right person. There is no point doing all this work to find you have been working on the wrong person.

For a start make a note on a piece of paper of the actual place you normally see them at. This might be at work or it might be a local coffee shop, or on a bus or train. Then make a note of the features that stand out the most.

For example, you may be drawn to the colour of their hair, or a specific mannerism, or they way they talk. Make a written note of several of these points. Another reason for doing this is that you are telling your mind you are serious….that this is an important project for you personally.

If when you are doing your influencing your image of the person starts to fade away then you can recapture it by starting again at the place where you normally see them and build back up from there. Mentally work through your written characteristics until you have built up a gestalt once again.

If you are trying to attract a new unknown partner into your life by using this process to bring someone "out of the woodwork" then you will not have an existing picture.

In this case you write down the approximate characteristics of the type of individual you want to meet. Do not however be too precise otherwise your field of potential candidates will be too narrow and your mind may be unable to create the necessary desire among this restricted handful of people.

If for example you are specifically stuck on the idea of a partner with blond hair then you may miss out on a more easily influenced but totally acceptable partner with dark hair.

Likewise if you ask for a person in a very narrow age group such as 35-40 you also create the same restrictions. It is much better to ask for a contact in the 30-45 age group.

This will give your mind more leeway in the number of potential people it can communicate with.

REMOTE VIEWERS AND INTENT

The remote viewers have found that the mind will follow strict instructions when it comes to remote viewing and remote influencing.

This professional group of people have found that the word "Intent" is the critical factor in mind work. If you convince your mind that you have an absolute intent to influence another person, by researching out details of their gestalt in advance, then it will take you seriously. The average mindset is used to us "wishing" things would happen.

Wishes are a non-emotive, non-specific non-command to the mind. When you prove to it that your desire to influence another person is not merely a "wish", then it will listen and act on instructions.

Once you have practiced and successfully used influencing techniques in a predetermined and planned manner then you will find yourself able to do the same thing almost instantaneously and without planning (such as in a supermarket)........because your mind has been conditioned to take your influencing seriously.

SUBJECTIVE COMMUNICATION

Clients who are familiar with Subjective Communication (a mild form of remote influencing) will be aware that the best time to affect another individual is at night during their dream periods. You program yourself (as you go to sleep) to wake up at the best possible time to mentally communicate with them then you do your "attraction" program.

Because of the emotive and acceptable nature of this type of programming (every normal individual wants love and affection) then you can break through to another persons mind at any time basically.......because most unattached individuals be amenable to this type of suggestion.

If I woke up in the middle of the night to find that a caring, loving unknown female was influencing me I would probably be quite flattered and somewhat delighted!

Unless of course it was the female dog next door which has taken quite a shine toward me!

Please be aware that the effect on the other person may not be dramatic........they may not instantly jump into your arms. But next time you see them you might just notice that they are somewhat friendlier.

And after a while they might well feel like jumping onto your lap but good manners and natural caution prevents them from doing this.

This is where your follow-up is vitally important. If you treat them with disdain, display uncouth manners or make ambiguous sexual innuendoes you will scare them off permanently.

Likewise, if you make an obvious pass at them or otherwise "come on" too strongly you may also scare them away.

The secret is to be very friendly and helpful....without expressing undue interest. Let nature take its course....let the relationship evolve naturally. Once it is underway your initial "spadework" is complete.

If they turn out to be the wrong person for you then a potential friendship will probably not evolve and they will quietly disappear out of your life.

The person that you are influencing will feel that their sudden interest in you is their own idea.

They will be totally unaware that it all originated in your mind....... unless you tell them! And if you do that....you will lose them forever, because nobody likes to feel that they have been manipulated.

You must keep the whole process secret. And I mean secret....don't even tell your dog!

If you are attempting to influence a person who you see regularly, say on the morning bus, then it may take some time for that person to react toward you.

Be patient. You might catch them looking at you and if they do just smile in a friendly manner. Don't go over and try to chat them up. It may be that you are both incompatible and if you realise that this is the case do not try and force the relationship.

But if the other person persists in showing an interest then all you can do is let nature take its course, as I mentioned before.

It is a proven fact that the last thing you think about before you go to sleep tends to carry over into your dreams. So if you are thinking about this special person you are likely to dream about them.

They will probably start to wonder why you have become so appealing but it is important not to try to force a relationship.

The trick is to be friendly, caring and sympathetic.

When you are first talking to them don't start raving on about yourself......display a genuine interest in what they have to say. Initially you should do more listening than talking.

The person you are influencing may be naturally shy and reluctant to approach you for this reason, even though they may want to. Make it easy for them by being friendly and helpful, but don't stare at them or exhibit too much interest.

Shy people tend to scare off easily.

Start off by being friendly and let it build from there.

If you are already married and have a partner who you are trying to influence then the procedure is different. You will already have close contact with this person so when you find that they become more amorous you will be able to handle the situation easily.

THE PROCESS

The visualisation/imagining process itself must be done in a quiet peaceful place.

It is probably better to do this in a dim light or in the dark.

You simply get yourself comfortable, close your eyes and start the process. Make sure you are in a situation where the telephone, doorbell, or noisy kids or neighbours will not distract you.

It is sometimes a good idea to listen to peaceful low-level music through a pair of headphones. If you have a tape of Pan-Flute music or seashore sounds this is better still. Eventually you will get to the point where you can go and sit in the bathroom and spend only a few minutes influencing an interesting person you have only just met....maybe at a party or function.

After you have developed your skills through practice you will be able to influence a person very quickly in this manner.

It may be better to do your influencing while you are in a sitting position......perhaps sitting up in bed. This is in case you fall asleep unexpectedly.

What you will be doing with this process is building an inner mental picture of a future reality. A reality that you desire to happen.

You are sharing this reality with the person of your choice and providing they feel comfortable with it......they are likely to accept it.

FIRST STEPS

The first thing to do is generate a mental gestalt of the person you are interested in.

If you have trouble with this remember the things you have noted down....such as the way they laugh or the colour of their hair.

You see yourself with this person as if it were happening in real life.

Remember when you focus intently on another individual you affect their brain waves and blood pressure.

You picture yourself with the person you desire in a very friendly non-threatening situation. Do not under any circumstances visualize them in a sensually amorous situation unless you are already closely connected with them, maybe as a husband or wife.

If you have already met or briefly talked to this person try and relive that event.

Try and remember the details and "live" through them again. It doesn't matter if you can't remember everything that happened. Just picture the person talking and the way they looked.

You might find yourself slipping into a daydream about them which is excellent because this will break through to their subconscious mind and impart your message quicker than normal. If you have met this individual on the bus or train then picture them in that same situation. They will be used to travelling by bus or train so won't feel threatened.

But if you start to picture them in a hot and erotic situation in your bedroom, they will be subconsciously uneasy and you will probably scare them off.

It is important to mentally place them in a situation that they are used to and feel happy with. If you are trying to influence someone you have only briefly glimpsed you will obviously have no idea of what it is they are comfortable with, so it will be best to picture them in a mutually acceptable place such as under a palm tree on a beautiful beach.

Most people like the concept of a romantic beach so this would be non-threatening.

If you already know the person quite well and have been in close proximity you might recall how they smell. And if you have touched them you might be able to recall how they felt. The more you can use in relation to your 5 senses the better your mental influencing will be.

If you are trying to influence an existing partner into becoming more amorous then you will probably be totally familiar with their feel, smell and overall appearance. You will also be familiar with how they sound when they talk.

This will give you quite an advantage when you are doing your "imagining" as there will be a number of familiar items you can easily picture in your minds eye.

REVIVING AN EXISTING RELATIONSHIP

If you are already in a relationship but things are not going well then you can use a more sensual form of mental influencing.

However you must not under any circumstances use the technique described below on a new contact.

This is the actual influencing for an existing partner:

If you imagine them in a swimming suit lying on a towel under a palm tree then you can now start to imagine you softly stroking their body with light, slow touches from your fingers. You will already be familiar with the type of touching your partner likes.

See yourself doing this in a non-threatening manner.

If possible "feel" your fingers stroking their body.

Now if you are doing this in the alpha state they will probably sense a slight tingling and start thinking of you. However if you do this in a theta state it will be as if you actually touched them and they might sit up suddenly to see who it was.

So if you are able to use the theta state then be extra cautious.

When you are mentally imagining someone with as much detail as you can muster....you are affecting them. If you add sensual touching in a non-threatening manner then you raise erotic feelings in that person and because of the connectedness of your two minds they will associate those pleasurable feelings with you!

Basically they become "turned on" in a very subtle and agreeable way.

Most normal active human beings appreciate the feeling of being aroused because this is the way nature intended it. It makes one feel warm and "glowy" when they are mildly aroused.

I personally have never met anyone who does not appreciate this feeling of erotic warmth.

When you imagine yourself being in a friendly relaxed place like a tropical beach, your mind easily slips into alpha. But if you imagine clearly the normal place you work or your normal home environment then your mind may have difficulty attaining the alpha state as there are a certain number of stresses associated with your work and home environment.

Therefore you mentally put yourself in an imagined peaceful place which has no historical stresses as far as you are concerned.

It is a good idea to spend a few days practicing your imaginary "safe" place so that you get the mental feel of it.

Picture the palm trees, the beach, the climate, etc. as clearly as you can.

Of course you may choose some scene other than a beach.

Maybe there was a peaceful place you used to visit as a child, which brings back fond memories. It might be a locality such as a bubbling brook or a peaceful stream.

Any environment which is serene and which you are familiar with would be suitable.

In fact it may be a place you have never visited but only "imagined" as your ideal spot.

Maybe you can cut a coloured picture out of a magazine which depicts such a setting.

I personally use a very beautiful spot on the North Shore beach above Noosa Heads in Queensland, Australia.

Each time I 4WD up this beach I tend to gravitate toward this particular spot.

It is my mental "escape" place, which I use any time I want to do a peaceful visualisation for some of my theta experiments.

The most important thing though is not to use your office or home to do these remote influencing projects.

One of the most important aspects of remote influencing is the feel of touch. It is important that you develop a "feel" of touching and stroking your existing partner.

In fact this can be more important than the actual visualisation.

You should imagine them as having the minimal clothing on. You use your imagined hand to gently stroke their arms then legs. Imagine your touch as slow and gentle. Mentally feel this touch if possible.

If you have trouble with this you can practice the sense of touch by visualising your self touching the soft fur of a cat, then an iceblock, then a glass window, etc.

You can touch these real objects first if you like then touch them again with your eyes closed. So if you are touching and stroking a pane of window glass you do this first with your eyes open then with them closed. Try and remember the feel. You might also touch a warm surface then do this again with your eyes closed. When you are touching another person you will normally detect a feeling of warmth.

So when you are stroking this imagined person sense the warmth from their body, the feel of their skin….and better still the pleasurable reaction from their body as you touch them.

Once you are comfortable with this basic touching you can then progress on to touching and stroking the more erotic parts of their body. You also might like to add mental kissing to this. Imagine yourself kissing their body…imagine the feel and taste.

Better still, imagine their reaction.

I want to stress that the above erotic process must only be applied to an existing partner who is already used to erotic activities with you. If you try this on a total stranger you will probably scare them off for life!

When you mentally "touch" someone in this manner you are creating a tremendously strong and very powerful link to that person. It is the way humans were designed to react to each other and happens at a subconscious level constantly between people.

The process I am explaining has been in existence since time began… there is nothing new about it. People erotically affect other people all the time. It is the way subconscious minds work. So if you are having philosophical troubles with what you are reading then please realize that you are involved in it all anyway, whether you agree with it or not.

What is new about all this is that it wasn't until quite recently that a handful of researchers became aware of actually what was happening and how it worked.

That is, the significance of subjective erotic communication had not been realised.

This report is designed to explain how to use and enhance the effect of this inherent natural human mental reaction.

But a lot of people will be very nervous about this concept so you must never mention it to anyone, particularly the person you are trying to influence.

The bottom line is to pretend you are actually there and proceed through all the touching, massaging and kissing that your existing partner is used to.

The interesting thing about this mental process is that many of us do this anyway.

It is a form of erotic day-dreaming. The only difference is that we are now doing it in a controlled and directed manner.

The big trick is not to rush things. If you are used to a passionate session lasting 15 minutes then make your mental session last 2-3 times as long. This is vitally important.

It is also important when doing these extended "sessions" that you do not become too excited yourself, otherwise you will leave the alpha/theta state and return to wide-awake beta. If you do feel yourself becoming aroused channel this energy toward your mental partner.

At the end of your session "see" your partner hugging and cuddling you. Respond in the same way.

If you are already married and have been using this influencing to try and rekindle a dying romance, then you are already in a position where you have close contact with that person and you will usually be the one they turn to with their sudden increased passion.

You are creating your own reality by mentally "practicing" a fully fledged romantic relationship in advance. You are covering all details and aspects of it in advance by mentally "sharing" it with your existing partner.

NEW AND EXISTING CASUAL RELATIONSHIPS

Once you have established contact with a new partner and the relationship is flourishing then there is probably no need to keep up the influencing, unless the relationship starts to falter. However should you become careless and by acting like an idiot treat your partner with disdain, the new relationship will fail of its own accord.

No amount of mind power can overcome bad manners and poor social skills.

Once you carry out these exercises a few times you will probably note that the next time you physically see this new potential partner they may give you a quizzical look....one of puzzlement and interest. You may note that their body language is strange and you will probably find that they are quite receptive if you should go over and talk to them.

You will also probably notice that they appear to be waiting for you to say or do something. That is, they are open to an approach from you.

What has happened is that they have developed a subconscious interest in you but may be reluctant to make any "move" because they cannot quite understand their feelings. Something does not feel quite the same but they cannot put their finger on it.

However if you then make a polite non-threatening move you will likely find this quite acceptable.

You might suggest a coffee or a light lunch in a place of their choice. Do not attempt to persuade them to come to a place of your choice.... this might be seen as subconsciously threatening. Whatever you do or say......leave them feeling comfortable.

The feelings they start to have about you will appear to come from within their own body and mind. They will have no idea that these influences are external unless you tell them.

I should point out here that there is no way you can mentally persuade another individual to do things with you that they would not normally do of their own volition. That is, you will not have them in a hypnotic trance.

However providing you are physically and socially acceptable to them you should experience no problems. Don't forget that 99% of all individuals desire affection and romance. It is just that you are using controlled mental techniques to provide what they desire. If for example you are chasing a particularly attractive man....along with half the other girls in the office.......then you are the one who will win his affections......all else being equal.

SUBJECTIVE EROTIC COMMUNICATION

If you want to contact this other person during their normal dream periods at night then you use the standard pre-programmed alpha technique as follows:

As you are going to sleep at night keep repeating over and over to yourself ……*"I will wake up at the best time for contact with (their name or general description) and I will remember why I have woken up"*……….

When you wake up some time during the night you will then run through your influencing program as described earlier. It is probably best to sit up in bed to do this and maybe leave the bed light on…..so you don't accidentally fall back to sleep.

What will happen is that the other person will start to dream about you and this attraction will play on their subconscious mind.

It may even be more effective to do your influencing during the night as you will capture their full attention during their non-stressed dream periods.

You may have to keep this influencing up for several days, or a week, or maybe even longer before the other person lets you know that they are available.

The main sign is that they will become more affectionate toward you.

They will be comfortable near you, providing you don't scare them away with macho talk or neurotic behaviour. It might be that they consider you "not their type" so you will have this mental hurdle to overcome first.

Another good idea is to do your influencing as you fall asleep at night. This line of thinking is likely to carry over into the first few moments of sleep which is in the theta area. As such you will add a burst of theta energy to your message and this will really break through to them.

OTHER INFLUENCING CONCEPTS

If you want to use this influencing technique for things other than romance then you use exactly the same techniques. Suppose you wanted a promotion at work then you would clearly visualise your boss clapping you on your back and congratulating you.

You picture the event as having happened.

See yourself phoning your wife/husband to tell them the good news.

See yourself doing all the things that you would do if you actually got the promotion. In this case however you would not use a palm covered beach as a scenario…….you would use the place where the boss feels most comfortable…..his or her own office!

This is the place where they feel in control.

Let us suppose you wanted a new car.

You would picture the car yard where the vehicle of your choice is on display.

You would "see" the salesman demonstrating the car and eventually handing you the keys. You see yourself drive away to show the car to your friends. However you would not attempt to picture where the money is going to come from to pay for this. Let your mind psychokinetically arrange this in its own way.

During your "picturing" you would notice the smell of the new upholstery, the feel of the steering wheel, the sound of the engine, etc.

Once you have done your projective influencing then stop thinking about it.

If you keep consciously thinking about your desire then you are indicating to your subconscious a "future tense" with regard to manifestation. That is.....you are retaining the thought on the "wish list" rather than treating it as having happened.

I have noticed this consistently with the slots.....if I constantly use PK to try and affect the machine nothing happens. But if I give the machine a full on "PK blast" then let go the thought...it often pays out. This is what happens when you play a machine for some time with an increasing level of frustration (masses of theta waves) then decide to give it one more spin and walk away in disgust.

You often find to your amazement that the machine pays out significantly on this final spin. This is your conscious mind "letting go".

Your mind will produce results providing your desire is focused and filled with emotion. Emotion is the driving force and fortunately it is human nature to become emotional about eroticism.

SUCCESS LIMITING FACTORS AND SUMMARY

If after a couple of weeks of influencing another person nothing appears to be happening then it is likely that this person is not for you.

It may be nothing to do with the way you look or act but more to do with their own personal belief system. They may have religious restrictions or peer group restrictions. Or they may simply have been "burnt" in a previous physical relationship and need time out for a while.

There also may be a maturity problem where they feel you are out of their preferred age group and they would be concerned about what their friends and family would say and think.

You may want to give the mind power a break for a few days then start again. This will give the other persons subconscious mind time to settle down.

The overall thing is to visualise that the other person feels comfortable and non-threatened in your presence. It is most important to create scenarios that feel safe and accommodate the expectations of the other person.

The technique can also be used to meet new unknown people and is really an advanced version of Subjective Communication.

In this case you would clearly imagine the type of person you would like to meet.

Do not be too specific otherwise your choice of potential partners will be limited. In this case you visualise them in a scenario which you normally frequent....such as a nightclub.

It is important to visualise a public place that your potential partner would normally visit.

You visualise this desirable individual appearing in front of you and talking to you. What this does is pull potential partners out of the woodwork and gives you a chance to meet them. For reasons that they don't understand they will be attracted to you and all you have to do is be friendly and non-threatening.

If the locality is a club which has dancing then so much the better because they will probably not object to dancing with you and this gives you bodily contact. You will then be able to sense their true reaction to you.

There is one word of caution I can offer however and this is watch out for a married person merely looking for a fling.

When influencing unknown potential partners you are likely to attract people in this category. It is their desire to have an affair and their subconscious can be ready and willing to accept any likely candidate that comes along. That is.....YOU!

THE DANGERS OF AMOROUS REMOTE INFLUENCING

The only real danger is that you will influence someone to the point where they simply will not leave you alone. In the case of a woman she may attract someone who turns out to be a stalker, or in the case of a guy he may attract a lady who develops a neurotic obsession with him.

The easiest thing to do in either case is another batch of remote influencing where you mentally portray yourself as being unfriendly, bossy, neurotic, uncouth, sexually cold, or just plain obnoxious.

If all else fails mentally impart to them that you may have given them an infectious disease. Visualise clearly the medical implications and outcome for that person.

If that doesn't reduce their ardour to zero I don't know what will!!

FINAL SUMMARY

Relax into an alpha or theta state.

Place the person in a mental environment that they would normally feel comfortable with.

If the person is a new contact then use a mutually non-threatening environment such as a beach or stream.

If the person is already well known to you then use the mental environment that they are used to, such as their office.

Use imaginary finger and massage touches on the person and mentally see them responding. You only do this with an existing partner.

Proceed further with imaginary oral contact and intimate touching.

Carry on this procedure for 2-3 times longer than you would do in real life.

At the finish of your influencing session see them hugging and thanking you.

Good luck !!!

22

TIME, SPACE, MATTER, ENERGY, CONSCIOUSNESS AND INTENT

Several hundred years ago scientists considered that the weight of an object was fixed and absolute. Then Isaac Newton demonstrated that an object weighed less at the top of a mountain than it did at sea level, where gravity was stronger. (Weight is a measure of the force that gravity exerts on an object). So a new term was coined ..... mass. The mass of an object was considered constant, but its weight varied with height. The higher the object above the earth's surface, the less was the effect of gravity, hence the less its weight. But height did not affect the "mass" of an object.

So for a long time mass was considered absolute. Then along came Einstein with his relativity theory. He proved that mass actually varies depending on the speed it was traveling. The closer a mass gets to the speed of light (186,000 miles per second) the greater its mass becomes. When it reaches the speed of light its mass becomes infinite and as it would take an infinite force to accelerate an infinite mass then nothing solid can exceed the speed of light.

So speed became more important than mass which had become more important than weight.

At the same time Einstein found that when an object travels very fast, close to the speed of light, time slows down so the astronauts who traveled to the moon and back have aged a fraction of a second less than us earthbound mortals. If an astronaut traveled outward for 5 years at near the speed of light and then turned around and made the same journey back to earth he would be 10 years older. But on earth something like 50 - 100 years would have passed.

So everything is relative to speed. Both time and mass are determined by speed.

Nothing in our universe is quite what it seems. The mindpower gurus who can operate mentally in theta or some other altered consciousness state believe that they enter a time-free zone where they can see past/present/future events with equal clarity. It has always been considered that time flows forward, like an arrow from a bow but the relatively new science of Quantum Physics indicates that it may well flow in the opposite direction also. And the more the scientific world delves into the strangeness of Quantum Physics, the weirder are the things being discovered.

It basically started out with the aperture test whereby a stream of light is shone thru a narrow slit on to a screen. The light either showed up as a particle image on the screen or as a waveform, depending on what the experimenter expected! And there is now a line of thought that wonders if the normal state of events is the waveform, which materialises into particle form only when required by consciousness.

When one considers the vast empty spaces inside supposedly solid matter, there may be some merit in this particle materialisation concept. If you think about all the planets in our solar system and the vast distances between them, then reduce the size of our solar system down to that of an atom, it becomes easier to comprehend the spaces inside each atom. In fact, 99.99999999999......% of a supposedly solid object is space. It has been estimated that if all the "spaces" in the known universe were removed and only "solid" material left, then you could hold this in the palm of your hand.

The piece of paper you are holding in front of you at this instant is made up of mainly blank space. It consists of subatomic particles with vast spaces around them. In fact the whole known universe .... and everything in it .... is made up of the same material ..... subatomic particles. If you raise your eyes from this page and look around you, everything you see is made of subatomic particles, even your pet cat, which is mainly empty space. (Something you've always suspected!) Everything is the same ..... except ..... Human Consciousness !!

CONSCIOUS AWARENESS IS A "STAND-ALONE" EVENT.

Obviously this consciousness is a superior event compared to all the mundane subatomic sameness surrounding it. No wonder that controlled consciousness can influence the lifeless brethren we call inert matter! That is, there is no reason whatsoever why a human mind cannot control matter. The main reason we can't do it, is because we don't expect to!

This situation is the same as the scientists with the aperture test..... they get what they expect in the way of results. It takes a major change in the mental operating process to be able to influence matter to the point where you can bend a spoon with mind-power alone, but the process can be learnt! If you think deeply about this, you will probably conclude that there is no reason why the superior stand-alone event of consciousness should not be able to directly influence the atomic structure of lifeless matter.

Einstein has proven that energy and mass are interchangable (as in a nuclear reaction) and various universities and laboratories have been able to either measure or calculate the force generated by a human mind (as in psychokinetic experiments). The obvious conclusion here is that, as mass and energy are interchangable, the energy generated by human consciousness can be converted into its mass equivalent, the format of which is controlled and directed by the most extraordinary of higher-consciousness processes ..... VISUALISATION !!!

When a human mind clearly and continually visualises an end result, with deep emotion and concentrated intent, then the formatted energy generated is converted into its mass equivalent - ie. the result desired. As strange as this may sound, it is scientifically feasible and generally accepted as truth among the mind power people and top motivators.

In our universe .... nothing is what it seems!!

When we are born we are totally unprogrammed. We are like a computer without the software. As we grow we are trained to recognise a common reality. That is, every sane human being adopts a "common denominator" when it comes to reality. The "window of reality" is basically the same for the entire human race. Your reality training teaches you that mankind cannot walk on white hot coals with a temperature 5 times that of boiling water! Yet it is done! The same training tells you that you cannot bend metal with your mind. Yet there are at least two "schools" in the US teaching just this. Everybody "knows" that you cannot sit in a chair, relax, and clearly visualise some distant scene, in past, present or future time with a high degree of accuracy. Yet there are people who do this remote viewing for a living! Major corporations employ them to fill in information gaps.

The reality window, as we accept it, is no longer valid.

Under certain conditions, your mind can "escape" from the restriction of this universal window. And as an increasing number of individuals experience these "impossible" alternatives, universal human consciousness changes. When a critical number of people can achieve these alternative realities, then, like the 100th monkey theory, everyone will suddenly "know" that these things can be done. Sheldrake's Morphogenic Field theory explains how this is achieved in real life.

Nothing is what it seems !!!

For the past 100 years or so western civilisation has been technology orientated. The higher the technology, the better we like it. But technology is logic based. And our logic is based on our reality window. If we become aware of a different form of technology which is not only outside our logic base, but also can't be replicated reliably and worse still, cannot be measured on conventional instruments, then we panic! It is outside our reality window. But such technologies already exist. They are the science of the 21st century! An example of one such technology using touch-sensing is explained below.

For example it has always been considered that time is a constant. That is, the seconds, minutes and hours tick along at the same speed for everyone.

But an extremely clever device has been invented which measures micro-small distortions in time. When a small mechanical or chemical event is examined it has been found that time is thin around the "cause" and dense around the resultant event. It seems that time may be variable !!

NOTHING IS WHAT IT SEEMS !!!!!!

And if you'd like a real life example of this strange mind technology, which appears to be based on INTENT, then read the following:

THE AMAZING HIERONYMOUS MACHINE

On September 27th, 1949 a US patent was granted for a radically unusual detection and analysis device. It was assigned to one Dr. Thomas Galen Hieronymous of ADVANCED SCIENCES RESEARCH AND DEVELOPMENT INC. at Lakemont, Georgia.

This machine incorporated a tactile sensor which caused a change of sensation in the operators fingertips when it was tuned to resonance with the object being analyzed.

Until this point the standard instrument indicator mechanism had been an audible sound or a visual indicator such as a needle deflection (as in a multimeter) or a flashing light. (There was one that worked on smell too.......usually when a device containing a power transformer was plugged into the wrong voltage!)

Hieronymous came up with something totally different. His device worked on the sense of TOUCH. That is, when the circuitry sensed a "signal" the otherwise smooth connection between the operators fingers and a "touch pad" became "tacky" or suddenly developed a "sticky" feel. The effect was rapid enough to prove useful as an alternative measuring mechanism.

Hieronymous indicated that the device was intended for the detection and analysis of minerals utilizing a new aspect of the physical universe which he called "eloptic radiation".

The device uses a very basic pickup coil, a simple 3 transistor amplifier (instead of valves) and a tuning device consisting of a rotating optical prism.

The output sensing "touch pad" was described as a TACTILE DETECTOR.

The sample of metal or mineral to be analyzed is placed within the "sensing coil" and the mechanism is "tuned" with the rotating prism. The signal is then amplified (and there is something very strange about this which I'll explain later) and the output is fed to a flat wound coil of wire underneath a flat square of glass or plastic. This is the touch pad. The fingertips are placed lightly on this pad and slowly moved back and forth while the tuning prism is being rotated. When the circuit is "resonant" (for want of a better word) the feeling between the fingertips and the touchpad changes.

The dial of the machine is pre-calibrated for various known elements so when the sample of an unknown substance is placed in the pickup coil the presence of specific elements can be fairly accurately determined. Not only this but the actual percentage of materials can be determined.

Sounds ridiculous....doesn't it?

Well....around 25 years ago when I owned an electronics design lab one of our regular customers (a physics tutor at the local university) bought in one of these machines and after demonstrating it asked me what I thought of it.

I can tell you now I didn't think of it. The machine was obviously a fake.

Only problem was...I could make it work accurately. So could my co-designers.

This caused mass consternation in our laboratory. We built one ourselves and I had trouble stopping the staff from playing with it when they were supposed to be working on time-sensitive circuit designs.

The device does not appear to operate on any known principle of physics but oddly enough in the past 25 years I have heard very little about it. At the time we assumed that this was some major breakthrough however little appears to have come of it.

There is basically no reason for it to work at all......but it does! Thousands of these devices have been built over the years and most operators appear to get passable results. Even profound skeptics have had success in some instances. (We were in this category!)

The sensing pad appears to produce a slightly different sensation for different people....but the recurring comment was that it felt like the pad had suddenly been covered in tar when the circuit was tuned. When it was detuned the "sticky" feeling disappeared and the original "smooth feeling" returned.

The other strange thing about this device is that the circuit components are totally non-critical. Any broadband medium frequency amplifier will do. The pickup coil is not critical....and neither is the touch sensor pad.

Once the machine is calibrated, say, for gold, then any other person operating the device will get a response for gold at exactly the same prism setting. That is, the tactile response will occur at the same place on the pre-calibrated dial.

Figure that one out!   (I can't!)

But....if you think all of the above is a bit far fetched and ridiculous.... you'll be even more stunned as you read the following:

Around 2 months after the physics tutor introduced us to the Hieronymous Machine he wandered in with another of these devices. He told us that this one was an improved model and asked if we would like to try it. By this time my super-skeptical staff were thoroughly puzzled and seemed quite keen to "give it a go".

We got the same results as before, with each of the staff noticing the "tacky" effect at the correct pre-calibrated points when different minerals were inserted into the pickup coil. We all agreed it worked at least as accurately as the earlier model. At this point the owner undid the screws on the top of the device and removed the lid....and we all did something we never should have done......

We looked inside......

All the circuitry had been removed and in its place was a CIRCUIT DIAGRAM drawn on a piece of white card. The wires from the input coil were attached to the edge of this card to coincide with the circuit diagram input....and likewise with the output connection. The diagram included the standard symbol for a battery.

That is...the entire "innards" was merely a circuit diagram.

Now I want you to picture this: Here were four of the top electronic designers in the country, who specialized in designing circuitry that other people found too complicated to tackle. We had in front of us a circuit diagram which was acting as if it were a bunch of transistors and capacitors. It was totally beyond anything we had collectively experienced. Then the physics tutor really upset us. He asked us to each try the "machine" once more to ascertain that it was really working. It was. He then took a rubber eraser out of his pocket and rubbed out the schematic battery symbol, so that the circuit diagram had no apparent battery. He then asked us all to try the machine again. IT DIDN'T WORK!

He then redrew the battery symbol in...and... it WORKED AGAIN!

All this in front of intelligent well-educated top flight electronic designers.

In recent years I have thought deeply about this device and concluded it worked on HUMAN INTENT. It used the power of symbols to create a bridge in the operators mind somehow.

I have never seen one of these devices since that day.....and I'm not sure if I want to. But if this subject is of interest....and you want to build one of these "impossible" machines, then you might like to get hold of a paperback book by rocket engineer G.H. Stine which gives precise constructional details for these Hieronymous devices plus other psychokinetic devices. It's called MIND MACHINES YOU CAN BUILD and it's published in the USA by TOP OF THE MOUNTAIN PUBLICATIONS....Florida.

There are many strange anomalies out there in the world of mind-power. And I'm certain there are many more waiting to be discovered.

23

THE LAW OF
ATTRACTION

**If we apply our mind correctly we can become <u>anybody we
wish</u>.**

Everything that happens to you is caused by what is in your mind.

That is….what you expect to happen to you.

Your mind is like a mental magnet attracting to it that which it has
been preprogrammed to attract.

You become what you consistently think about. Your thoughts become
your future reality.

This has been known for hundreds of years but was kept as fairly
secretive knowledge until around 50 years ago when a few deep thinking
individuals published data on this phenomenon. The dedicated mind-
power people picked up on it some 25 years ago and since then it has
slowly seeped into public awareness.

I was personally made aware of this concept in 1970 and have been
using it ever since with sometimes quite outstanding results. In fact the
vast majority of success I have had since then can be put down to utilizing
the Law of Attraction.

If you think personal abundance your mind will provide it. But is you think fearful thoughts then you mind will attract fearful situations.

You have to focus on what you want. Do not focus on what you don't want because the Law of Attraction is working for you one hundred percent of the time, 24 hours a day.

The vast majority of individuals think in a confused manner because their thoughts are not focused on a specific end result.

You have probably noticed yourself that is you focus intently on some event with deep passion and strong emotion then it tends to happen the way you want.

Almost every sane individual has had a positive event like this happen to them in the past.

Negative individuals may find them difficult to recall but that successful event will be there somewhere.

Your life is a physical manifestation of your existing thought patterns.

We do not understand how this process works but most people don't understand how a TV works.....and they still use one!!

The Law of Attraction works slowly, not usually instantly.

If the required results happened instantly you would rightfully regard this as a miracle.

In fact many years ago I had a required event happen in three days. It was so fast that I had trouble believing it. I went from stony broke to having $40,000 in my bank account in three days flat! I still find this result incredible when I think back on it.

I was in a totally desperate situation and focused non-stop on the result I needed. And it worked!!

Look hard at your current position. It has evolved from your previous thought processes.

If you want to change your future from the path it is currently on then you will find that it takes a little effort to set up a new "mental regime". The average person has an estimated 50,000 to 60,000 individual thought processes per day. Usually confused waffly thoughts with no coherent pattern.

Good positive feelings make you feel good while bad thoughts usually make you feel depressed.

The trick here is to think deeply about all the good things that have happened in your life and project them into the future. Expect these good events to happen frequently in the future.

If after you get out of bed in the morning negative unwelcome events start to happen then do something that makes you feel cheerful and positive. Maybe play music you particularly enjoy or go into a shop and buy that item you have been thinking about for some time.

That is.....break the negative pattern.

Picture exactly what it is you want. Think carefully about it and write it down. Cut pictures of a similar item out of a magazine and place it where you can see it daily, maybe on your fridge door or the inside of your bathroom door.

Throw up pictures in your minds eye of this desired event or object.

Daydream about it. This can be an extremely powerful use of the Law of Attraction.

While you are daydreaming you are usually in the alpha state and if you are throwing up pictures of what you want then you are really forcing your message into the universe.

You need to generate feelings and emotions related to your requirements.

Life is like taking a night flight in a commercial aircraft. You know where you want to go and despite the fact that you can't actually experience your journey visually the competent people in the cockpit get you there. You are not aware of all the tricky processes involved in night flying but you have total confidence in the end process.

All you had to do was to determine where you wanted to be on a specific day or time.

When you visualize an end result with deep yearning and emotion your journey starts. Suddenly out of the blue you arrive......sometimes quite suddenly and unexpectedly.

The trick is to generate the mental picture, the absolute yearning and the deep emotion.

Then everything happens automatically.

Unfortunately a lot of individuals start out correctly then let their attention wander so the mind gets conflicting messages. Or they become bored with the process or otherwise lose interest. Unless you focus intently on the desired outcome right through to the end the Law of Attraction will not work.

Some individuals can attract regular car parks.....right where they want them……even in busy traffic periods. I used to do this consistently which never ceased to amaze my fellow passengers.

Other people are quite surprised when just after thinking deeply about a friend….that friend rings them out of the blue!

These are examples of the Law of Attraction and Subjective Communication at work.

In exactly the same manner you can attract debt…..or no debt. The choice is yours.

Your overall health and financial situation are the result of your previous dedicated thought patterns. So if you're not happy….change your thinking.

One of the best tricks to really get yourself fired up is to make a written list of previous successes. Dwell on these for a while then make a list of exactly what it is you want out of life. Set up your mental program to encompass your new list and keep mentally referring back to your older success list. In effect you will be projecting these previous successes into your future.

If you analyse your past thoroughly you will probably be quite amazed at the number of successes you have had. The mind tends to forget these and focus only on the negative events. Tie your past successes and your new required successes together in one mental image which will flow into the future.

VISUALISE INTENTLY WITH DEEP FOCUS, POWERFUL FEELING AND THE STRONGEST EMOTION YOU CAN MUSTER.

Don't be surprised if a near miracle occurs and the desired event materializes spontaneously in the most unexpected manner!!

You figure out exactly what it is you want then via your mental processing turn it over to the universe. Let the universe figure out how to achieve it. Don't try to help in the actual materialization methodology.

There are millions of individuals alive today who have successfully made this process work for them. You read about these successes every day in the newspapers.

Nature is naturally abundant and life is intended to be the same.

WHAT EVER THE MIND OF MAN CAN CONCEIVE
AND BELIEVE, IT CAN ACHIEVE.

24

SUMMARY

The material you have just read is the result of over 20 years of serious mind power research. For years I ran a research laboratory with a small dedicated staff. We made some amazing "world first" discoveries. One of these was the profound realization that luck is an individual's personal resonance with the environment. We soon realized that luck is totally controlled by the individuals mind and in any given situation each and every human mind is capable of manifesting enormous runs of luck.

Some people are naturally lucky in that they are more closely resonant with their environment than others.

However we also found that luck tends to fade in and out in some sort of rhythm and in some cases can be predicted and enhanced.

The human mind is capable of accessing events in the distant future and past. It appears to be in subconscious contact with all other minds and shares racial and current knowledge.

This is automatically processed below our threshold of awareness.

The Russian States were doing serious telepathy experiments in the 1960's. Much of their research was sponsored by the Iron Curtain Governments. They produced quite stunning results in some of their experiments. They basically proved that under certain conditions in-dividuals could telepathically communicate with each other, sometimes below the level of conscious awareness. The initial motivation apparently was to telepathically communicate with their underwater submarines. Standard radio communication was not possible underwater. There are reports of experimentation with orbiting spacecraft also.

It is interesting to note that the Russian public in general believe that telepathy exists as opposed to western society individuals who in general don't believe in it.

The western world never experimented in this manner because of lack of government encouragement and sponsorship. It was left to a handful of private western organizations to do this research using their own limited funds.

It slowly dawned on the American Government that Russia was light-years ahead of them in psychic research and they scurried to catch up. Remote Viewing and other disciplines were hence born sponsored in part by the government via the military.

There is a slowly expanding awareness among the western public that the mind is capable of far more than we have believed. Closed minds are beginning to open.

Quantum physicists are discovering that consciousness appears to have a noticeable affect on sub-atomic particles and in fact focused conscious-ness may actually help convert matter from its basic energy units. These are stunning concepts.

Matter in effect becomes solidified energy in the same manner that steam can be snap-frozen into solid ice.

And you are capable of sharing in this ground breaking research be-cause you already own the necessary laboratory.....*your own mind* !!!

Those dedicated mind researchers like myself who have spent years learning how to drop to low delta brain frequencies (while still retaining conscious beta awareness) all report that the delta experience is a marvel-ous personal event. While in deep delta I have to give myself hypnotic commands if I wish to move a muscle otherwise I am too relaxed to do so. If I want to change the position of a leg I instruct my mind to "move my leg". If I want to open my eyes to make an observation I need to issue the instruction "open eyes".

Likewise for closing them. In fact I have noticed a very strange occurrence here. If after my eyes are open I try to close then without the hypnotic command then my stomach "lurches". That is….it jumps. I think this is one of the main Chakra points. I have no explanation for this.

The problem with delta is that you can get so low that you interfere with your "core" memory, to use a computer term. I have heard of some nasty side effects from delta practitioners.

To all intents and purposes medium to deep theta will give you all the benefits you need. There is no practical advantage to lowering your brain frequencies any further.

Burst of theta caused by anger or frustration can often produce psychokinetic effects.

You might have noticed this when gambling at slot machines. You might have played one particular machine for a while and had almost no wins. You decide to give up in disgust and frustration. You give the machine one more spin before moving to another one and to your pleasant surprise it pays you a good win. This is theta based psychokinetics at work triggering off a "burst of luck".

The lighter state of alpha is the daydream state which we drop into many times in the average day. You can achieve a lot of beneficial effects using this light state without spending several years learning deep theta.

Deep delta took me around 10 years of constant daily practice. You have to be really serious about mind-power if you want to play round with delta.

As mentioned in the chapter on Alpha the easiest way you can learn Alpha techniques at home is to make yourself a training cassette. After a while you ignore the cassette and practice the Alpha induction technique mentally.

After several months of constant practice you will find that you can induce the Alpha state quite rapidly and once you have thoroughly learned the technique you will have it for the rest of your life.

It's rather like learning to ride a pushbike. Even if you don't ride a bike for 20 years or more you will find that you quickly recapture the skill because it has been ingrained into your system.

As you practice your Alpha skills you will find that you drop lower and lower in brain frequency (while still maintaining conscious awareness) until you start to reach down to the top of the Theta range. The ability to drop to these lower brain frequency levels while maintaining conscious Beta awareness is often referred to *as mind awake body asleep.*

It is a very peaceful enjoyable experience and has been used by eastern civilizations for hundreds of years.

As with all new training exercises you must not stress your development. If you do an aerobics course you start out in an easy manner then progress on to the harder material.

It is exactly the same with personal mind-power programs. You start off gently and give the program plenty of breaks so your mind can slowly adjust to it. Remember your mind has operated in a fixed pattern for many years and it may rebel if you try to advance it too rapidly.

You will be slowly teaching your mind what you expect of it. Quite naturally there will be some resistance at first but after a while the new programming will be accepted.

When I first started learning Alpha I would close my eyes and press the eyelids with my thumbs. After a short period of time I would perceive flashes of iridescent blue or mauve colours which I told my mind to associate with Alpha. After a few weeks I was able to trigger the Alpha state off fairly quickly by merely pressing my eyelids for 30 seconds or so. I found this fairly handy when I was playing slot machines late at night waiting for a predicted luck cycle to occur. I would become tired so I would retire to the nearest bathroom and while sitting in the most comfortable position I could achieve relax and press my eyelids to induce Alpha. After 10 minutes I would stand up and return to the casino feeling somewhat refreshed. I also used this method while I was driving long distances in Australia. I would pull over to a lay by and use this method to induce Alpha for 10-15 minutes. I would then feel reasonably fresh for the next couple of hours. Some of these trips that I did were extremely long involving up to 30 hours continuous driving and my Alpha relaxation helped immensely.

These trips were mainly to the South Australian Opal mining town of Coober Pedy.

We used remote viewing and pendulum techniques to locate the "potch" that signified opal deposits. We located quite a lot of potch deposits and some of it contained valuable opal. Without these mind power techniques we would have had no better chance than any of the hundreds of other hopeful opal miners. Our techniques gave us an advantage over the others which paid off in cold hard cash. Our team was only there part time for 15 months and we found more potch than many of those who had been exploring for 10 years or more. We lived underground due to the dessert heat and I found the experience very fulfilling. We had no TV signal out there so when we had guests and visitors we gave them a small pickaxe and they tapped away at our lounge wall of clay which we had left uncovered. It was always possible that they might find a small amount of opal so it kept them amused!

Personal mind-power gives you a feeling of control. You tend to feel that you are not alone in the universe because it "connects" you. Once you have successfully tried some of the processes in this book your self confidence increases and you tend to suffer less stress.

The more you experiment the better life becomes. You also become increasingly aware of things happening around you which you would normally have ignored. Your general awareness and intuition improve particularly if you have been practicing remote viewing techniques. Remote viewing is really just controlled intuition. The more you practice this discipline the better your everyday intuition becomes. And this enhanced ability tends to stay with you for the rest of your life!

In all the years I have been involved with mind-power I have never come across any downside. That is there have been no negative aspects that caused me concern.

I did run into a few problems with my deep delta experiments but once I was made aware of the situation I desisted for a while.

It is for this reason that I recommend that readers of this book focus on alpha and theta only.

Once you get right into your meditation practice you will probably start to become aware of strange synchronistic events that you would otherwise have not noticed.

These events in your life have probably always been there but you have not become aware of them. Once you become aware and start to think deeply about their possible significance you may find that they tend to lead you in a specific direction in life......usually to your advantage.

IGNORE THESE SIGNPOSTS AT YOUR OWN PERIL !!!

So if a series of strange semi-connected (synchronistic) events occur pay particular attention as this is likely to be your subconscious giving you directions.

A lot of individuals start off their mind practice programs then give up on them fairly quickly. It appears that they expect "instant" results and this doesn't normally happen except with Subjective Communication which can quite often miraculously work the first time you try it.

The trick is to keep practicing your chosen mind discipline. Even if you become bored with the process **keep at it.**

In due course you will notice the process starting to work.

I had a lot of trouble when I first started dream control experiments. I fed a repeating message on to a cassette tape calling for a specific style of dream. I played this tape as I went to sleep at night and waited breathlessly for results. Nothing happened for a while and it wasn't until the tenth night that I had the required dream. I was able to remember it quite vividly in the morning.

My point here is that you have to persevere if you want serious results.

Sometimes the required events happen so rapidly you regard them as miracles!

But most often they happen in their own good time.

It is very important that while you are running personal mind enhancement programs you do not tell others about it. Almost invariably you will receive negative feedback and sometimes outright hostility. And you can point out to intensely religious individuals that God gave us these potential abilities but we normally don't bother to use them!

The world of applied mind-power can be quite strange. As in the Law of Attraction whereby you attract positive events you will find that other potential mind-power graduates suddenly appear in your life. No particular reason. They just appear.

It is likely that as we are all subconsciously connected then some of these individuals feel compelled to be at a certain place at a certain time……and "accidentally" run into you.

This has happened so many times in my life that I have ceased being amazed.

Like minds tend to gravitate together.

When I was running my advanced mind seminars in Australia a few years ago individuals who I had never heard of contacted me out of the blue to buy a seminar ticket. They had heard about my seminars from a "friend of a friend" and felt compelled to attend. These seminars were almost always booked out yet I did virtually no promotional advertising.

This was direct mind-to-mind contact and it appears to work extremely well among the mind-power enthusiasts.

Once you become deeply involved in the mind field you can expect some very strange experiences in that strangers will arrive unexpectedly to help fulfill your dreams. Required events will "just happen" in a way that will sometimes leave you breathless.

People you have never met before will go totally out of their way to help you. At first you might be somewhat suspicious and find the situation unnerving but after a while you will grow used to these strange events and learn to expect them in the future.

The Law of Attraction appears to work in a vastly stronger manner among individuals involved in mind-power, probably because we are dealing with mind enhancement processes which subconsciously attract like minds.

I have had the most extraordinary contacts with other individuals......
just when I needed them the most.

At one point I was trying to find a copy of an out-of-print book relating to psychic discoveries in Russia. I had tried all my email contacts and library services without success. Anyway a couple of months later I was driving on a long trip in Australia and as I passed through a township I noticed a small café which stood out for some reason and I decided to stop for a sandwich. I bought the sandwich and walked outside and noticed a secondhand bookshop right next door. I walked in and started to browse through the books when to my utter amazement I discovered a copy of the book I had been searching for. Not only that but it was in almost mint condition.

I was seriously impressed with the way my mind manipulated events to supply me with that rare book!!

Once you start on your mind programs it may take a little while for things to start to "fire" up but then again you might achieve fairly rapid "spontaneous" results.

I have seen some amazing results from the first-time use of Subjective Communication.

Quite often you may experience the "novice effect" whereby you achieve spectacular results on the first try. Then results drop off dramatically and recover slowly over the months. This is sometimes referred to as "beginners luck".

The point here is that the beginner has a burst of luck on their first try and this would give them confidence for the future. At least they know what results to expect down the line.

Experiment carefully with the mind programs of your choice. If you notice any unwelcome side effects such as tiredness or mild confusion then back off for a short period. Remote Viewing can rip mental energy out of your system to the point where you can become quite confused for a short period afterwards. Your conscious awareness can fly right out the window and you will need an extended quiet period to recover.

If we are in a normal health condition our consciousness awareness is usually fairly consistent but if we are suffering from ill health or some form of mental stress then we can make bad mistakes based on the fact that our conscious awareness drops way down the scale. This happens too when we are overtired.

It is often misunderstood that while our IQ factor (intelligence quotient) remains fairly constant our CA (conscious awareness factor) varies all over the place. I have made some serious mistakes under these conditions then next day wondered what was the matter with me for this sudden burst of "stupidity".

The trick is to become consciously aware of your limitations and adjust your activities to allow for your CA.

Experiment carefully......have fun....and aim for the stars!!!!!!

The day you start your mind enhancement program is the day your life changes forever.

BONUS INFORMATION

Over the years I have written a number of reports that have helped the readers enjoy a better lifestyle by removing the confusion from their lives and clarifying their aims.

Four of the best reports appear on the following pages. These are a free bonus for readers of this book.

GROUND ZERO

STRUGGLE VERSUS SUCCESS

COME ALIVE!

HOW TO HAVE A FANTASTIC DAY.... every day!!

GROUND ZERO
A BREATH OF FRESH AIR

HAVE YOU EVER WATCHED A CHILD GROW THROUGH ITS FORMATIVE PERIOD FROM 2-5 YEARS OF AGE?

When the child first awakens in the morning it feels a sense of magic and wonderment in the air. Everything is larger than life to a young child. Every fresh awakening promises new joys....new hopes....new wonders.... and new fascinations. To a toddler, each new day brings the promise of magic!

Until they enter the schooling system. Where over a period of 12 years or so they are taught the basic survival requirements of the society in which they live........and........existing knowledge! Near the end of their schooling they are given exams and if they have absorbed enough conventional existing knowledge ...they pass!

They emerge from the schooling system with little idea of how to create new concepts.

It is comparable to the situation of a baker making bread. The dough mixture is malleable, flexible and easily molded......just like a child's mind. The dough is kneaded and placed in bread moulds..then cooked. Every loaf that emerges from the oven has the same shape..the same texture.... the same smell...the same consistency....and the same end purpose in it's life.

SOUNDS LIKE THE SCHOOLING PROCESS....DOESN'T IT?

Creativity, originality and uniqueness are not part of our learning system.....we lost those abilities as a child.

But....we can recapture them.....by intentionally exposing ourselves to fresh, exciting new concepts.

The human mind was designed to be creative.........but our mundane, mind-numbing upbringing suppresses this creativity and causes frustration and unhappiness.

Watch a young child awaken in the morning. They stretch...take a deep breath of fresh air...and open their eyes...to an exciting world of magical happenings.

How long since YOU took a breath of fresh air ???

Where are you in life at the moment?

Maybe things have gone well for you in the past.....but maybe now they've lost their "fizz".

Maybe you've been "burnt" so much with the passage of life that your emotions have gone numb. Or perhaps things have just gone "stale" because there are no new challenges. Or perhaps the people in your environment are negative....and it's rubbing off on you.

It might even be that things have come unstuck and you're back at square one. Perhaps some of the decisions you made in the past have proven to be wrong and you're regretting some of the things you have done in the past.

If so...there is one very important thing to remember......

...when you were born you did not come with an instruction manual.

You were dumped on this planet and shoved through the schooling system. Then......you were left on your own. And you are not alone. There are hundreds of thousands just like you.

If you find yourself currently in a position you'd rather not be in... there is only one mindset you can adopt. You must realize that everything that has happened to you up to now....has been your learning curve. If you grab a piece of paper and draw a straight line in the middle of the page...from the left hand edge to the right hand edge...then everything that has happened to you up to now is below that line.

Your future is above that line.

The decisions you make right now will affect that space above the horizontal line. Any serious decision you make in the next 24 hours may well have repercussions years from now. So any important lifestyle decision must be made in a clear state of mind...without confusion and without mental conflict.

If you are unhappy about life at the moment..there is a simple ...but extraordinarily effective process you can evoke to improve things...out of sight!

The process is called.........GROUND ZERO.

Make a list of all the things you are currently doing which create your current lifestyle. Then ruthlessly divide these items into two groups. The first group will contain all those basic items which are necessary for your existence on the planet. The second group will contain the items which are superfluous to this existence.

Look very carefully at this second group and mentally cut out items that are really not necessary in your life.

If you have trouble with this consider how your life would change radically if you felt sudden heart pains...and after visiting a specialist were told that you had an incurable disease and had only 6-8 weeks to live.

YOU WOULD PLACE A DIFFERENT PRIORITY ON THINGS... WOULDN'T YOU?

The point of all this is to analyze what is really necessary in your life... then cut out all those items which are holding you back emotionally and financially.

It is an indisputable fact that each and every human being....at any one point in time...... is either doing that which makes them the happiest....or that which makes them the least unhappy.

And most people are involved in the second item........doing things which make them the least unhappy.

WHICH ONE DESCRIBES YOU THE BEST AT THE MOMENT?

If you analyze your lists very carefully....you might recognize the items that are causing emotional baggage in your life. That is...items that have become a habit in your life but have no real foundation in logical reality. Ask yourself why you do some of the things you do. Were you pressured to do them by someone else....and have they since become a pointless habit? Did they seem like a good idea at the time.....but have now become a burden. Question yourself....be brutal!

It is your life....you only have one of it......you deserve to experience profound happiness and peace-of-mind. And these mental states come from within...very seldom from outside.

If these desirable states aren't currently part of your make-up....then it may be that you are carrying too much excess emotional baggage and your priorities in your every-day life are confused.

What can you do about it? Better still...what do you intend to do about it? Are you seriously unhappy with the way things are? Do you want a change?

If so...the change must come from within. You have gone through your learning curve in life...you have made your serious mistakes. These are all below the line on your piece of paper.

The rest of your life is.....above the line.

Start off today...do something different. Do something you would not normally consider doing. Something different. Any little thing. Surprise yourself! Look for the magic in life......see things as little children see them....

Take a breath of fresh air......the rest of your life is...yours!!

STRUGGLE VERSUS SUCCESS

There will come a point in your life when you feel the need to look at WHY some people have continuous success and why others don't, despite their best intentions!

It is a fact that some people are into continuous struggle - it has become their normal day-to-day mental state. These people, in general, are not successful for any length of time.

If you take a hard look at the people who form the society around you, it will become obvious that there are 2 basic kinds of people - those who are into struggle and those who are into success! Those who are into success accept struggle only on a short term basis and then are mentally and emotionally prepared to accept and enjoy all the fruits of success when it arrives! However- those who are into struggle accept it as a permanent condition and if by accident they become successful will mentally self-destruct until they return to the level of struggle which their environment and belief system has trained them for, and which they have accepted as "normal". Many misguided parents tell their children that "struggle is noble" and infer that successful people are liars, cheats, and have probably "ripped people off" to get where they are. I was told this as a child by my relatives and it took me until the age of 30 to overcome this mental conditioning!

If you plant a flower or vegetable seed it usually grows to full size as nature intended. It does not normally half grow and stay that way for months. Nature intended it to have a SUCCESSFUL growth cycle and that is usually what happens!

Success is an inherent part of nature!

And so it is with human beings! We were intended to enjoy the abundance that nature provides!

If we are NOT successful, there is a 90% chance that our own internal belief system is the cause. Some people complain that they have had a life of "bad luck". Well, luck is where opportunity meets preparation! Bad luck is where opportunity meets lack of preparation and indifference!

Every time I have met a person who complains about "bad luck" I have found out that in general these people are born losers"! Of course, occasionally a bit of bad luck does happen (even to me!) but it does n't happen every day of the week, month after month. If it did, I would have to naturally assume that some nut case had made up a doll that looked like me and as a hobby spent all his spare time sticking pins into it!

Occasionally we get locked into a business or personal situation which seems to be out of control but it is a fact that there is always a way out of any given situation. Of course, there is always a price to pay! But if you stand still and do nothing there is also a price to pay! Usually mental anguish! If you can look at your problems from a lateral thinking point of view, a spectacular spontaneous solution will usually present itself! All it then takes is action! This is the point where the "born loser" does nothing ....and of course suffers more "bad luck".

On the other hand, the person who is success orientated sees the answer to their problems and seizes it! The solution required may be a radical one and might be right outside your comfort zone"! But this is the price you have to pay to solve you problem. Friends and associates around you may disagree with your proposed solution, but they aren't wearing the problem, so ignore them! You have to be emotionally strong about this, but successful people always are!

Strugglers have no emotional strength and determination - their emotions flop around the parking lot like a tribe of demented Mexican jumping beans!

The choice of whether you make something out of life is yours alone! No one else can determine it for you!

Your attitude toward success is critical to your success!!

COME ALIVE!
STRETCH YOURSELF AND LIVE LIFE!

BORING - MUNDANE - NON EXCITING - DULL - DRAB.. ...

That is the way 80% of Westerners describe their lives ... and another 10% won't admit it. Less than an estimated 10% of our citizens consider their lifestyle acceptable and pleasant.   -
That is - only one in ten people are satisfied with their lot in life. Some consider it exciting - others merely consider it as non-boring!

And what is it that causes this 10% of the population personal satisfaction?

Simple .....they are prepared to live outside their own personal comfort zone. If you do NOTHING to stretch your talents, thinking patterns, knowledge, experience, and inter-action with others, you are living INSIDE your own comfort zone. You are living on your own personal Island....welcome to boredom!!

But, if you are prepared to push yourself slightly, life takes on a new meaning. Take the true example of a lady whose husband died and left her all alone in the world. Her kids were grown up and were involved in their own life. She had made few outside friends as she had been totally involved in her husbands work. For three years she virtually did nothing socially but suddenly she "flicked" into a different mind-state. She joined a dance club and an up-market singles organization. Now, 12 months later, she is an excellent dancer and is also secretary of the singles club. But most importantly, she is enjoying the life that used to pass her by. She pushed herself outside the security of her personal comfort zone - she took the first step to a better life!

The simplest way to "break out" is to join a club - any club - but obviously one that appeals to you. Clubs are basically groups of like-minded people who do things that they would not do if left to their own devices. Make sense?? Virtually all clubs have a couple of dynamic members who DO things. Quite often these are the same people who initially formed the club. These people "push" others along with their enthusiasm. The net result is that you do things you wouldn't normally do. If you don't want to join a group like this but you want to extend yourself personally, then the simplest way is to set a few personal goals which push you outside your aura of comfort.

For example, if you feel uncomfortable driving your car in heavy traffic and big cities, take a few days off and do just that! Push yourself. If you are a shy, nervous type and want to gain massive dollops of self confidence very quickly - take a hot-air balloon ride, or approach a rappelling club for a trial rope descent down a 20ft cliff face, or take a ride on the back of a commercial Harley Davidson motor bike, or take a helicopter flight, or, if you're really daring do a tandem parachute jump. Some of these ideas might sound a bit radical (or maybe a bit tame!) but if you've never been involved in anything like this before it will give you such a giant "buzz" you will remember it for years.. AND .... you will feel really good about yourself.

Let me give you a personal example of what I mean: Many years ago I did a trading/exchange deal which left me with a number of small lower priced items, one of which was a fairly old jet ski. Now I was NOT a good swimmer and felt very nervous if I got out of my depth in water, so the idea of falling off the ski in 20ft of water was somewhat daunting. However I donned the life-jacket and started the engine. I was decidedly nervous, not about the ski, but about the water. After a couple of weeks it suddenly dawned on me that I was not only staying upright on the machine (it was one of those stand-up models) without any fear but I had occasionally forgotten to put my life jacket on! In view of the fact I was being "dumped" in the water regularly I was rather amazed that my fear had been so easily overcome! And the funny thing was I didn't notice it happening - it sort of crept up subconsciously!

Shortly after that I took up scuba diving - something I'd always been keen on but my nervousness of the water deterred me. Seeing I've mentioned all this, I may as well tell you about another experience I had many, many years ago. I'd always had this urge to do a parachute jump, and because my parents were dead against, I went ahead and did it! And, it was so totally amazing that skydiving became my weekend relaxation for nearly 10 years. Which is even more surprising - because I was terrified of heights. Let me just say that with skydiving there is virtually NO sensation of height or falling - the overall sensation is one of floating! (And you can't drown!)

These are classic examples of facing your fears .... step by step.

What I'm saying is that if you want to improve your satisfaction in life, tackle those things you wouldn't normally do! You don't have to go "overboard" - just tackle things slowly and deliberately. Each achievement, no matter how minor, will give you an inner glow of satisfaction.

If you don't continually step outside your security zone, things will become mundane! And the interesting thing is that as you join into an increasing number of outside activities, you will meet more and more like minded people - who will carry you along with their enthusiasm. Be aware thought, that when you intentionally embark on "pushing" your comfort zone, you will receive quite a lot of implied criticism from well meaning - but boring - friends. You may have to leave them behind as you develop a new range of contacts!

It is a fact that your immediate circle of friends are probably all inside your current comfort zone. New, as yet undiscovered friends.... are not! So, push yourself to look for them. Once you start on this course of action, it's a lot easier than it looks!

See you at the next national skydiving champs!

HOW TO HAVE A FANTASTIC DAY.... EVERY DAY!!

This is a short compilation of lateral style affirmations.....the idea is to print a copy and read it every morning just after you wake up.

What are your first thoughts in the morning - the very first thoughts that go thru your mind as you come awake?

They are likely to be either positive...or negative!

If they're positive about the coming day they will be along the line of.... "Wow......another glorious day.....I can't wait to get into it!

OR....

If they're negative they'll go like this...... Oh boy! Here we go again! Why did I have to wake up? Look at all the garbage I've got to get thru today...what a bore. How long can I stay in bed before I have to get up? Etc...etc.

If this negativity fills your thoughts....congratulations...you'll be among 95% of the population who wake up feeling the same way.

So...what can be done about it?

That's easy! As you're waking up you are passing thru a light alpha semi-hypnotic stage and your mind is highly susceptible to suggestion. Any serious mind-set that you adopt at this critical time.....is likely to set the tone of your day...and stay with you all day.

If, immediately upon wakening, you fill your mind with positively charged thoughts, your mind-set is likely to remain positive all day long.

The following material is simple and easy to read. It will make the day look more acceptable....even challenging!

Read these inspirations every morning just after you wake up.... NOT 5 minutes later, but IMMEDIATELY you awaken. While you are in a sleepy state, your subconscious mind will accept the following suggestive concepts much more readily...and ACT on them!

STRENGTH

Dawn is when your vitality surges! If you really want to vitalize yourself...
walk at dawn! The forest - the beach - the country. Some isolated place
where you can breath and think clearly. Absorb the peace and serenity
while you're burning off calories and toning your system. You'll feel better mentally and physically.

SERENITY

During the course of the day take segments of time to slow your
thoughts. Avoid doing things at triple speed to suit someone else's time
schedule. Never let yourself be rushed - correct decisions are difficult
under pressure. Develop an effortless lifestyle and mode of operation.
You'll be far more relaxed and happier - and you'll probably achieve a
lot more.

FREEDOM

True freedom is where you feel in control - and get out of bed in the morning raring to go. True freedom is when others have stopped trying to manipulate you. True freedom is the ultimate human experience....but until
you have experienced a lack of freedom you can't really appreciate it. True
freedom is the ability to manipulate your own life ...the way you want it.
If you haven't got it....then work toward it!

CHALLENGE

Constantly stress your own personal comfort zone - or you will become
stale. Do things that make you think...and that make your heart beat faster.
Push yourself to do things that you've always wanted to do.
Plan it! Make a project of it! Give yourself a time-limit for achieving it.
A challenge has to be believed in and followed thru to its successful conclusion. The personal satisfaction gained from achieving even the simplest goal will be a reward in itself.

THE WAVE-EFFECT

Watch a surfer riding a wave - it looks effortless. Now watch another surfer trying to catch a wave - either too soon or too late. They

expand a massive amount of energy to attain any form of result. Opportunities are like this. If you catch the right opportunity at the right time - you have a fairly effortless ride. All you have to do is "keep your balance". If you approach an opportunity with common sense and commercial reality the chances of success are greatly enhanced. But the "wave-effect" takes practice. Every time you get caught off balance....try again until you succeed. Learning from your failures will eventually lead to your success. Watch for those wave-effect opportunities. When one appears..catch it and ride it carefully.

NEGATIVITY

If you have people around you who are perpetually negative....gently ease them out of your existence. It is difficult enough to get ahead without handicapping yourself. You are basically a product of your environment...and the easiest way to change this is to change the influences of your current environment. If you're not happy with the mental input you are receiving ....change the transmitting source! For your own well-being, you will have to make firm definite decisions about the type of people you really need in your life. And to succeed and become free....you will have to stand by those decisions. When it comes to friends and associates it is a fact of life that quality is better than quantity!

RESTRICTIONS

Unless you're in an institution you have very few real restrictions. Most of our restrictions and limitations arc those that we place on ourselves. A restriction is the assumption that a certain course of action must be maintained. If you stop and analyze your assumptions, you will quite often find that there are alternative courses of action which are more satisfying and applicable. If you really think things thru you will probably conclude that most of your restrictions are imposed by your own subconscious mind-set. Are they real.....or have they formed thru habit and indifference?

MENTAL RESONANCE

There is an important mechanical/acoustical/electrical effect called resonance. If you tap an empty wineglass with a pencil it "rings" at its natural resonant frequency. It requires a lot more energy to make it ring at any other pitch. The mind works in a similar way. If you become involved with an occupation or activity that "pleases" your mind, it will slip into a "resonant" mode and very little mental energy is required to achieve results. Alternatively if you are doing something you don't like, massive amounts of mental energy are sometimes expended to achieve even mediocre results. If your waking activities are done in a state of mental resonance you are in harmony with your environment and your lifestyle will reflect this. If you can achieve this state of mental resonance in your everyday affairs....you will quickly attain almost total freedom from stress and anxiety...and have energy to "burn" at the end of the day!

DESIRE

If you have a burning desire in life....a total obsession....something which occupies your thoughts virtually every waking hour...then you will be working in a "mental resonance" mode. You are at a mental peak and life will take on a new slant. You are focused! Your yearnings are centered. Find something to get obsessed with. Figure out what interests you the most and get involved....100% !!! When you do this the world will look different.....it will look more interesting. Your life will develop a new meaning......because.......you have a mission and a purpose!

BELIEFS

Your current mind-set has evolved from.......all of the things that you have ever believed in! If you carefully analyze each and every major belief that you currently have...you will probably conclude that some of them are totally without foundation! These are.......beliefs without a reality foundation! Isn't it time you....cleaned out the garbage? Some of these beliefs may have been installed in childhood....or by peer groups. In fact....they may not be your beliefs at all! They may be someone else's beliefs...that you have accepted and adopted.

Do what you feel and believe in.....not what peer groups do and expect! Start today!!!

PROBLEMS

There is one certain way to mask a problem.......create a bigger one! Many people go thru life doing exactly this...but the original problem still remains. If you have a problem......face it!!! Start an action-plan to solve it. The fact that you are doing something will release some of your built up tension and concern.....and the deeper you delve into the problem... the more it will fall apart. If possible, break the problem into its individual parts and attack each part separately. It may even transpire that the real problem was not exactly what you thought it was! You won't know.....until you face it!!

The idea of reading these inspirations each morning while you're still in an alpha state is to slowly impinge them upon your subconscious.... where they will take hold and become part of your personal philosophy. Alternatively you can record them onto a cassette and play it each morning just after you wake up. You will probably find that this produces better results as you will be able to maintain your sleepy alpha state without having to focus and concentrate on written words.

You will probably notice a difference within a few days....and within 2-3 weeks you just might find that the world looks more interesting....and less stressful!

Those readers interested in a substantial amount of free follow-up information can contact the author at either of the following email addresses -
mindtech@vanuatu.com.vu
jimfrancis@bigpond.com

Printed by BoD™in Norderstedt, Germany